THE
ENCOUNTER
GAME

THE ENCOUNTER GAME

Bruce L. Maliver, Ph.D.

STEIN AND DAY/*Publishers*/NewYork

First published in 1973
Copyright © 1973 by Bruce L. Maliver
Library of Congress Catalog Card No. 72-160352
All rights reserved
Published simultaneously in Canada by Saunders of Toronto, Ltd.
Designed by David Miller
Printed in the United States of America
Stein and Day/*Publishers*/7 East 48 Street, New York, N.Y. 10017
ISBN 0-8128-1423-1

This book is dedicated to several people, since my love for each of them is different—

To the memory of my mother, to my Aunt Pearl and my sister Robin; and

To Lynn: for loving me, especially the part of me that this book represents; and

To Susan: for loving me, and especially for not being too impressed with that part.

Contents

Foreword

Any writer attempting to evaluate an ideology owes his readers an "up-front" statement of his own ideological position. So I'll borrow a piece of encounter game ritual right now and say, in good ungrammatical encounter style, "This is how I feel and where I'm at."

I've been participating in, observing, discussing, criticising, and writing about the encounter group movement since 1968. At that time, nearing the end of my postdoctoral training and having been in private practice for about five years, I approached the movement from the vantage point of a psychologist and psychoanalyst.

My experience with groups dates from the very beginning of my career as a professional psychologist. Indeed, there has not been a time in the last twelve years when I was not responsible for leading at least one ongoing group of one sort or another. My private practice has always included both individual and group psychotherapy.

After four years of training in individual psychoanalysis and psychotherapy, I undertook a two-year program in group psychotherapy. Partly because the encounter world seemed to offer many innovative, useful techniques and ideas, I participated in and led a variety of encounter and sensitivity training groups in schools, in conference settings, in private practice, in drug rehabilitation centers, and in growth centers.

I took a critical position almost at once, and found myself one of the few professionals with that stance. During those years I had the opportunity to interact with many of the "stars" of the encounter movement. I found them personally likable, though almost invariably fanatic on the subject of groups. Ultimately I got bored with their rhetoric, their arguments, and their ritualistic claims of a new openness and a humanistic world revolution.

Late in 1970 I decided to sum up my position in an article for the public, expecting that afterwards I would be done with the matter. But once that article appeared in the *New York Times Magazine* (January 3, 1971), just the opposite occurred. The piece seemed to allow considerable negative sentiment toward the encounter movement to surface. Members of the public contacted me with their own horror stories. A number of professional groups and publishers requested that I go further into the topic, and the result is this book.

This is not a technical book, though I was frequently tempted to document my points with references from the professional literature; to cite in good academic style all the lines of argument, subtle nuances, and exceptions to every point; and to present and assess all of the "relevant research." Ultimately my editors convinced me that while such weighty evidence has a place in the professional literature, it is a crushing bore to most readers.

There is one thing that I would have liked to do but could not. The scientist in me would have liked to have grant support to carry out systematic observations and data collection on a sizable random sample of encounter group participants interviewed and studied in depth by a team of researchers. In short, good social science field methodology.

That was not possible. Instead, I used my own interviews and experiences, pieced together what I saw as common themes, and drew my own conclusions from these observations. My method, then, was that of the clinician and critic.

Though I am very much committed to the use of groups as a modality for human change and growth, my commitment carries with it what I hope is a keen awareness of the limitations, dangers, and drawbacks in any group process. Groups are not magical. In fact, the laws of group dynamics can easily be understood by anybody willing to devote the necessary time and study. People in a group for the first time, or who have had very limited experiences in groups, often leave with what has been called the delusion of uniqueness—"What happened in my group was so warm, so unusual, so exciting, it simply must have been a unique phenomenon."

This is a delusion; moving from group to group, you find the same kinds of revelations and emotional interchanges; the same kinds of fears, intimacies, and human contacts. They are a part of what is called by professionals "group process," and in fact they can very much be planned, stimulated or suppressed, focused or allowed to occur at random.

The group psychotherapist spends his training time and professional development perfecting the skills necessary to make sure that what happens in his groups is not random and haphazard, but in accordance with a treatment plan aimed at facilitating growth and personality change *specific* to the needs of his individual patients.

The main cause for my concern about the encounter movement is that I have repeatedly seen the artificial, the shoddy, and the absurd being mistaken for the significant. It is precisely because the ideology that surrounds encounter groups so often becomes destructive when translated into action that I believe it deserves careful scrutiny by an informed public.

It is my hope that exploring the negative side of this complex cultural phenomenon will have several results: first, players of the game will be warned of the dangers and exploitations possible. Second, since there seem to be clear-cut positive effects for some participants, I hope that sufficient public scrutiny can help clean up the encounter house, so to speak, and salvage—and place in an appropriate perspective—whatever real value may reside in the movement's activities.

Interactions and discussions with many people helped me crystalize my views. I wish to thank them all. And though they don't agree with my position, many encounterists deserve thanks as well. It's impossible to name all who've helped in different ways, but the list includes Lenny Blank, Dan Casriel, Magda Denes, Bob Goldfarb, Graham Finney, Berta Isaacs, Mort Lieberman, Clem Loew, Rollo May, Stu Miller, Betsy Mintz, Jean Munzer, John Pierrakos, Carl Rogers, Martin Shepard, Bill Schutz, Harold Trigg, Howard Yahm. Jeffrey Atlas and Frank Dworkin helped with technical points of law and accountancy. Luz Gunsberg deserves a monument for turning my multicolored, pasted and patched, dogeared drafts into a readable manuscript. Al Rosenblatt taught me a lot about writing during the preparation of the *New York Times* piece; Renni Browne and Mike Hamilton continued that job, and faithfully rode herd on my tendency to write psychological jargon instead of plain English.

BLM

East Hampton, L. I.
August 1972

THE ENCOUNTER GAME

1

Panacea or Snake Oil?

Julia was thirty-two years old, attractive, unmarried, and had recently ended a lengthy and unsatisfying love affair. She was lonely and increasingly depressed about her social life. Since her depressions were recurrent, Julia thought she needed some kind of therapy, but she didn't know what kind. She shared her concern with a few friends, even telling them that she'd thought of suicide. One friend told her about encounter groups run in New York City by a founder of the Synanon method of group confrontation.

She decided it was worth a try. Unlike most new players of the encounter game, she was given a fifteen-minute "screening" interview with a psychiatrist, after which she was placed in a group of about twelve people which met for several hours each weekday evening under the leadership of a "paraprofessional."

She had paid fifteen dollars in advance for the fifteen-minute interview; the group sessions cost fifteen dollars for each two hours, and that seemed cheap compared to what she imagined to be the cost of individual attention from a licensed psychotherapist.

The group's participants, who ranged in age from their teens to their sixties, varied each evening, as did the leaders. But as the weeks passed, Julia made a few friends among those who came fairly regularly.

The sessions were unlike anything she had ever experienced. "I'm learning how to get out my feelings and be angry," she told a girl friend. "And the amazing part is that, despite the anger, the people in the group draw closer to one another."

Three months later, Julia killed herself by swallowing several dozen sleeping pills.

Though I've changed her name here, Julia was a real person; it was she who first made me aware of the dangers of a phenomenon that has, in one form or another, invaded nearly every segment of our society today: the group-experience encounter culture, which promises that if human beings can only be more open with each other, all will be right with them and the world.

In different ways, that is what the various groups try to accomplish. Unfortunately, things just don't happen so easily. What *has* happened is the emergence of a cult preaching humanism and openness and cloaking itself in an aura of pseudopsychotherapy. Julia, an acquaintance of mine, had called to ask my opinion of encounter techniques before joining her group. At that time I knew little about them, but what she described during that conversation sounded so unconventional and so lacking in the elements of good psychotherapy that I warned her against joining. Her death in the late spring of 1968 prompted me to start my own professional investigation of the cult.

Along with the "Human Growth Centers"—which is what many of the organizations that thrive on the cult call themselves—churches, public schools, universities, prisons, and corporations are all running encounter and sensitivity-training groups. Known variously as sensitivity groups, T-groups ("T" for training), growth laboratories, and communications labs, they may last anywhere from a few hours to several weeks full time; they may meet only once or continue regularly for a year or more. Few of the people who lead these and other groups have any professional credentials or training. Frequently their only qualification is that they have participated in enough groups to have acquired a certain professional veneer. Training for such leaders, referred to in different parts of the country as "facilitators," "trainers," "leaders," or "paraprofessionals," rarely lasts as long as six months—three months as a participant and three as a co-leader. In many cases leaders have opened up shop after participating in only two or three encounter sessions themselves.

Encounter "groupers" include just about everyone: teachers, students, business executives, housewives, criminals, policemen, drug addicts, doctors, lawyers. So many people participate (better than six million was the estimate made in 1969 by the eminent psychologist Warren Bennis) that organizing and leading encounter groups has become fantastically profitable for some operators. At least one growth center has gone public, recently—its stock opened at five dollars and within a few weeks was trading at eighteen dollars per share.

While the profit motive is sometimes an important part of the game, the psychologically seductive tactics within the group themselves are the reason most of the players keep coming back.

Julia's group presented her with the idea that deep inside she was boiling with anger. It was her fear and suppression of this anger that made her depressed, she was told, and in order to get better she would have to "get in touch with" that anger.

One of her sessions went something like this: "Let's get out some of that anger," said a group leader. "First, Julia, I want you to acknowledge it." "I'm angry," Julia answered in a querulous tone, as if not quite certain of what she was saying.

"I don't believe you," the leader said. "Make me believe it!"

Goaded by her leader and the rest of her group, Julia shouted "I'm angry" in a louder and louder voice; the group shouted, "More, more, you're not angry enough!" Julia continued to escalate her intensity until she was shrieking at the top of her lungs, *"I'm angry! I'm angry! I'm angry!"* and was finally reduced to hysterical, sobbing exhaustion. At this point, typically, other group members might say to her, "That's good, you got a lot out," or hold her in their arms and stroke her. But someone else, either the leader or another grouper, might not be quite satisfied. "No," he would say, "you didn't get it all out. There must be more. Try again."

And Julia tried again, and again, and again, each time embarking on an anger-expressing cycle which left her exhausted. At some point, the group was satisfied and transferred its attention to the next grouper. After a number of such sessions, Julia found that her long-standing depression had actually lifted and, she said to a friend, "I'm happier than I've ever been."

To a trained psychologist, Julia's new-found happiness would have been a danger signal. He would have been aware of the high risk of suicide among people who, after being lifted from a severe depression, experience sharp disappointment. But Julia's group leaders had no professional training. And her disappointment came quickly.

She had begun an affair with one of the leaders. Meeting him at a time when she felt encouraged by her therapy, she responded to him intensely. Her disappointment came when she found out he was having affairs with several other girls he'd met in the same way. Apparently Julia's leader took very seriously the encounter culture directive to "act out" feelings. And he probably believed that having sexual intercourse as often as he could helped everybody's therapy, including his own.

Further, I'm certain that Julia's group doesn't know to this day that she is dead, since most of the encounter organizations make little or no effort to keep tabs on those passing through. If her group does keep records, Julia probably is listed as having stopped coming.

I started with the case of Julia because I think it illustrates the worst aspects of the encounter movement:

First, Julia clearly was looking for and needed psychotherapy, and was sold encounter as a form of psychotherapy. While many group leaders and growth centers have learned to hedge about whether or not they are offering "therapy," others—like Julia's—openly make such claims.

Second, it is clear that the professional planning and responsibility that ordinarily protect a patient in psychotherapy were not available to Julia. There was no professional psychotherapist responsible for her treatment (except for the initial "screening" interview). No reliable therapeutic relationship could have developed in the many different groups in which she participated, since the cast of characters changed each time. Nor could there have been much in the way of carry-over for Julia as she went from group to group and leader to leader.

Third, the group style to which she was exposed is called "psychological karate," the form of encounter that is probably most devastating to people whose emotional state is fragile. We will talk about this style later; at this point it is sufficient to indicate that its specific purpose is to rip away people's customary emotional defenses. Proponents of this Synanon-type encounter acknowledge that it is designed to make people "briefly psychotic," in the naïve view that by recognizing their pathological sides, people will automatically become healthy.

Fourth, contrary to the claims of encounter advocates that their brand of therapy is cheaper—when they do admit that they are selling a form of psychotherapy—the fees that Julia paid to join a group run by a nonprofessional leader were actually equal to or higher than fees charged by accredited and often senior members of the mental-health professions.

Fifth, these first glimpses of the group process in Julia's case illustrate how a supposedly humanistic, honest, intimate, and concerned style of "relatedness" can be a kind of psychological tyranny, with group members being coerced to express emotions that the group arbitrarily demands, in conformity with the common encounter-game notion that the expression of emotions is in itself curative. This idea has been disproved again and again in empirical research on psychological change.

Sixth, the absence of a trained professional who could keep tabs on Julia's reactions while she was being put through severe psychological stress was an invitation for trouble. She was intentionally put through emotional surgery; and in any surgery, there must be a certain amount of risk. In fact, psychological incisions can be risky even at the hands of the most highly trained professional. To perform any other kind of surgery without postoperative facilities would be clearly criminal, yet psychological surgery without follow-up is commonplace in the encounter world.

Seventh, Julia's affair with one of her leaders is unfortunately characteristic of the mores and style of sexuality among players in the encounter game. The intimacy generated by therapy procedures often provokes sexual feelings in both therapist and patient. Knowing that such feelings are most often an artifact of the therapy, professionals are trained not to act on their sexual impulses with patients, but rather to examine with the patient the implications of those feelings. Should a therapist become sexually involved with a patient, his behavior is censured by his fellow professionals as unethical. Further, such a therapist has an obligation to refer the patient elsewhere instead of pursuing a "sexual" therapy. No such ethical constraints bind the nonprofessional encounter group leader, whose philosophy of reacting spontaneously often places a premium on sex between leader and group members, as well as between group members.

Finally, the failure to keep records or to hold themselves in any way accountable for the "treatment" offered is a hallmark of the encounter world. The do-your-own-thing approach—and we'll see further examples as we go on—is carried to the point where no person has any responsibility for what he does to others.

Evidence now coming to light shows that the encounter game can be a dangerous one, one that is really an insidious form of psychological hoax. Not only do the groups fail to deliver what they promise, they often play on human foibles and needs—with the result that people are sucked into emotionally or physically damaging situations that they cannot cope with.

Although objective research often lags behind cultural changes, at least one broad-scale study of the encounter phenomenon points out that approximately 10 percent of participants risk significant emotional damage. This study, carried out by a prestigious research team at Stanford University's Medical School, shows further that the participants may not directly connect their symptoms with the encounter group; that most participants will go away feeling satisfied with the experience and, in fact, feeling that they have changed in some substantial way, but that their subjective reports of change diminish dramatically six months after the encounter group experience; and, finally, that other people who know these participants will not perceive them as changed. In short, it may very well be that the average encounter grouper is running at least a one-in-ten risk of severe anxiety, agitation, and depression in return for a brief illusion that he is different.

Government and professional organizations are beginning to take an interest in protecting the public from the abuses that can result from the encounter game. The American Group Psychotherapy Association has issued a position paper which includes the statement that "if encounter were a drug it would clearly be banned from the market."

In May 1971 the New York City Council, acting in conjunction with members of the New York State Assembly, held open public hearings on encounter groups in an attempt to determine whether ethical abuses were of such an order as to indicate a need for new consumer-protection legislation. While the findings of those hearings were inconclusive, since then reporters have discovered that a number of encounter organizations are affiliated with unaccredited colleges known as diploma mills in the United States and Canada. The encounterists were planning to set up a network of encounter "clinics," located in church basements and staffed by their own instant Ph.D.'s and bogus clergymen.

It is now quite clear that the encounter game is a broad-scale and complex social movement encompassing characteristics of religious revivalism, antiestablishment political and social attitudes, new sexual and social mores, and a heady brand of anti-rationalism. The encounter game, accordingly, has its own ground rules, its own principles for play; its sandlot versions as well as its major-league versions; its superstars, and young kids eager to emulate them; its casual players, and encounter bums who travel great distances to the latest or hottest game.

In fact, the encounter game is so diverse that one might question at the outset whether it has any unifying significance or ideology. But though there are myriad ways to play, the same ideology is present in every group of players and serves to explain what seem to be vast differences in the behavior of groups, or chance-determined and seemingly unique interchanges between individuals.

To understand the game we must understand the ideology and its resulting rituals and ground rules, since the players explain their behavior in terms of that ideology. And, like other complex ideologies, this one carries with it certain intrinsically irrational articles of faith which serve to unite the true believers against the Philistines.

I view the encounter game phenomenon as part of a social movement having at its core the irrational—and perhaps uniquely American—idea that people can be run through an emotional production line and come out with instant change and growth. Looking at segments of American culture through the encounter lens may bring into sharper focus the antirational, anti-intellectual trend evident to many current observers.

While the encounter game has its grisly and at times fatal side, it also has all the fun, hoopla, magic, and excitement of a circus. Let's take a look at that side first.

2

Bill Schutz and the Flying Circus

My second exposure to the encounter movement's handling of people took place a few months after Julia's death, when I attended an all-day workshop or "microlab" run by members of the staff of the Esalen Institute.

A microlab may be viewed as the basic public-arena play in the encounter game. Originally designed as a sampler of the whole range of encounter techniques, it actually offers a highly compressed cafeteria of emotional experiences. The way microlabs are set up, they can hardly fail to have an emotional impact on some if not all of the participants. Probably more people have experienced the encounter game through microlabs than through any other single form of encounter; and for many, the taste of excitement and instant intimacy that microlabs offer serves to bait the hook that keeps them coming back for more.

The first microlab group I attended was large, about two hundred people. (I don't know what the highest gate figures are, but microlabs of seven or eight hundred people have been staged.) We'd paid twenty-five dollars each to gather in one of the ballrooms of the Jack Tar Hotel in San Francisco. Almost all of us present were psychologists, since this microlab was billed as an "all-day workshop" for members of the American Psychological Association, during its annual convention. Our leader was William C. Schutz, Ph.D., one of the brightest lights at Esalen and probably the country's best-known exponent of encounter techniques. To a large extent, Schutz developed and shaped the microlab script that most other encounter game pros have copied.

At that time Schutz had a beard, though he has since shaved it off. Though he is neither, he looked rather gentle and accessible with the beard; without it there's a tough quality to the set of his jaw. He's a bald, handsome, solid-looking man who seemed younger than his forty-five years. That day he wore a brightly colored turtleneck and a pair of equally colorful slacks, and seemed entirely composed, comfortable, and free of anxiety.

In our stockinged feet—after being given the usual encounter game warning that we were each responsible for our own physical safety, while at the same time being asked to suspend all critical judgment—we were led through a series of games calculated in the jargon of encountering to "increase awareness," "stimulate emotional growth," and "promote interpersonal communications."

First came a warm-up technique for releasing tension (and establishing a base line of group conformity and control). Each person was asked to stand and scream as loudly and mindlessly as he could, and, of course, all two hundred of us screaming at once made quite a din. For many it probably was the first time they'd made such a noise since they were children. "Now wave your arms," Schutz (from a little raised platform) yelled above the din, "and jump up and down in your places." Off we went again, the noise and vigor of our massed activity generating enough human energy to shake the hotel's foundation.

"Now be quiet, very still, and go into yourself. Take a sounding of how you feel, of where you're at. Feel your whole body," Schutz said. The silence seemed louder than the noise, as each of us felt his physiological "awareness" markedly increased.

Next we went back to screaming again. The alternation between the screaming/jumping and silence/contemplation has a clear-cut hypnotic effect, of course, and one of the critical elements in any hypnotic induction is the instruction to pay attention to sensory experience. Doing so almost automatically alters one's ordinary state of consciousness, and certainly provides the subjective feeling that strange and wonderful things are happening.

Breaking into the final silence, Schutz told us to introduce ourselves to one another without speaking or uttering a sound, and to express through our eyes what we were feeling.

This led to a period of touching—shaking hands, placing a hand to a face or one cheek to another; hugging; patting fannies; grasping each other's shoulders—whatever each person wanted.

After this, more silent nonverbal inspection, so that except for an occasional outburst of embarrassed laughter the only sound was the shuffling of feet as we groupers made contact with first one person, then another.

Those touch contacts, for some, seemed espeically warm and new. I am sure that the newness and the excitement—as well as the embarrassment—resulted from our heightened awareness, an effect that such group hypnotic techniques can be relied upon to generate. All two hundred of us were following the Pied Piper with enthusiasm by this point. Schutz made sure that these "interpersonal" contacts did not go on too long. The idea was not really to get to know anybody, but to develop a sense of community with everybody; you touched a beard or inspected a face or patted a fanny and smiled about it, and then were instructed rather quickly to move on.

Now Schutz stationed ten people a few feet apart along the walls and asked the rest of us to form a line in front of each of them. Once we were lined up, the instructions were simple: ask yourself how dominant or submissive you feel, and, using your own judgment, place yourself in the appropriate spot in your line, with the most dominant person at the front. "Of course, someone else may not agree with you, and if he's in your spot, get him out of there," Schutz urged.

The fights that followed were amazing not only for their sheer violence but because, in many cases, women fought like tigers for those front, "dominant" spots. Those willing to join the fray experienced a great deal of roughhouse pleasure; those at the submissive end talked embarrassedly, or looked on with envy at the bolder ones. At the rear of one line two people actually got into a heated argument over who was more submissive! Occasionally you could see someone from the submissive end shuck his trepidation and go charging into battle at the head of his line. Sometimes two or three "dominants" would gang up on a real fighter, subdue him, and drag him off to the submissive end— allowing a sneaky middler, finding himself in the top spot by default, to enjoy his moment of glory before the gang returned. At that point he might choose to fight, or step meekly aside.

At this point, little more than thirty minutes after the microlab began, the excitement of the group was palpable. We had already dared to attempt the forbidden if not the impossible. We had jumped, screamed, and touched; we had fought; we had stood in silence and contemplated. All this had helped create a feeling of exhilaration and camaraderie that came from having experienced so much together. Most of us would have followed any suggestion Schutz made, and the anticipation of the pleasure to come was intense.

Now we were ready for the real stuff: "interpersonal honesty."

Schutz views honesty as the key ingredient in man's salvation, the cardinal virtue which, if only practiced widely enough, would repair the ills of mankind. Taking this ideal as a mandate for messianic manipulation, Schutz divided us into smaller, more intimate groups of five—"half men and half women," he said, in what I later learned is one of his standard jokes. We were told to sit down and discuss the feelings we'd experienced. It is this small-group-sitting-on-the-floor-sharing-feelings that is often called the "basic encounter group." The premium placed on honesty and being "with it" emerges quickly in this setting, and "honesty" usually means acknowledging uncomfortable, embarrassing, or socially unacceptable feelings—while the rest of the group watches to make sure you don't cop out.

The idea is to state exactly what you're feeling and to be as candid and open as you can. What this came to in our group was some admissions of weakness and discomfort about their lack of dominance from two of the men. A couple of women expressed interest in the men's feelings and shared their own reactions to dominant men vs. submissive men. One woman said she had wanted to compete in the dominance lineup, but had feared getting beaten up or hurt.

After a few minutes of this general encountering, Schutz indicated from the platform that each person was to take turns sitting toe to toe or knee to knee with every other member of his small group, look directly into his eyes, and express whatever he had felt about that person in the last few minutes of general talk. Most of the details of that particular small encounter group have long since been fused in my mind with hundreds of later encounter experiences. But one memory stands out very vividly.

There was an attractive young blonde in the group who had indicated that this was her first go at encounter. She was obviously enjoying all that honesty and directness, and as she moved from person to person, she would give each of the men a big hug and kiss. It didn't take more than a few seconds of her tongue in my mouth before I recognized the kiss she gave me as deliberately sexual.

A little while later, when we were again sharing feelings as a group, it became clear that all of the men had had the same experience with this woman. Until that point I had not been too emotionally involved in the activities or the feeling exchanged and, indeed, had been criticized for being remote, not "with-it." My response had been that I really was expressing what I was feeling, and if I wasn't feeling much, then "that's where I was at," in encounter lingo.

But when I realized that this woman had sexually turned on each man in the group, I got angry. And when it came my turn to confront her, I told her how I felt about being part of her group tease.

She got embarrassed and upset, having apparently hoped to hide from the group as a whole her play with each of the men. She explained that her husband was in a different minigroup, sitting a few yards away from us, and that for her the experience of some sexuality with other men was exciting, an experience she had thought would be "useful." She had evidently failed to consider that these sexual exchanges would involve other people, who might have feelings themselves.

Needless to say, the honesty of my exchange with her earned us both points in our minigroup. I was suddenly elevated from "aloof, intellectual bastard" to "really open and direct, sensitive, capable-of-expressing-anger *soul.*" While I didn't fully understand it then, I'd had my first taste of encounter group pressure toward conformity to emotional expectations. Evidently I was somewhat less than human until I expressed something the group could use to consider me human. Once I'd paid my emotional dues, I was okay.

With the emphasis on the here and now, you can run out of things to talk about very quickly—especially since the relationships in the group have no real history, indeed no real purpose other than the mutual analysis of quick impressions.

As a result the leader must constantly create new emotional or sensory experiences for analysis and criticism by the group. And so, after a few minutes of this "honest interchange," we were put through such activities as arm wrestling or "falling," to give us some more experiences we could "interchange honestly."

During the arm wrestling we were each to scream and shout into our opponent's face; this was supposed to help us tap primitive levels of aggression, anger, and competitiveness. For some, something like that did seem to occur—at least, they seemed to get into the spirit of the thing, if noise and red faces are the proof of primitive aggression. Others wrestled with a few tentative grunts, or just plain wrestled, and I suppose we'd have to infer that they missed their golden opportunity to get in touch with the primordial rage residing in ancestral parts of their unconscious minds.

As for falling, that's a bit more likely to tap long-forgotten fears. Each of us was told to keel over backward, knees locked and arms slightly away from the body so that the person (hopefully) waiting to catch you could break your fall by grabbing you under the arms. For most adults, falling is one of those frightening experiences we presumably mastered as children and have outgrown. But even divers have trouble coping with the fear of back dives, and amusement parks capitalize on such fears by offering rides that create the sensation of falling.

This apparently simple exercise, then, really played on one of our deepest fears, though presented within the barest of conceptual frameworks: trust. The exercise was supposed to confront each person with his willingness to trust others to take care of him. It did seem to do that for many of us, and there were obvious differences in our readiness to let ourselves fall, depending on the attributes we ascribed to the sex, size, or presumed reliability of the catcher. Some people found it an easy thing to do, regardless of who the catcher was; some could easily trust males to catch them but not females (though the physical strength of the catcher is largely irrelevant); some made a good show of letting go but actually broke their own falls by stepping backward; and some would not even try, having been brought to the edge of panic just by watching others do it, and knowing that they too were expected to fall.

Some encounterists heighten the fear potential of this exercise by having the faller tip over backward from the edge of a table or windowsill, while several other groupers line up to catch him. Catchers seem to take seriously their obligation to catch, and until quite recently, with all of the thousands of falls there had not been a known instance of intentional failure to catch. In one recent microlab, however, a catcher decided to see how he would feel if he were intentionally untrustworthy. The faller wasn't badly hurt, I'm told, and they reportedly had a fine encounter as a result of the incident.

After the arm-wrestling and falling, Schutz led the group through several other games—"rock 'n' rolling," "breaking in" and "breaking out"—and then reassembled the small groups, for discussion of individual reactions.

These games were supposed to help us start to change lifelong personality patterns. In the "rock 'n' rolling," for example, one person stood with eyes closed, knees locked, and body straight but limp while the group formed a circle around him. The person in the center was passed around, all hands supporting and twisting him like a slow-moving top. Once sufficiently relaxed and disoriented, the person was tipped over and lifted as high as the group's arms would reach, slowly rocked back and forth, and gently lowered to the floor. The process is supposed to help the subject get in touch with early childhood feelings of dependency and long-forgotten memories of being lifted and cradled. For some it appeared to do just that; for others it seemed like a great way to emulate a sack of potatoes. For the most part it's an easy trip, though at other times I've seen this game generate vivid recollections of a childhood surgery experience, with its terror and pain.

"Breaking in" aims at the sense of being excluded. Schutz asked for volunteers who'd suffered from feelings of social isolation. A demonstration group formed a tight close circle with arms around each other's shoulders. The outcast in each case fought his way in, pitting his strength against that of the group trying to keep him out. Some got in by attacking at knee level. One chap picked out what he figured would be the weakest link—a slight young woman clutching a frightened-looking librarian type—and barreled through between them. Another stalked outside of the circle and finally charged. Using the locked arms as though they were ladder rungs, he vaulted himself over the top, amid great cheers for his bravery and ingenuity. Such success was supposed to prove that if you try hard enough, you can get into any group; hence feelings of being excluded should disappear.

Schutz next led us in a few rounds of "breaking out" of a circle—supposedly a way of overcoming feelings of inhibition due to social rules and constraints.

The absurdity of these facile solutions to complex human experiences is apparent, yet in the heat of the moment they actually seemed plausible. Schutz always called the tune, telling us each time we re-formed the encounter groups to express our feelings either verbally or without words, with each member encountering, eyeball to eyeball, first one person and then another.

"Now I want you all, without saying a word, to point to the person in your group to whom you feel closest," Schutz said in his soft, rich baritone. Arms rose and swung around; fingers pointed. "And now point out the person you feel most remote from," the voice intoned, repeating for emphasis: "The person you feel most distant from."

In each small group arms swung every which way to new positions of rest. Some relieved groupers found that they had not been singled out. Others, not so lucky, had been chosen by three or even four members of their small group.

Several seconds passed before anyone beyond her own group noticed that a thin girl who had been pointed to by several people was trembling. Her face was quite pale, her lips pressed together in a tight line as she struggled for control of her body. She huddled up and shook with a violence all the more frightening because she did not utter a sound.

Several "facilitators" sprang to the girl's side. Most of these are women in their early twenties who travel with Schutz and are being trained by Esalen as group leaders. They are referred to, possibly with their emergency service function in mind, as the Flying Circus. While the groups went on, they held the girl closely and caressed her for almost an hour until she was once again calm and "in contact."

Later, Schutz had the girl describe her experience for the rest of us. She said that when the others had pointed at her she felt herself alone at the end of a long, dark tunnel; that she was terrorized by the thought that she would never be in touch with people again.

Bill Schutz at one point asked if there were two people in any of the minigroups who had been especially distant from one another or had failed to settle a conflict. He selected two men first, had us all clear a path from one end of the room to the other, and instructed these two to walk toward each other in "High Noon" fashion and confront each other nonverbally. The shorter one began by slapping the bigger guy; when he got little response, he slapped harder and harder until the bigger one finally let loose and belted him. In a matter of seconds they were punching, kicking, rolling on the floor. The fight went on for some time, with the smaller guy obviously getting the worst of it, but fighting on gamely to the point where many of us were enormously relieved when he finally quit. He didn't just quit, incidentally. When he got up, he gave his bigger opponent a hug—to many in the audience it appeared to be a gesture of good sportsmanship, but to me it seemed more like the ritual submission gesture of one animal bested by another.

As the day-long microlab progressed, several serious fights were triggered by such "games" as breaking in, breaking out, and "high noon." We were told not to stop them, incidentally: Schutz's rationale is that minor physical injuries are psychologically worthwhile, and he later acknowledged the history of sprains, bruises, and occasional broken bones at Esalen and other growth centers.

While apparently giving more emphasis than most encounterists to the body, Schutz seems in fact to operate on the principle that personality and psychological factors take precedence over the physical; if you have to hurt your body to help your psyche, so what? In this way he and many of the other encounter game people actually reverse the priorities more commonly held in our culture. While whether or not to endure physical pain is certainly a choice each of us may make for himself, in a microlab you find the decision has been made for you by the group, the leader— indeed, the encounter culture. Never mind the "you're responsible for yourself" warning: when you've been encountering intensely for several hours, following instructions in a semitrance, having suspended "critical judgment" and allowed yourself to experience a wide range of emotions, you are not really in a position to walk away easily from a confrontation like a "high noon" setup. And if your opposite member begins to express himself nonverbally by using his fists, you have the choice of hitting back, using the "Esalen copout" (a hug), or announcing your cowardice to two hundred onlookers. Most self-respecting males will, of course, fight under these circumstances.

After another round of sharing our feelings about what we'd seen, we broke for lunch, and the break came as a welcome "decompression" to all.

It happened that I had an acquaintance who knew Suki Miller, a member of the Flying Circus. We chatted, liked each other, and she invited me to lunch with the staff. Some of the in-group's luncheon conversation was a little surprising. At one point Bill joked about how nice it was that there were no broken bones so far that day. The group laughed, and I couldn't be sure whether they were kidding or not. (I later learned it was no joke.) At lunch I asked a few of my New York psychologist-style questions about research, screening, controls, and results at Esalen. The reactions included derisive laughter, since my questions really came out of what hard-core encounterists call the "mind-fucking" intellectual realm of the East Coast.

When the microlab resumed after lunch we took an extended "body trip," all two hundred of us lying on the floor and imagining that we were entering our bodies and exploring them.

We had moved into another range of encounter game procedures, using fantasy. This particular body trip, coming as it did after the morning's emotionally exhausting physical experiences, seemed like a snap at first. We were snuggled up pretty close, most of us had an arm draped over another grouper or were holding hands with a newly made but usually nameless friend—an air of comfort prevailed during the silent trip.

After several minutes Bill Schutz suggested that those who cared to should tell us about their trip. And so, still prone, we listened to one woman tell us she'd entered her body through her vagina and found it so warm and comforting she didn't want to leave it. Another said she'd explored her lungs and found them filthy and smoke-filled, and become afraid that she couldn't get out. An intriguing array of fantasies were displayed, including being caught in blood vessels, and coursing along out of control propelled by each pulsebeat; being "stuck" in a librarylike room behind the eyeballs; being digested and ground to feces in the lower intestines. Certainly many of these trips had emotional significance for their owners, but it soon became obvious that an air of competitive showmanship had taken over: subtle kudos were awarded to whoever could tell the most vivid or unusual story.

Back in the small groups we continued to focus on the body in a different way. Schutz instructed us to "go around" in our mini-encounter groups and describe in turn the parts of our bodies we liked most, and those we were most displeased with or ashamed of. Of course, this caused a lot of embarrassment and discomfort, but after sharing these taboo feelings most groupers experienced a sense of relief and pleasure—and quickly became convinced of the uniquely intimate value of the encounter group.

For many, the high point of the day came next. Schutz moved us into it masterfully. He began by talking about our bodily experiences, telling us how much of his concern about human growth was centered on the use of our forgotten bodies rather than our minds. Into this set speech he dropped a few goodies such as reactionary concern about nudity being too sexual when we all know we needn't be ashamed of our bodies; the unfortunate lack of feedback opportunities as to how we carry and use our bodies; the recent benefits that had accrued to participants in nude marathons. By the time he'd gotten to this point several members of the group had already begun to remove most of their clothes, with Schutz playing the reluctant but tolerant parent encouraging this spontaneous surge toward freedom.

Paul Bindrim, who claims the paternity of the nude encounters, and who was a participant in this group, announced that he did not wear underwear—was that all right with Bill? Schutz said it was fine with him, but since we were in a midtown hotel it might be best if we kept the stripping to the shorts or bra-and-panties level. From the encounter point of view, this copout is really an indefensible failure to stand against the rising tide of conformity, but I guess even the most intrepid player accepts social limits at times.

At least three fourths of those present stripped down to their underwear. Some were quite matter-of-fact, others went into a playful striptease, or covered their anxiety with jokes. Some became visibly upset; I remember one young woman who was in tears at the prospect until she asked someone if she "had to do it," and was told that she needn't. She was so caught up in the group pressure that she wasn't sure she could trust the man who told her she didn't have to strip.

Once in this half-clad condition, we were asked to make systematic, detailed observations of each other's bodies, pointing out to their owners such manifestations as hunched shoulders, irregular postures, and fat concentrations.

Schutz, a pretty solid-looking physical specimen, entirely comfortable in his white briefs, presented what struck me as an antiquated, simplistic theory of the relationship between mind and body. He demonstrated certain postures and body types and explained their origins in terms of lifelong patterns of handling sexual and aggressive feelings. Thus, according to Schutz, guys with overdeveloped chests puff out from a need to compensate for "weak guts"; people with fat distributed around their hips and thighs have constricted the movements of the pelvis to avoid too much sexual stimulation. Schutz had us all demonstrate the veracity of this thesis to our own satisfaction by leading us in a few bumps, grinds, and pelvic thrusts, clinching his argument by pointing out how sexy and pleasureful those movements are.

In all, while several people were shaken up by this public seminudity, I suspect that the greatest degree of amazement and consternation was experienced by the hotel's kitchen staff, several of whom were peeking through the kitchen doors; they were shoved away several times by a few hairy-chested men in jockey shorts who evidently felt protective of the intimacy the two hundred others were experiencing.

One other observation is worth noting: most people look better with their clothes on.

After dinner we resumed for the "cognitive" part of the daylong workshop. This is, of course, a distasteful necessity to the encounterists since rationality, the conventions of science, and the protections of ethical constraints are viewed as uncomfortable limitations on the individual freedom so cherished in the encounter world.

In this group, because we were meeting as a semiofficial part of the annual conference of the American Psychological Association's Division of Psychotherapy, we were treated to some variations on the usual stand-up-and-be-counted confessional routine that Schutz leads at the end of his open encounters. It was different this time because this was basically a scientific group, and the encounterists have always been eager to gain acceptance and make converts within the ranks of the mental-health professions. The act was, I'm sure, played with special care.

Thanks, presumably, to the heady effects of the excitation, the seminudity, the new physical and emotional experiences, and the "intimacy," by evening this group of two hundred psychologists had largely thrown their objectivity to the wind. They were just about ready to believe that encounter was here to revolutionize the world, and many were looking for ways to get on the bandwagon.

At the time I was surprised at the way several of my New York friends and associates, whom I knew to be far better trained than most other psychologists at the conference, could so easily be swept up in the experience—so easily, so quickly, and so uncritically. Since then, I've seen this bandwagon effect happen in every kind of group, and I know that the enthusiasm is in part a response to pressures for group conformity and in part a natural excitement that comes from breaking a few social taboos. I should add that I've seen many of these same converts lose their faith; in fact, they seem a bit embarrassed to think back to their seminude enthusiasm for the encounter game.

The usual postencounter format involves eliciting accounts of subjective experiences and "feeling statements"—but no questions. To players of the encounter game, questions largely demonstrate the emotional impoverishment of the questioner. All questions are thought to be concealed statements, and the usual routine is for the leader (or one of his mimickers) to say, "Make that question into a statement about how you feel." If you fall for that gambit, you're lost, because it overrides anything remotely like the pursuit of knowledge, and leaves feelings as the only admissible reality for the group's consideration.

Because of the cues from Schutz, anyone who asked a question in that microlab was immediately hissed or shouted down with comments like: "Intellectual!" "Obsessive-compulsive!" "Sit down!" "Too cerebral!" "Get out of your head. Say what your gut says!" Schutz would respond with, "How do you feel?" One man said, "I'm not feeling—I want to know that answer!" And Schutz broke up the audience (and shot down the questioner) with, "Oh, I see—you feel curious."

But by the time evening came around, I and one or two others had some serious questions to ask Schutz. We asked, for example, what was done at Esalen about screening. (Answer: nothing.) I asked whether encounter groups were not advisable for people with any particular problems. (Answer: no. Encounter is suitable for everybody; we don't think about psychopathology; diagnoses are inaccurate anyway, and reasoning that way is not health-inducing—indeed, it tends to keep people sick.)

I asked about injuries and suicides, the case of Julia still fresh in my mind. Suicides were denied, but Schutz later grudgingly acknowledged that there were injuries. He rather cleverly placed them in a context that made them seem necessary if participants are to arrive at new levels of psychological growth. This argument raises a host of questions; most particularly, do the changes that supposedly justify the physical injuries really occur? But in the encounter postmortems the level of discourse is most often limited to reports of the individual person who has "changed." Schutz cited some examples, including a confession of infidelity that led to a wife's knocking two teeth out of her man's mouth, which "cleared the air" between them and, of course, saved the marriage.

The fundamental question, of course, was (and is): Can you prove it? Fortunately that tradition runs pretty deeply in scientifically trained psychologists, and as the pressure mounted Schutz began to show a little discomfort. When asked about diagnostic criteria—whether he thought of encounter as a treatment method; how he explained those personality changes he was describing; what follow-ups were done—he finally got angry and said, "Well, psychoanalysis hasn't proved itself either."

That made *me* angry. Only in retrospect did I realize that I'd gotten my first taste of defend-encounter-by-attacking-psycho-analysis, a favorite technique in the encounter game. While I hadn't then thought through all the nuances of the gambit, I knew something was wrong with it. I said, "Listen, psychoanalysis is not presenting here, you are. This is Division 29 of the A.P.A., and we operate under a code of ethical standards. Those ethical standards require us not to introduce new methods of treatment until they are sufficiently tested and until there is a reasonable reason to expect they will be of help. Now I want to know what you've done to test the method, and how do you know it works for anybody? What research procedures and what controls are you using?"

Schutz backed down a little, allowing that perhaps there were some topics to be researched, and that Esalen was "planning" to set up some long-range research projects. That was some four years ago, and only recently has anyone undertaken that responsibility. Certainly, though Esalen has at times billed itself as a research institution, it does not function that way. When you discuss this point with encounter game players now, they have a whole range of reasons why research doesn't prove anything anyway; but at this particular workshop Schutz and his Flying Circus placated the audience by indicating that research was in the works.

The Flying Circus team of facilitators came in for some criticism that night, too. They included Suki Miller, Stu Miller, Pamela Portugal (Schutz's principal girlfriend of that period), as well as several other Esalen "residents in training" and hangers-on. During the day they had helped to demonstrate the more complicated encounter games, helped to line us up or divide us into groups, and, perhaps most interestingly, had moved from minigroup to minigroup serving as stimulants, provocateurs, and catalysts for the process.

Often they would slip into a circle and let fly a provocative statement—occasionally missing what was going on so completely that they were summarily ejected, though most groups tended to assume that they knew what they were doing.

In one group a recently widowed woman in her mid-thirties had "opened up." She had been talking quite painfully and with considerable difficulty about her feelings about her future and her own lack of self-esteem. Pamela, a dark-haired, top-heavy facilitator, popped in toward the end of this, and, assuming the woman to be talking about sexual attractiveness, threw in a few things like, had she ever had an orgasm, who would she like to sleep with in the group, and, really, you're very attractive anyway. Pamela's "facilitation" did something, all right. It made the young widow sorry she'd ever started talking about what was really bothering her, and gave her instead the excuse to avoid any real effort to get some help from others.

This one-day demonstration microlab was my first exposure to Bill Schutz. I found him a fascinating character, especially since I felt that he had given an extraordinary, indeed, a bravura performance. He was "on" from about nine in the morning until ten or eleven that night, with meals his only interruptions. With all of my psychoanalytic training, presumed perspicacity, and hound-dog nose for anxiety, I could detect only that one moment when he lost his cool.

Reasoning from this, I decided he must be a psychopath—you know, one of those guys with no anxiety who, because of the absence of guilt and ordinary moral constraints, become thieves, heads of large corporations, or political figures. Only psychopaths and actors, most clinicians will tell you, can function in such surroundings so long and so well without any apparent anxiety or guilt.

I've changed my view of Bill Schutz quite a bit since then for many reasons. First, what I didn't know then was how many times he had been through such performances before. I doubt if even he knows at this point, but several hundred is probably an underestimate. So part of what I was seeing was the bored, flat, cool, though manifestly alert and interested, rather workmanlike performance that one can find in actors doing their thousandth performance in a Broadway play.

Since then, I've gotten to know him a little better through his participation in two encounter vs. psychotherapy conferences, and through some brief social contacts.

I doubt if anyone gets to know Schutz very well. He has described himself as shy, and explained that he wanted to become famous so that people would recognize him and approach him socially, thereby saving him the discomfort of introducing himself. Certainly he seems much less comfortable in a one-to-one situation than when leading a large group. Many microlab participants have ended the day feeling that they had a personal relationship with Schutz, only to be brought up short by his remote response to their ecstatic thanks at the end of the day.

Schutz got his moment of fame as a result of the success of his second book, *Joy—Expanding Human Awareness,* probably the best seller of the encounter movement. Schutz's encounter books have not been especially well reviewed, either in the popular press or in the professional journals. Rather, reviewers tend to point to his superficiality, outmoded theories, and cookbook approach to emotional salvation—as do serious critics of the movement in general.

Schutz places great stress on openness; one of his definitions of "open encounter" requires that it be open to all philosophical systems, just as Esalen itself supposedly is. It seems to me that in this lies one of Schutz's greatest faults, a fault endemic in the encounter culture: the idea that all systems are created equal. Hence Schutz, in what becomes a parody of intellectual freedom, tries to absorb into the "open" encounter ideology anything that anyone ever found valuable. Just as closed systems of thought falter by being too narrow, encounter buckles under the weight of being indiscriminately all-inclusive.

The "you're-responsible-for-yourself" ethic often seems to go beyond the point of liberty, indeed of liberalism, to license: specifically, the license of almost any form of behavior the leader feels inclined to try on the group. A heady power, and one that in the view of at least some observers has gone to Schutz's head many times. For a guy who describes himself as having had difficulty in initiating actions, there must be considerable satisfaction in signaling several hundred people to jump, shout, and hug, and have them respond with military immediacy. Of course, if he's bothered by it, one way to handle the conflict is to tell them—and perhaps to believe—that he's not responsible for the fact that they obey. This morality is a curious reversal of a moral problem most often considered in military or governmental terms. There each defendant says, "I'm not responsible—I was just doing my duty and following orders." Here, in the encounter game, the reversal comes out as, "I'm just making suggestions—you don't have to obey if you don't want to."

Schutz demonstrates his megalomaniacal tendency when he writes of his vision of a tearful, tender encounter group between future American and future Soviet leaders. The absurd dialogue that flows from this and other such fantastical events may have been included in Schutz's book for laughs. From what I've seen, though, under the false humility and gentle humor, Schutz and other encounterists take their mission quite seriously.

Disarming in his humility, Schutz clearly manages to get his way with groups. On the more direct one-to-one level, he's far less comfortable; and in those situations where he was a subordinate, he caused his supervisors considerable consternation. The Esalen culture seems to have been the perfect soil for his personality, and the Flying Circus circuit seems to have provided him with the brief intimacies with which he has said he's most comfortable.

My own impression is that Bill Schutz is a pretty lonely guy. At one recent conference in New York, he described himself as a "burnt-out case," and with years of constant encountering and daily intense human interactions, it's little wonder that there is not much left for him in the way of emotional experience. As though to confirm his disclosure, several hours later I noticed him at the bar, alone and looking quite depressed.

Whatever his own emotional struggles are, and however he has been affected by his leadership in the encounter world, he deserves recognition, not so much for the psychology and philosophy that he promulgates—that's clearly faulty—and not for his writings or recastings of other people's techniques—that borders on theft in the opinion of many—but rather for the personal bravery that he has many times demonstrated in his battle to lead a cultural change. His importance in the encounter movement derives from the fact that his behavior—humble yet flamboyant, honest yet manipulative—provides a model not only for participants in his groups, but for other group leaders as well.

As important as Schutz's cultural hero status is, he did not make Esalen; Esalen made Schutz. In return, Schutz's stage presence caused a brief but important publicity "boomlet" for Esalen. His microlabs clearly have a central role in the circus, but they make up only a small part of the entire carnival.

3

The Gospel According to Esalen

Esalen is the rock on which the Church of the Encounter was built. The new religion was founded with the scars and joys of a strange mélange of contributors. The Orient was there, complete with intuitive wisdom achieved through meditation; the corporate boardroom appeared, with profit world practicality and quotas on emotional output. The radical therapies contributed a sneer for the prestige of the Freudian establishment, despite their eagerness for legitimization. The body cultists, with their suntanned health, added a vision of salvation through the physical senses—the mind, in their view, having failed to fulfill man's potential.

Like other religions, the encounter game has its Jerusalem: Esalen. Geographically, Esalen occupies one of the most beautiful sites imaginable. And it represents one of those peculiar confluences of history in which a man and a piece of land come together and create a force strong enough to change a culture.

The man is Michael Murphy; the place, of course, Big Sur. Murphy is a tall, fair, quiet, friendly man who has been described as resembling "the angelic brother" in *East of Eden.* More than anyone else the founding father of the cult, Murphy had an excellent academic, sports, and fraternity record at Stanford and is now about forty.

A professor of Eastern philosophy, Frederic Spiegelberg, turned Murphy on to the Orient. He dropped out of his fraternity, started meditating and studying Eastern religions and psychology. After Stanford he went into the army, where he ended up doing psychological testing. Stu Miller, now Esalen's vice-president, told me:

After the service, he came back to this country and started meditating six to eight hours a day. He supported himself as a bellhop. His parents were upset—this was in the fifties. He went on like this for about ten years. Then he spent a year and a half in India at an unusual Ashram which tries to make a synthesis between Eastern and Western traditions. When he was thirty, his grandmother died and left him the property at Big Sur.

Murphy's grandfather, a physician, had bought the place because of the sulphur baths, intending to turn it into a health spa. The property came with a run-down hotel and some cabins, but because of its physical beauty, its nine acres, and the fact that it's the only commercially zoned property for ten miles in either direction along the coast, it's easily worth a million dollars.

Murphy had started at Stanford graduate school in philosophy but left because he found it sterile. He met Dick Price, a Harvard graduate student who was also taken with Eastern ideas. Murphy is, and especially at that time was, the world's most unworldly man. He had the property but didn't know what to do with it. Finally in 1962 he got the idea of holding seminars there to explore Eastern and Western psychology, religion, and philosophy.

He began by sending out about fifteen or twenty letters to people like Huxley, Watts, Bucky Fuller, asking them to come to Big Sur to explore their potential. They all came and gave weekend seminars. From 1962 to 1965 Dick and Mike lived there with no salary. Mike's basically an ascetic with one sport jacket and one pair of shoes; Dick's the same way.

The early Esalen brochures indicate the scope of the intellectual and religious potpourri which has given the encounter movement its unique flavor. In a 1963 brochure for "Big Sur Hot Springs," the only one of the thirteen seminars that could even remotely be considered a precursor for encounter was called "Leadership Training in Group Dynamics." Religion was covered in such seminars as "The Vision of Sri Aurobindo" and "A Weekend Retreat for Prayer and Meditation." There were seminars in poetry and in the expansion of consciousness through art, body movement, and exercises, and psychedelic drugs. The two-day seminars cost as little as four dollars each, and room and board ran about ten dollars a person per day.

A little more than a year later the name "Esalen Institute" made its appearance in the program, although "Big Sur Hot Springs" still appeared in larger type. The brochure had grown larger and now featured such names as Alan Watts, Joan Baez, Frederic Spiegelberg, Bernard Gunther, Fritz Perls, Ken Kesey, Virginia Satir, Charlotte Selver, and S. I. Hayakawa. As these and other notables joined the Esalen group, the fees began to get as high as $150 to $170 per person for a five-day stay.

From the start the emphasis on body movement was mixed with encounter. "Our gestures and posture, the way we sit and stand and move in relation to others, the way we talk—all of these are fundamental to our relationships with self and other people," says a program for the early encounter workshops. In a workshop called "The Concept of the Subtle Body," led by Frederic Spiegelberg, Esalen offered no less than

> An examination of the Indian concept of "sukshma sharirasthula sharira," often translated from the Sanskrit as "inner and outer" or "subtle and gross bodies," and of how this concept relates to modes of perception and feeling, to experience of the body and the body image, to yogic and psychedelic experience, and to Indian art, surrealism, abstract expressionism and the later work of Picasso.

Speaking of this period, Stu Miller said:

> As people began to come to Big Sur, Mike and Dick began to hear more about various techniques for developing consciousness, expanding awareness, helping people achieve joy, etc. Because they had no disciplinary boundaries, they were able to break through and discover these new techniques. Mike attended his first encounter group at the Highlands Inn in Carmel [it was probably called sensitivity-training or T-group then] and had a peak experience. He came out of it very enthusiastic about encounter techniques.

As a result of Murphy's experience, the relatively tame verbal, businessman-oriented T-group theories and practices became part of the Esalen program. At first, the verbal sessions devoted to ideas and research issues were separate from what came to be called the "experiential sessions." By the following year, the fusion of body, mind, and mysticism was almost complete, and the Esalen brochures employed a variety of Madison Avenue techniques to sell the heady mix. Larger and much more attractive, the 1965 brochure begins:

> Within a single lifetime, our physical environment has been changed almost beyond recognition. But there has been little corresponding change in how we, as individuals, relate to the world and experience reality. Such a change is inevitable, however—indeed, it is imminent. New tools and techniques of the human potentiality—generally unknown to the public and to much of the intellectual community—are already at hand; many more are presently under development.

By 1965 the Esalen group included leaders in psychology such as Rollo May, Gardner Murphy, Carl Rogers, and B. F. Skinner; Bishop James Pike joined Alan Watts in a workshop blending Eastern and Western religious mysticism; J. B. Rhine offered ESP and mental telepathy; several Indian musicians and temple dancers performed; a harpist gave a concert. LSD, then in its heyday, received attention in a seminar called "LSD and Human Potential."

By 1966, the encounter game had grown so rapidly that "advanced creative encounter" was offered for those who had already been through basic encounter. The body seemed to outrank other specialties, accounting for almost 20 percent of the workshops. Abraham Maslow, Michael Polanyi, and Bill Schutz made their Esalen debuts.

By 1967 encounter had become big; Bill Schutz occupied the inside cover of the Esalen brochure. Now called "More Joy," his workshop included "body movement, body awareness, fantasy, psychodrama, and the microlab." The blurb also promised: "There will be some exploration of media such as poetry, drama improvisation, and creative thinking." Just in case things got dull.

Reading these brochures, it seems remarkable that the same mind-expanding interaction can be described in so many ways, yet still sound the same. In all cases the brochures promised that "the spectrum of the participant's experience and self-expression" would be expanded. Each participant was expected to have gone through basic encounter or sensitivity-training groups, to be sympathetic to the supernatural and open to Eastern mysticism, and to be eager to "increase the natural range and freedom of body functioning, strengthen the sense of personal identity, and work toward spontaneous nonverbal expression."

Stu Miller has said, "Esalen is a very complex institution, sort of like a college. There's a part of Mike Murphy that is very proper, that is embarrassed by people like Bill Schutz, Fritz Perls, and Ida Rolf; but he's big enough to say that these people do have something, that they deserve a forum, and he gives it to them. This is why he's the center of Esalen and why Esalen never could have happened without him. It's also the reason why other growth centers have a hard time—because they don't have him."

Esalen spokesmen frequently point out that encounter has never made up more than 15 percent of their program. Of course, that depends on what is meant by encounter. Strictly speaking, workshops labeled "encounter" probably make up only that percentage of Esalen programs. But if you consider encounter an ideology, an amalgam of Eastern religious themes, body activities, a new educational scene, and radical therapies, then except for an occasional visitor with a distinctly different identification (such as Buckminster Fuller), Esalen is 100 percent encounter.

In April 1970, and again in April 1971, Esalen Institute came east and staged three-day exhibitions of psychological and physical awareness techniques in what must have been the record encounter game playoffs of all time.

Months before each exhibition, people in the fields of education, health, and industrial personnel began to receive multiple mailings of the brightly colored Esalen announcements, which, when opened to their full 16 x 22 inches, could double as posters. In a letter on the back of the flier, Stu Miller stated that the experiential disciplines which "many people have found to be exciting and helpful in their lives," would be available. Miller also noted that, besides their eagerness to raise money "for research and scholarships," the Esalen leaders were coming to New York in order to provide people on the East Coast "a chance to sample, first hand, what Esalen is about and to see for themselves . . . that life can be much richer than any of us had previously thought."

That richness of life was being offered at the Hotel Diplomat on Forty-third Street, just east of Broadway. Once the scene of elegant affairs, the Diplomat now seemed faded and dingy. Esalen had sold far too many tickets for the Diplomat's limited facilities. There were no reserved seats at any of the workshops, nor was anyone about to say when a room was full. For the crowd to move from one demonstration to another required designating one stairway as "up" and the only other one as "down."

The Esalen leaders had made a vain attempt to transport California to New York. The occasional person in conservative dress stood out among the more frequent dungarees, tie-dyed shirts, Indian dresses, and love beads. The crowd was almost entirely white, primarily young (late teens to late twenties); peace signs and long hair were everywhere. "Beautiful," "dynamite," "relating," "open," "heavy trip," "out of sight," were the words most often overheard. But although the New Yorkers emulated the California style, they couldn't quite pull it off.

On Friday night Bernard Gunther, Esalen's chief expert on massage and body conditioning, warmed up the crowd with a sensory awakening demonstration. Soon everybody was jumping around, running, skipping, and hopping in waves from one end of the Grand Ballroom to the other. By midnight, when the first evening's program was officially over, lots of new "intimate relationships" had been started, though any number of vague lonely wanderers were seen floating around the hotel looking for someone to make contact with.

The real encounter demonstration began the next morning when Bill Schutz made his only appearance in the 1970 exhibition. He led an open encounter much like the one I'd attended in San Francisco, and it seemed as though most of the four thousand people who'd registered were present. The apportionment of space was a good indicator of what Esalen and the crowd considered important: the bigger rooms were always used for the experiential sessions. Even so, after several hours of intense relating, the hundreds of people crowded into these poorly ventilated rooms created a hot, damp, sweaty, locker-room stench.

When not engaged in the various encounter games, most players behaved like the slightly disoriented teachers, social workers, and students they actually were the rest of the year. The fee for that weekend of intimacy training was $75, or $35 by the day. There were many discussions of how much money Esalen was making, but few players seemed resentful. If Miller's estimate of four thousand players in 1970 is correct, the gross must have been $300,000. At the mailing rate of 1.6 cents, Esalen would have paid only $1600 to mail 100,000 announcements; and even with liberal estimates of the other costs, they should probably have cleared close to $250,000.

While the whole convention had a distinct air of commercialism, Esalen leaders did draw the line at one moneymaking opportunity. According to Stu Miller, resplendent in a red velvet jacket, the producers of the film *Woodstock* had approached him and other Esalen leaders with the idea of filming the entire weekend and releasing it commercially. Certainly the exhibition did have the quality of another Woodstock, and it was easy to see why the producers felt they'd have a market for their film. But the Esalen leaders, always wary of the press, films, and tape recordings, said no.

When I asked some encounter leaders why freedom of the press was being curtailed in the free atmosphere of an Esalen-sponsored public event, their answer was something to the effect that people would be hampered from developing intimacies if they knew that others were taking pictures of them. From my own observations I knew that those engaged in intimacies, whether necking, eyeball-staring, or touching, were far too busy to either notice or care about anyone snapping their picture. I'm quite sure that encounter pros merely wanted to avoid examination of their practices by anyone who did not participate in them.

Almost every one of the session leaders attempted to conjure up microlab intimacy. And, regardless of the topic for the microlab, the leader would begin with some version of the usual Esalen injunction, "Everyone is responsible for himself, and nobody has to do what he doesn't want to do." George I. Brown, author of *Human Teaching for Human Learning,* and one of Esalen's less flamboyant leaders, did a workshop at the Esalen II Benefit in New York, working with teachers and guidance counselors. He stated the usual warning, and added: "This is a very subtle ground rule, because it means that whatever you do, or whatever happens to you in terms of your experience here, is really your responsibility. If you do something, it's your responsibility; if you don't do something, it's also your responsibility."

Brown went on to suggest that each person in the group introduce himself to another in what he called "a special way"—namely, to introduce himself by bragging about something. When my turn came, I gave my name and indicated that I didn't feel like bragging. Even though I was exercising the permission explicitly granted by Brown not five minutes before, other members of the group quickly reacted with questions like, "Aren't you going to tell us *anything* about yourself?" and "Why don't you share yourself with us?"

Morris Parloff, writing in the *International Journal of Group Psychotherapy* in 1970, commented, "The mere announcement that participants are free to decline participation is no assurance that the rights of the nonconformist will be protected. Free choice can only be exercised when the individual is not threatened by humiliation, reprisal, rejection, or ridicule."

A highlight of the Esalen II weekend was a lecture entitled "Mental Health; Continuous Satori-Samadhi," given by John Lilly, M.D., whose pathfinding research on dolphins once made him one of America's best known and most respected scientists. A thin, fair-headed, soft-spoken man, Lilly typified the encounter game's quest for otherworldly fulfillment in a mathematical description of levels of psychic awareness derived from his own drug trips.

He started by flatly informing the audience which appeared especially young and drug-oriented that they were all at level 48, because they were attentive and ready to learn. He then went on to describe level 24, where feelings operate more strongly but not exclusively. Then he continued:

Level 12 is the level of enjoyment and bliss. In Indian yoga terminology this is Samadhi Amanda—the blissful Samadhi. This is where you are still in your body; you feel the energies coming from other people, you see the energies, experience them. Those of you who have taken psychedelic trips know this state. It is the first stage of the acid trip—a good trip, not the down trip. Another experience you probably have had which gives you a 12 is sexual activity with the right partner. There are other ways of getting to it but 12 is a state which we normally do not experience unless we're on a vacation.

We were all told that we could get out of our bodies to level 6, and that it would be a familiar departure for those who'd had "far-out drug trips," or sexual trips. Clearly, the loss of what is technically called "body ego" was being described. When he got to level 3, Lilly started to explain the altered state of consciousness but finally said it would be impossible to describe "merging with the astral bodies" verbally.

But of course, there's a bad side too—

When you start heading for 96 you are going down. When you get to levels higher than 48 you are going *down*. 96 is what happens to the ordinary man when he's drunk too much. 196 means you're a living ball of pain, and so on.

As if to confirm my feeling about the religious nature of the encounter game, the 1971 Esalen show offered two different services on Sunday morning, each of which reflected an important component of the encounter ideology.

The Grand Ballroom of the Diplomat, recently crowded with groupers struggling in a dominance lineup and screaming at the top of their lungs, became strangely beautiful during Alan Watts' Aquarian Age Religious Service. Watts is a master dramatist whose study of the Eastern religions has helped him develop a presentation which could capture the hearts of any audience. In the darkened room that Sunday morning, the participants sat cross-legged on the floor, with hushed expectancy. Dressed in slacks and a sports shirt, Watts presented an introductory discussion of meditation, religion, consciousness, and the search for inner peace. After he'd set the intellectual and spiritual tone, he disappeared behind the curtains and reappeared shortly in a flowing yellow robe. He is a tall, thin man, ascetic and stately in his movements, and his proud bearing commands instant attention from a large audience. At his side were two girls also dressed in Indian robes. Incense was burning, and a variety of Indian brass instruments would occasionally sound.

Without the excitement that accompanies the search for inner peace in so many of the Esalen demonstrations, Watts' ceremony had a calm and quiet tone. A few trained musicians in the crowd served as harmonizers, and Watts, with his resonant voice, had little trouble in leading the group in singing the Hari Krishna, some oriental chants, or mantras, and several versions of "Hallelujah."

Meanwhile, downstairs in the also darkened Crystal Room, three dropouts from America's leading religions held a "Sunday Morning Service." Harvey Koch, Sam Keen, and Richard Rubenstein, all Ph.D.'s, spoke to the audience about their own childhood experiences with religion and related tales of the "true" religion—religion that goes beyond the confines of any organized church. And not far away were a discussion of Gestalt therapy, a rolfing demonstration, and a lecture on brainwave feedback. Best of all for mainstream encounter religionists, in a basement alcove called the Palm Room, John Heider was presenting what he called the "Frontiers of Encounter Technique," but what boiled down to deep-breathing exercises and standing with one's eyes closed, feeling imaginary baskets in the air.

Many other growth centers have modeled themselves after Esalen. In 1967 there were some forty growth centers in the United States. A year later the number had grown to eighty-five; and by 1971, according to the Association for Humanistic Psychology, there were 163 growth centers in the United States, eight in Canada, and nine in other countries including Germany, Mexico, Belgium, England, and Australia.

In the United States, encounter has spread from the West Coast eastward. Although the movement is large in terms of the number of people involved, the number of leaders is relatively small, since a given leader's activities can account for several thousand encounters per year. The number of encounter leaders who are widely recognized is smaller still. After establishing a reputation they, like Bill Schutz and other Flying Circus members, travel the encounter circuit regularly. The brochures of all of the growth centers include the same vague promises of growth, personal enhancement, and personal development. The language always features the same set of key words, and each growth center may be viewed as a local house of worship for this new religion.

Here are some growth centers which have developed on the Esalen model, with excerpts from their liturgies:

The nonprofit, tax-exempt Aureon Institute, with offices in New York City and a 130-acre retreat near Woodstock, New York, offers one of the broadest ranges of programs in the East. Founded mainly by Harold Streitfeld, Ph.D., Aureon's aim is to "uncover and maximize man's inherent resources for living life to the fullest." Its founders see the program as an "ongoing experience, ever-changing and ever-growing," and acknowledge that their "programs make use of therapeutic methods from psychiatry and psychology," as well as "games" derived from the theater, dance, religion, and art. Most recently Aureon's copywriter came up with a gem: clients may choose from the tasty mental delights of the Aureon "psychomat."

Nominally under the supervision of several degreed professionals, Aureon has offered weekend workshops in the country bearing such titles as "The Dynamics of Psychosynthesis" (emphasizing "methods for developing will, empathy, imagination and intuition"); "The Joys of Play" (an opportunity to bring one "closer to the spontaneous, free-creative expression of the long-forgotten child within"); and "Quest for Zest—for the Unattached, Either Single or Divorced" ("more zest can be put into everyday life by helping males and females gain self-confidence and skills they need to tune-in on each other, communicate and cooperate, and let their spirits soar"). Cost for an Aureon weekend, meals included, runs from $76 to $86—about the same as a weekend at Grossinger's, the Concord, or other nearby Catskills resorts. Aureon also offers two-week workshops at $450 per person or $800 per couple, marathons, and ongoing groups that meet weekly (with a choice of "bio-energetic, eclectic, Synanon type, or Fritz Perls' Gestalt approach").

Quest, a profit-making operation in Washington, D.C., keeps the people on its mailing list off balance by never sending them two pieces of mail the same size or shape. Along with the usual range of workshops, marathons, and "drop-in encounters," Quest offers continuing encounter workshops for those who wish to examine themselves "through interpersonal interactions at levels deeper than those of conventional relationships." The groups which are limited to twelve members, meet once a week, with new members added as old ones drop out. The cost is $50 for four sessions, but drop-in encounters are also available at $7 to $9 per session.

In addition to the usual array of visitors from Esalen and the rest of the encounter circuit, Quest offers encounters on the beach at Ocean City, Maryland, in a houseboat on the Potomac, and under sail in the Chesapeake Bay. One February participants were invited to fly to Miami, board a seventy-foot yacht, and sail the surrounding waters for five days of encountering—"truly a voyage of discovery."

One of the group leaders at Quest is a movie star who has a doctor of divinity degree and is qualified to teach Kundalini Yoga. Corinne Calvet, the Quest brochure tells us, "received the name Karuma, meaning Compassion, from Satchidananda, one of her teachers who, along with Yogananda and Yogi Bhagan, have been influential in developing Miss Calvet's spiritual life." Miss Calvet leads a workshop called "The Spiritual Path," in which participants are guided to "a deeper understanding and a clearer vision of their own paths."

Like a few other growth centers, Quest offers "individual consultation" to people "who wish an ongoing experience" in "self-actualization" via "techniques of humanistic psychology." Quest does not call its program psychotherapy, and adds that it is "not for extremely emotionally disturbed persons."

Anthos, in New York City, also offers "Individual Counseling," but they like to use two counselors at a time for each player. They state that these three-party sessions "will combine the focus and intimacy of the classic analytic session with the more active and dynamic structures of the group process."

To a large extent, Anthos' program reflects the thinking of Martin Shepard, M.D., who, except for one chemist-turned-dentist-turned-encounter-leader, is the only staff member with any professional training. Shepard pretends to pass his training on to Anthos' staff. In addition to the full range of growth center offerings, Shepard, who calls himself "boy psychiatrist"—and who is known as much for the *Time* magazine picture of him with an encounter group participant, both nude, as for his attacks on conventional therapy—has led Anthos into the most openly anti-psychotherapy stance yet taken by any growth center. He leads "a series for dropouts . . . who have endured traditional psycho-therapies and found them wanting." Shepard's alternative is a week-long encounter session every three months for a year, with "specific self-development programs . . . for each group member to work on in the months between sessions." The fee is $950.

Paul Bindrim and Associates, based in Los Angeles, specializes in nude encounters held in swimming pools. Participants are assured that once nude in the warm pool, they will be "gently held, rocked, and massaged, permitting regression and release of 'intense infantile' emotions. This condition of weightlessness, womblike warmth, seems to reawaken the profound trust in life lost since infancy. . . . Emotional releases may then resolve into peak experiences with breakthroughs into new depths of inner strength, beauty, and human understanding." Bindrim promises that the process "is particularly useful for those who wish to develop their capacity for emotional relationships, accept and respect their bodies, become more at ease in touching people, and improve their sexual relationships." Cost: ninety-five dollars for a twenty-hour session.

Bindrim is quite the individual entrepreneur, though his shop is classed among the growth centers. None of his brochures seems to identify his "associates"; rather, they offer for sale or rental an array of reprints, tape seminars in how to have a peak experience (at fifteen dollars a reel), and his by now famous twenty-five-minute film showing a nude marathon. Mostly Bindrim is to be seen exposing himself to new nude groups on the growth-center circuit, but if you can't catch his act on tour, you need only tear off the bottom of a flier and enclose a check.

A recent Bindrim flier announced the opening of the first Humanitarium:

> *WHAT IS A HUMANITARIUM?* Most cities have an aquarium where nude fish can be seen in their natural environment. Mays Landing is the first city to have a humanitarium, a pool in which nude people may also be seen without distortions. This newly completed facility has been specially constructed to accommodate nude marathons. It is equipped

with underwater stereo sound and an underwater color-organ. Located within two hours' driving time from Washington or New York, it is also serviced by ground transportation from the Atlantic City and Philadelphia airports. This makes it possible for us to conduct effective sessions on the East Coast and we are now able to offer our services to growth centers and other organizations who wish to sponsor their own nude sessions.

The growth centers that have recently sprung up across the nation promise warmth, human contact, and personal growth. The names always have a ring of dedication to the worship of "human potential": The Center for the Whole Person (Philadelphia); Explorations Institute (Berkeley, California); and the Athena Center for Creative Living (with intimacy labs in Mexico and Aliquippa, Pennsylvania).

Several centers in New York have an interesting twist: GROW (Group Relations Ongoing Workshops), Groups for Meaningful Communications, and WILL (Workshop Institute for Living Learning). Like the other centers, they consider themselves educational institutions, but they structure their encounter programs somewhat like college courses and view themselves as teaching others to run encounter groups and growth centers. As a result, many people who run groups in New York claim as their credentials a course at one or the other of these places. GROW has recently begun to offer a mail-order-type Ph.D. course through an affiliation with Indiana Northern University. Two months after GROW announced this affiliation, officials of the New York State Education Department made it clear that these doctorates would not be acceptable for admission to state examinations leading to recognized professional standing.

More recently, investigative reporter Ralph Stowe of the Chicago *Tribune* (1972) unearthed the full story of I.N.U., which turns out to be little more than a few shacks and an old fire engine designated as the university's College of Fire Sciences. I.N.U.'s "president," Gordon DaCosta, gave himself the first Ph.D. awarded by his university, and has since gone on to add to his own credentials a divinity degree and a doctorate in science. DaCosta sits in an office piled high with legitimate college catalogs from which he works out bigger and better curricula, degrees, and impressive affiliations for his university, which is now interlocked with a fringe seminary, GROW in New York, and a Canadian diploma mill called Philathea College.

The worthy "doctors" at the helm of this operation have been busily building a financial empire. Extrapolating from the encounter-world notion that experience is equal to education, they've given a string of certificates to encounter participants which purportedly qualify them to treat mental illness with encounter methods. Not content to just collect fees for these diplomas and the group experiences, these operators developed a multimillion-dollar scheme to set up a nationwide string of clinics called Neighborhood Centers for Human Development in church basements, staffed by their graduates who would, of course, find a way to funnel fees back to the head office.

More than sixty "practitioners" with fraudulent credentials have turned up and the whole network is, at this writing, under investigation by the New York State Attorney General, the New York City Department of Consumer Affairs, and the Minister of Colleges and Universities in Ontario.

With countless variations, the number of growth centers continues to grow; but in each case the range of offerings is pretty much the same. The basic encounter comes first, with special groups for couples, singles, divorce contemplaters, etc. After that one learns through further encountering how to help others encounter. But from the proliferation of variations and combinations it is apparent that such encounters don't really satisfy. If basic encounter really succeeded, there'd be little need for Encounter II.

Evidently business in the encounter world has fallen off, and I've heard several encounter game stars jokingly say that the movement has passed its peak.

Attendance at the Esalen exhibitions fell from four thousand in 1970 to twenty-five hundred in 1971; of that number, I'd estimate that 15 to 20 percent had also attended the previous year. Repeaters or no, the drop-off in gate receipts probably meant a gross of $112,000 less than for the first show. The seminar business was slow all over the nation that year, and there was a falling off of every sort of educational and training activities, including college and graduate school applications.

But I believe that the real reason for the decreased attendance is that the encounter movement has peaked. When Esalen first came to New York in 1970, it was a new wave; but by 1971 it really seemed to be an old show. The discomfort of the Esalen people was evident in every medium—a few hastily arranged television interview shows, advertisements in the *Village Voice* and the *New York Times,* and spot announcements on the major New York radio stations. To pack in the last-minute crowd, the proceedings were broadcast live over radio. But despite the efforts of the Esalen leaders, the turnout was small, and there was no repeat performance in 1972.

While business may be declining at Esalen and the other major growth centers, most encounter leaders feel that the movement is just bracing for a surge into the hinterlands. One joke that briefly made the rounds among encounter leaders was that once Des Moines and Atlanta had growth centers (as they now do), the movement would be dead. The sense of being an elite was an important quality for the early encounter group leaders. And though the movement claims broad egalitarian goals, it appears that now the old pros are becoming jealous of the young upstarts.

4

Body Manipulators

Any social movement is shaped by its leaders. Their personalities affect their actions and their styles of communication, and to the extent that students, followers, and participants emulate their style, a social movement takes on the personality characteristics of its leaders.

The encounter game has the characteristics of not one but a blend of cults of personality. As I examined the game, the personalities of key encounter movement figures began to emerge as the driving forces in this psychological subculture.

This follow-the-leader process carries with it certain inherent errors. Since followers tend to be lesser men than leaders, their imitations tend to magnify the errors and limitations of the innovators. Further, in their reliance upon authority, imitators are subject to less self-criticism than innovators. History is full of examples, like the astronomers caught for centuries in the Aristotelian view of the earth as center of the universe, until Copernicus sweated out the modern view.

In my opinion we don't have any potential Copernicuses in the encounter game; as yet we don't even have any figures who have earned the more pedestrian but worthy rank of twentieth-century scientists. What we do have is a string of leaders, usually from the fringe of the mental-health field, who on the basis of their own informal experiments with people have created techniques, treated people with them, and disseminated their methods almost entirely without validating their results or subjecting their work to formal scientific scrutiny.

Operating outside the confines of medical, psychological, and scientific ethical traditions, the encounter game stars nevertheless claim the mantle of scientific authority for their "innovations," taking the stance that as professionals they have the right to develop new treatment methods. They seem more outspoken on that right than on the commensurate ethical obligation not to introduce treatment methods before they have been shown not to induce harm, and, further, shown to have a clear positive effect.

When the issue is treatment for disease, arguments can be made for both daring and cautious approaches. Certainly when a fatal illness is involved, few would question the need for experimentation by physicians and researchers. But we've learned from past errors, and under today's ethical and legal constraints no one would think of introducing a drug—no matter what the disease—unless it had been proven both nontoxic and beneficial in lower animals.

For the most part, encounterists don't openly claim to be treating any disease other than the human condition. Nor, as they grudgingly acknowledge, has there been any real proof that what they offer works. Certainly, the medical and scientific basis for their activities is shaky, to say the least.

If we grant the dubious right of a medical practitioner to introduce a new and as yet unproven technique on his own authority, we assume him to be qualified to make reasonably objective observations of his results and to report them to his colleagues for further scrutiny. It would strike most of us as absurd to grant that same right of clinical investigation to the patients and untrained followers of such an experimenter. Yet by and large that is the situation that prevails throughout the encounter world. With no more training than having participated in a few group experiences under the direction of those admittedly experimenting stars, countless numbers of untrained "leaders" have opened up shop, simply by imitating the leaders they've briefly observed. Interestingly enough, the stars encourage the imitation, probably because they need followers in order to maintain their own positions.

In this chapter and the next we'll take a look at the principal leader-models and some typical imitators. I've divided them into "body manipulators" and "word manipulators," more for the sake of clarity than because the distinction actually holds up throughout the encounter world. Actually, while these particular stars clearly lean in one direction or another, your local encounter entrepreneur is likely to create his own style—depending on whose workshops he happened to be in most recently, which star was ascending when he was at Esalen, and whose encounter style gave him the largest personal jolt when he was a participant.

Regardless of how the leaders try to achieve them, intense emotional experiences are "where it's at," as the most common encounter game cliché reminds us repeatedly. In every variation of encounter, from T-grouping for businessmen to religious ecstasy for third-world young adults, emotion is the path, if not the goal, of "growth." Every theory of human personality change has recognized, to one degree or another, the fact that emotions are crucial if the behavior of a group of its members is to be changed. All systems of educating the young or training adults—from ancient Sparta to American elementary schools, from Chinese Communist prison camps to Trappist monasteries—have tried for the maximum emotional impact on those to be molded.

No encounterist, of course, has formally studied the effects of expressing strong emotions in encounter groups. Nor has much recognition been given to the fact that emotional expression, however necessary, is only one factor in personality change. The focus of attention has simply been on stimulating the emotional responses of the group members, with the presumption that experiencing strong emotions in a group somehow facilitates changes in each person's range of emotional awareness of others and his ability to handle his own feelings.

Careful questioning of encounterists on this point brings out two central ideas: that emotional expression leads to personality changes, and that emotional expression is good in and of itself. The first has been proven untrue, the second is an oversimplification; yet in combination these two ideas form a powerful cornerstone in the encounter faith. As each player discovers these "truths" for himself, his conversion to encounter is solidified.

People obviously differ in the range of emotional experience they can comfortably tolerate. Since Freud, most observers have seen these differences in terms of personality development, and have recognized that emotional experiences too intense to be easily assimilated may be repressed. This is especially true of childhood experiences, when the resources for assimilation are less developed. Events that overload the child's emotional system become repressed, and the repression itself influences the subsequent receiving and sending of signals.

In psychotherapy, therapist and patient work toward increasing the patient's range of emotional control, both sending and receiving, and usually this is accomplished by examining those life instances in which the emotional controls failed to work. In most cases therapist and patient first attempt to arrive at an understanding of the problem, and then attempt remediation.

In the encounter world the same human limitation of emotional capacity is a primary issue. But since it is often assumed that everyone experiences pretty much the same limitations, the painstaking work of arriving at understanding a person's particular emotional capacities and limitations is passed over. Further, most encounterists prefer provoking emotional experiences *directly* to talking about emotions. The simplest way to do that is to do something—indeed, almost anything—to people's bodies.

All of the encounter games described in Chapter II are designed to—and do—provoke strong emotions. Most encounter leaders today use physical activity for this purpose. The games described above are the most common, but variations may include group massage, theater and dance techniques, children's games, "sculpting" of bodies into tableaux, and anything else that will stimulate a sensory response. Not content with setting up situations in which players interact emotionally, many encounterists adopt unusual subroutines in which leaders or other players directly manipulate the bodies of participants with a view toward generating more immediate reactions, more intense levels of response, and, hopefully, more rapid personality changes. The first of these systems is known as rolfing.

The radical process known as "structural integration," or "rolfing," largely developed by Dr. Ida Rolf, is an approach to the unlocking of neuroses through exercise and massages that is now being used quite extensively in the encounter world. Rolfing, as done by Rolf, is a series of deep and often painful massages of all the major muscle groups, including the face and mouth. At least in some cases, although without official sanction, rolfing has included penetration of any and all body orifices. In my first discussion of rolfing with Bill Schutz, he told me that in order to change the body's "integration and habitual carriage," rolfing should be done with delicate and sensitive fingers and a knowledge of musculature.

Shortly after that conversation a New York analyst, who preferred to remain anonymous, reported the case of a twenty-six-year-old girl who in her second rolfing session found those delicate and sensitive fingers inside her vagina and became severely psychotic. It seems that the man behind the fingers had not bothered to take a case history. If he had he might have hesitated, since the patient had previously been hospitalized for acute psychosis triggered by having been raped.

I mentioned this case in my *New York Times* article, and shortly after it appeared I got first a letter and then a telephone call from one of Ida Rolf's assistants. She started by saying, "We're not angry with you," and explained that she and Dr. Rolf felt that rolfing was being misused, mislabeled, and misapplied in the encounter world, primarily by Bill Schutz and the Esalen people. She then invited me to attend a workshop with Dr. Rolf, who would be in New York soon.

The workshop was held at Anthos, and its appearance there again points up the networklike nature of the encounter game and its playing fields. Anthos occupies the top floor of a rather dingy loft building on East Twenty-second Street in New York City. When I approached that Saturday morning a drunken man was asleep on the doorstep. Wine bottles and newspapers were scattered in the entrance to the building, and the smell of urine was unmistakable.

I rode up a creaky elevator and stepped into a different world. Anthos is decorated in a style that can only be called "growth center groovy." That means psychedelic posters on the walls, carpets and heavy pillows on the floor, almost no furniture, and raw pine collapsible doors so that the space can be expanded. Despite the encounter movement's manifestly liberated view of women, Anthos displays a garishly painted water cooler in the shape of a woman's body, with two spigots done up to resemble breasts and the catch basin as the mound of Venus. As I entered, a few minutes late, I heard a voice that I knew must be Ida Rolf's saying, " . . . and we're not interested in the orifices, we're interested in the whole man!"

Dr. Rolf was sitting in a director's chair with about thirty people on the floor at her feet. As no other chairs were in evidence, I pulled up an overstuffed pillow that seemed about eight feet long and snuggled down for the lecture demonstration.

Dr. Rolf, a white-haired woman in her late seventies, has about her the air of a person who has been involved with the body all her life: she exudes the kind of healthy old age one sometimes sees in tough old gym teachers and health-food fans.

Rolf earned her Ph.D. in 1920 at Columbia University in biochemistry and physiology. After a dozen years' work in biochemistry she started working in "applied physiology," and developed her system of manipulative techniques. Knowing her lack of a medical or even a chiropractic license, I assumed she must be very confident of her techniques, or very sure that she won't encounter a paranoid eager to sue her for bending a limb too hard. In terms of personality, Ida Rolf was dogmatic and autocratic, accepting no criticism and offering no answers to questions that she did not care for.

She spent the next several hours talking at the audience in clearly nonencounter style. Probably accustomed to a more interactive style of communication, the listeners sank lower and lower on the floor as they heard more and more hard-sell explanations of how many different ways rolfing is health-generating. Though attendees had spent forty-five dollars each to hear the lecture, they didn't seem turned on by it.

Basically what she described, redescribed, and overdescribed was a theory that could be put into one sentence: the body must line up straight to be healthy; most of us don't line up perpendicular to the floor, hence we're not healthy.

Rolfing, she said, is the solution. It is a series of ten hour-long sessions in which the patient—or victim—goes through "carefully graded" steps of body manipulations. Dr. Rolf explained that these manipulations are designed to stretch the fascia, the connective tissue between muscle and bone. This is done in such a way that the body "snaps back" into its natural, genetically ordained, healthy state. Each hour in the sequence has a different focus, the general idea being that every individual muscle group must be treated before the total body can reintegrate. Chiropractors and osteopaths have long worked on the principle that smaller areas of the fascia can be stretched, but Rolf decided that for the job to stick, the whole body must be dealt with lest some chronically defensive stance cause a given muscle group to tighten up again.

Dr. Rolf illustrated her talk with a series of line drawings of bodies, with boxes drawn around different segments. The boxes for a body that was out of alignment were stacked in a precariously balanced mound, and of course the rolfed body looked more solid with the stack of boxes lined up neatly. She used photographs and drawings to illustrate many postures in which the body is not perpendicular to the floor, explaining that when the body is out of alignment, the muscles and internal organs do not work with maximum efficiency and ease.

Dr. Rolf was annoyed with the few members of the audience who dared ask her questions. One that came up in several forms was, "How is this different from just good posture?" Dr. Rolf rather testily explained that posture is only the way one momentarily stands or walks or holds one's body, while rolfing changes the body's basic structure permanently.

I felt that her impatience with her questioners fit the role of the misunderstood scientific genius whose ideas are too new, too radical, and too much of a challenge for the scientific establishment to cope with. Continually annoyed by the stupidity of the questions, she kept responding with statements like, "It would take many years of intensive training before you could understand that."

Ever since the days of medicine shows, one type of stage direction has succeeded in convincing gullible audiences: look for yourselves and be convinced by your own eyes, your very own senses.

Dr. Rolf treated us to such evidence in two ways: during the morning lecture we saw numerous before-and-after photos; then, in the afternoon, we saw it all happen before our very eyes—a real live body was restructured.

It seems that it is customary for Dr. Rolf or her chiropractor son, Dr. Richard Demmerle, to take Polaroid snapshots of rolfing subjects. In many cases, his before-and-after shots showed a dramatic difference; for, as Dr. Rolf later mentioned, chiropractors often referred their "most difficult" cases to her, and the before shots often showed a rather distorted body. In comparison, the after shots seemed a vast improvement.

Perhaps because this "data gathering" seems to be the extent of the family's commitment to science, a great deal of busy activity surrounds the photographing of rolfing demonstrations, with "Dr. Dick," as his mother calls him, busily arranging his cameras and lining up the subject. One of the several volunteers had stripped down to his jockey shorts and was being photographed by Dr. Dick as we filed in. The group again sat on the floor, this time in Anthos' large skylighted room. The young man, called Steve, was almost naked; he seemed chilled and apprehensive when he made his appearance in the middle of the room. A mat had been laid out for him to stand on. His obvious discomfort occasioned a bit of compassionate good humor from the crowd. Certainly he had volunteered to place himself in an unusual situation, not the least of which must have included a sense of being a specimen on display.

Dr. Rolf did nothing to dispel such a sensation. She asked us to observe Steve's body very carefully, paying special attention to areas of disproportionate musculature and stance. She asked him to turn around slowly so that everybody could get a good look at him. A few questions and suggestions from Dr. Rolf led the audience to make observations about what they saw. For example, his right side seemed slightly more developed than his left side (not at all uncommon for a right-handed person); he held himself hunched slightly forward "as though in a protective stance"; and his breathing (like that of anyone undergoing some anxiety) was clearly from the chest and shoulders, not from the diaphragm. The man had seemed fairly well put together at the outset, but after this auction-block display he seemed to have shrunk a few inches and certainly was paler.

Dr. Dick, a blond, muscular man whose face remained devoid of expression throughout the demonstration, began by placing his arm under the back of the now prone Steve and tugging upward, at the same time pulling on the muscles at his sides. Steve began to emit grunts and growls of discomfort or pain. Then, with further proddings of his stomach, chest, rib cage, and spine, the first "amazing" result began to occur: his breathing seemed to come more from his diaphragm than from his chest. (Of course, if someone is immobilizing your chest by stretching it upward from the spine, it's a lot easier to breathe from the abdomen.) Dr. Dick seemed at first to be concentrating just on expanding that chest, but it wasn't long before Steve's arms were pulled, his feet prodded, his legs turned up and stretched, and the muscles around his hips, buttocks, and thighs pushed, elbowed, kneed, and shouldered by the brawny doctor into painfully new but "much better" positions. For example, after one of Steve's legs had been prodded and pulled upward well beyond its original limit, the arc of movement was compared with that of the unstretched limb. A stretched limb, we all saw, moves farther than an unstretched limb.

While this was going on Mother Ida and Dr. Dick would occasionally exchange commentaries on the location of the mysterious knots of tension in Steve's body. The language was rolfese mixed in with some basic anatomy of the spinal column. (Dr. Rolf: "I think it's between the fourth and fifth." Dr. Dick: "No, it's the fifth and sixth." Dr. Rolf: "Try it between the fourth and fifth and then spread and crease him out a bit, and see if you can get to it.")

Dr. Dick, sweating, blank-faced, working hard, continued to apply the force of his own thick but sensitive fingers, well-muscled arms, elbows, and even knees against the rather frail-looking young man being manipulated on the floor. There were moments when the scene looked like a bout between a professional wrestler and a sleeping paraplegic intellectual.

The group decision-making and evaluation process so familiar in the encounter world took place at the end of the demonstration. A few suggestions and queries to the audience by Dr. Rolf elicited several statements by the members about the amazing differences they could now see in Steve's body. These people, of course, had been watching for, awaiting, and expecting something to occur for five or six hours, and not surprisingly some of them found that Steve breathed differently, stood differently, seemed differently balanced, and even expressed dizziness upon getting up. We had all been with him during his travail, had heard his grunts of pain, and certainly we all hoped it had not been in vain.

Having been rolfed for an hour, Steve now seemed to be an entirely different physical specimen. He even said he felt better; I felt sure that after an hour of such treatment, just *stopping* would make one feel better. It also did not surprise me that he felt dizzy on getting up—almost anyone who undergoes that kind of physical stress would, and even psychoanalytic patients often feel dizzy when they get up from an hour on the couch. The audience, however, took the dizziness as proof of the treatment's success.

Few present were willing to raise the question of how long these effects would last. To my perhaps nonbody-oriented eye, not much had really happened. Of course, this was just the beginning, and if Steve or any of us wanted the whole trip, then nine more sessions and a healthy fee would be called for.

After we'd taken a break for a few minutes, we were divided into two groups—half to watch while the others lay down on the floor and participated in some rolfing warmup techniques. Part of the demonstration was having the prone players extend their arms straight out from the shoulders without looking. The observers readily spotted people who thought their arms were at right angles to their bodies, but who actually held them either high or low. This fairly common phenomenon—that perception of the upright is largely dependent on visual cues—was interpreted by most of the observers as proof of their need to be rolfed.

We then went through a series of brief exercises designed to confront each person with the limitations of his mucle movements. My understanding is that most people who are not active athletically do not utilize the full arc of potential movement, and that even many who *are* athletic become muscle-bound. So this demonstration, too, could hardly fail to make most of us feel like wrecks sadly in need of a little rolfing.

The *pièce de résistance* came as a result of what seemed like an extraordinary incident.

Earlier in the day, an anxious, pallid-looking man in his forties had approached me and said, "You're the guy who wrote the article in the *Times*, right?" When I said yes, he pulled up a chair, sat down, and began staring at me. When I asked him if he wanted to talk about the article, he said yes and again lapsed into a silent stare.

"What did you think of the article?" I asked.

"What do you think I thought?" he said.

"I don't know what you thought of it," I said. "You approached me."

"Well, I didn't like it," he finally said.

"What didn't you like about it?"

I could see him struggling with the temptation to say, "What do you think I didn't like about it?" but instead he said, "You obviously have never been in an encounter group; otherwise you couldn't write such a bad article."

I pointed out that the article clearly described groups in which I had participated.

"It must have been a brief encounter group."

"I've been in many groups, up to two weeks in length."

"You ought to have done more than observe. A good group would get you involved."

"I've done marathons. I've hugged and kissed, cried and fought. I've been the whole route, and I still think there's a lot wrong with encounter."

"Impossible!"

"Why—because I don't end up seeing it the way you do?"

"Yes, that's right." And with that he got up and left.

That afternoon, while Dr. Rolf was leading us in some simple hand exercises, this same man suddenly began to make all sorts of noises with his breathing and his lips.

Dr. Rolf and Dr. Dick rose quickly, went over, and started to comfort him. Beaming at the audience, Dr. Rolf asked the man what he felt.

"I'm having an abreaction," he said, using an outdated textbook word for the reliving of a traumatic situation. He explained that he had been given ether for a tonsillectomy at about age three. Sure enough, the snorting and exhaling appeared to be the echo of a childhood fight against an anesthesia mask. Dr. Rolf urged him to spit it out and push it away, and as he did so his breathing became more gentle. Then she and Dr. Dick gave him a few extra special kneadings and prods (I'd say somewhere between the seventh and twelfth).

Dr. Rolf told the audience that some of the rolfing exercises can cause the return of experiences that were repressed in childhood. She used this man's distress as further proof of the strength of rolfing; and sure enough after a short while Dr. Dick's sensitive and muscular fingers brought him back in contact with his surroundings.

The clincher came when someone later asked this fellow if he had ever remembered the experience with the anesthesia before. His answer: "Of course. I've worked it through in my analysis several times."

At no time during this demonstration did Ida Rolf state that her method was aimed at psychotherapy, but her brochure claims that "psychological improvement can certainly be expected." She has also said that her subjects show "invariable improvement in attitudes, and sometimes quite basic change" which "can be verified through accepted psychological tests." Yet in spite of her claims, it is significant that Rolf's studies have not been accepted for publication in any reputable scientific journal.

With very little research evidence, rolfers claim to be able to cure anything from spinal disturbance to hemorrhoids, neurosis to thyroid malfunction, asthma to ulcers. Julian Silverman, Esalen's new research director, has publicly stated that the value of rolfing is proven by changes in electromyographic records (the recording of the electrical activity of muscles) and in cortically evoked potentials (the electrical response of the brain to light flashes). But these research reports have never been made available to professionals who have asked for them.

Bio-energetics differs from rolfing in that the body is not directly handled, and also in that at least some bio-energetic therapists have attempted to fit their work into the context of the patient's life. In the encounter world, however, bio-energetics has degenerated into just another fad for instant growth.

Bio-energetics is loosely derived from the work of Wilhelm Reich, a student of Freud and a brilliant contributor to psychoanalytic theory in the early days. Following up some Freudian notions about sexual functioning, Reich studied the function of the orgasm and ultimately developed his theory of the "orgone," which he saw not only as the basic life force but as a force that could change a desert into a blooming garden and that lay at the core of hurricanes and celestial movements. Most Americans have heard of the orgone boxes—or, as Reich called them, orgone energy accumulators—which were designed to cure cancer, change the flow of physical energy within the body, and redirect sexual functioning.

My own interest in Reich stems from my senior year in college, when I had a friend who was a devoted patient of Reichian therapy. He had an orgone box in his house. I tried it once, but ultimately only felt a bit bored and sweaty sitting nude in this rather small lead-lined box. The principal effect seemed to be increased temperature, humidity, and stuffiness from breathing such a limited amount of air. Nevertheless, the account my friend told me of Reich's early history; his renown in intellectual circles; the dastardly handling he reportedly received at the hands of the United States Government, the Communists, the Fascists, and the medical and psychiatric professions; his death in a federal prison— all this had a strong intellectual and emotional appeal. Eventually, however, I came to realize that not every rejected innovator is rejected because he is right (try telling that to encounterists).

There is a revival of interest in Reich now, and perhaps scientific tests may yet establish his work as valuable. But so far nothing in the way of validation has appeared in a reputable journal.

Responding to a recent article on Reich, Dr. James A. Brussel, former Assistant Commissioner of New York State's Department of Mental Hygiene, reported complaints "made by relatives of cancer victims who had been subjected to Reich's fraud." According to Brussel, "Three of these [orgone treatment] centers were set up in Manhattan and Queens. They were run by psychiatrists not licensed to practice in New York. All but one had been discharged from mental institutional positions in other states . . . several deaths had been reported occurring in patients who, had they sought surgical assistance when their cancer was first discovered, might well have survived." The author of the article on Reich that stimulated this response, David Elkind, pointed out that Reich could not be held responsible for acts that he did not commit, even though they were done in the name of his theory.

The orgone theory has turned up recently in a new context, the encounter culture, only now it's known as "bio-energetics."

The two best-known leaders in bio-energetics are Alexander

Lowen, M.D., and John Pierrakos, M.D., both officers in a non-profit institute in New York called the Institute for Bio-energetic Analysis. Although billed as a research endeavor, the Institute has undertaken no controlled studies of its work, nor has it published any of its findings. Like most aspects of the encounter game, bio-energetics must be learned by participation.

At the 1971 New York Esalen affair, Pierrakos, a charming, handsome, personable showman with just enough of a Greek accent to enhance his attractiveness, spent several hours running the crowd through a demonstration that aroused everyone's orgone energy. He started off by showing some line drawings on slides of bodies with a blue "aura" drawn around them. He explained that the aura is the visible proof of the "fact" that each person generates an energy field, and that if this energy field does not flow correctly a variety of diseases will result.

Pierrakos proceeded to demonstrate; again the evidence of our own senses was to be the criterion. He presented some special photos of the skin at high magnification which showed what looked like spouts of gases coming out of the pores. These were "proof" of the aura; and as soon as we were told how to look for it between our fingers, several members of the crowd announced, "I see it! I see it!"

Even if the "aura" were a real phenomenon, it seemed to have little to do with the theory and the techniques that followed. Pierrakos explained that that energy in the body must flow in a figure eight if it is to function well. He briefly described some clinical examples, showed sketches of figures whose energy flows were supposedly blocked, and gave a few diagnoses. Then came the big stuff.

Pierrakos had earlier asked for volunteers, explaining with a chuckle that they would have to strip to their bras and panties (or shorts). It seemed unlikely that there would be a woman wearing a bra in that crowd, but two such women were among those who stepped forward.

The first woman was fortyish and not especially attractive. Pierrakos had her stand with her legs apart, knees bent forward, heels pointed inward, fists clenched and planted above her buttocks. This posture was supposed to cause vibrations in the thigh and calf muscles (which it did) and throughout her body (which it did not). According to Pierrakos, if a person's orgone energy is flowing properly this exercise will trigger fairly smooth, regular vibrations of the body at a rate that I would estimate at about two or three per second.

When this first woman did not vibrate correctly we were told that her energy was blocked, especially in the pelvis. She was dispatched to the care of two of Pierrakos' leotard-clad girls. They helped the woman to lean over backward, balancing her mid-section on a low stool. With her heels still on the floor, the woman was pushed and pulled a bit, and encouraged to continue vibrating, pushing at the floor through her heels and shouting.

Meanwhile, Pierrakos was working with the next volunteer, an attractive young Frenchwoman, whose embarrassment was even more pronounced because of the language barrier. Pierrakos made some observations about her posture—that she was a bit round-shouldered, arched her body forward, and did not seem to be standing with her feet on the ground—and then set her to vibrating. She also did it poorly, as in fact most people would, since the particular muscle groups that this exercise employs are rarely used in our society. Once her energy blocks had been pointed out, she too was assigned to a leotard-clad aide, and Pierrakos quickly forgot about these two volunteers.

Next Pierrakos asked us to move the furniture aside and stand in circles. We were told to begin with the knees-bent-thighs-aquiver posture; we all complied, with varying results. In each circle some members could be seen to really "get into it," eyes closed and vibrating regularly. Some half-heartedly and some with enthusiasm gave their obviously long unused bodies an irregular jerk or two. After a minute or two, Pierrakos instructed us to accompany our actions with sounds, and the result was a cacophony of rhythmic grunts and groans.

After a short warning about massive energy accumulation, Pierrakos had us lie down in wheellike circles on the floor, holding hands or with arms locked, legs bouncing at the knees. He quickly established a rhythm for us, encouraging us to keep the beat with grunts and shouts. With the rhythm established, Pierrakos began to interject shouts of "No!" "Mama!" and "Leave me alone!" The crowd picked up these words, and many individuals integrated them into the beat.

These childhood shouts seemed to trigger extreme distress in several participants, and soon about half a dozen people were hysterical. Much like Bill Schutz and his Flying Circus, Pierrakos responded to the signals of his aides and went to the side of those who'd lost control. With a comforting hand on a diaphragm, or a slowing of the person's bouncing knees, he calmed the overly upset.

But the aides were not the only ones who offered comfort to flipped-out bouncers. This crowd had had a weekend of Esalen encountering, and while Pierrakos looked on with approval, several co-bouncers could be seen to hug and protect people near them who needed help.

After more than half an hour of vibrating, Pierrakos asked the participants to form their circles, close their eyes, and feel the new energies coursing through their bodies. Fingertips, arms, legs— Pierrakos drew our attention to all of these, and everyone sensed that these parts were vibrating and felt different.

This experience in bio-energetics had been billed as a lecture demonstration; Pierrakos had promised at the start that there would be discussion and questions after the demonstration. But at the end he asked the group if they wanted to ask questions. One young man, representing the audience's sentiments, said, "Screw the questions!" and Pierrakos laughingly agreed.

These two body therapies, rolfing and bio-energetics, have some of the aspects of a play within a play in the encounter game. Both illustrate the importance of the body in the encounter game; both point to the manipulative specialist-working-on-patient motif; both point to the antirational, antiresearch theme; and both end up as oversimplified cures. Perhaps most important, advocates of both rolfing and bio-energetics claim to deplore the abuses of their methods in the encounter world, while actually encouraging such abuse by frequent demonstrations to encounter groups.

There might be some real value in both of these body technologies, though probably less than their proponents claim. Throughout the encounter game, many worthwhile techniques of human growth are thrown into the mix and get lost among the less reliable ones. The context in which an idea, a procedure, or a technique appears makes it valid or renders it absurd. As used in the encounter game, rolfing and bio-energetics fail to achieve any enduring changes and encourage the continued acceptance of transitory, dramatic emotional experiences.

The body manipulators are at one end of the encounter spectrum; as mentioned earlier, any local encounterist is likely to try his hand at these rolfing and bio-energetics techniques once he's experienced them, or if he's looking for something new to offer. These two techniques are disowned by the more conservative stars of the encounter game. Carl Rogers has said, "I deplore the games and gimmicks that have come to play such a large part in many groups and the manipulation which often accompanies their use. I too am concerned about . . . the use of untested approaches like bio-energetics, rolfing, and the like." Others, like Bill Schutz, have approved and adopted them.

But some encounter game players have found it easier to respect our cultural taboo about touching bodies and imitate the leaders at the word-and-gesture end of the encounter spectrum. Let's now turn our attention to those types—leaders who are more typical of the encounter ideology and more widespread numerically.

5

Word Manipulators

Far easier to imitate than the body benders are the leaders who by direction and example encourage group members to shout, scream, fantasize out loud, or simply explain how they feel to other group members. The varieties of verbal ritual in the encounter game are legion, and in fact most of what happens in encounter groups is talk—talk in a more personal style than is customary in our culture, talk laced with self-explanation and reactions to others ("feedback"). The language tends to be more "honest" than participants would ordinarily dare; since honesty is the most widely known characteristic of encounter groups, it is the most widely expected, encouraged, and rewarded. Most players of the encounter game tend to think of it as a talk activity, remembering not what was said but the impact; and, interestingly, they often overestimate the impact as though they'd forgotten the old saw about sticks and stones.

Actually, words are probably both more and less powerful than many of us think. We tend not to say the things we think and feel about others, usually out of a fear of retribution that gets rationalized into not wanting to hurt the other person. And given the notion that words can devastate, most of us prefer that the other person not be too direct, either.

Clinical experience with the power of words shows that people can take much more honesty than they think, and can in turn learn to be more honest about what they feel. What's needed is called a climate of psychological safety, which changes the social reward system from the usual acceptance of protective dissembling to a system where uncomfortable perceptions can be shared. The hope is that such honesty, if offered without censure or coercion, can provide people with data which will shed light on their own behavior, their impact on others, and their understanding of how others experience events in their lives.

That hope is often realized, and the good that does lie in the encounter game, it seems to me, comes from that very process—when it works. If in fact the majority of encounter leaders were able to achieve and sustain such climates of psychological safety, and concentrated their efforts in that direction, there would be little need for this book.

But the fact is that arriving at that kind of safety-honesty balance in a group is a very complex process, not easily or often achieved, and not easily maintained once achieved. Most group leaders do not have the necessary understanding of human behavior, group dynamics, and the complex needs of people undergoing emotional change to come anywhere close to achieving that climate.

Without the climate of psychological safety, leaders are often left with a hollow parody of a group psychotherapy experience; and too often, unskilled leaders try to remedy the situation by suggestion, coercion, manipulation, games, or gimmicks. When in doubt about what's going on and what to do, an unskilled leader will often introduce a nonverbal technique, or aim to create an emotional reaction. The skilled leader will usually sit back and try to understand, or perhaps enlist the group's aid in understanding what's happening. But on countless occasions I asked encounter leaders why they did or said a particular thing, only to find that they were operating out of a desire to "keep the group going," or because they didn't know how to handle what was happening to their own feelings or those of the group members.

The title of this chapter may need some clarification. By "word manipulators," I don't mean people who never use body techniques and games. Most encounter leaders do at times use body games, sometimes advisedly and sometimes not. Further, I don't mean that words are played with or that group members are "manipulated" into saying things they would not ordinarily say. Sometimes those things happen, sadly, and sometimes not. Finally, I'm not using "manipulation" here in the sense of covert control or deceit—that happens much too often for my taste, but it isn't limited to encounter groups.

What I am trying to parcel out of the spectrum of leadership styles are the leaders who see verbal expression and interaction as primary—leaders who rely on talk to generate "growth." Language always has a certain measure of emotion—as listeners we can pretty well agree on the emotion, or lack of it, that a speaker communicates, even though what we perceive may not in fact be what he is feeling. And, accordingly, "talk" is used here to include not just words, but the emotional communications, including the body gestures and signals, that go with the words.

Most leaders have found out through experience or imitation that a certain style will prove workable for most groups, and that style quickly becomes a basic weapon in their arsenal. For the most part group leaders take a soft-spoken, unassuming, guilelessly open and intimate tone. Most likely they'll start off by just saying hello, introducing themselves, or perhaps saying something to the effect that "Our purpose will be to get to know each other and look at ourselves in a different way, to experience ourselves and to enjoy relating as a group." They are then likely to add, usually quite explicitly, that they'd like the cooperation of the group, but of course each person is free not to cooperate or not to go along with any given game suggested. "Each person is responsible for himself" leads the participants to believe that they have done the whole thing, taken new steps on their own initiative, and acted autonomously. Once players have accepted these ground rules they subject themselves to the agenda and controls set down by the leader, and are halfway to the belief that they've had a profound emotional experience.

W. H. Blanchard, writing in the January 1970 issue of *Psychology Today*, pointed out this process of submission to the leader and the fulfillment of expected emotional experiences:

> . . . in the typical group, the pressure to experience awareness is enormous, and the urge to fake it is almost irresistible. Most group members have been coached by friends and promotional brochures: they believe that a peak experience is not only desirable but necessary if one is to have fullest happiness and mental health. They are programmed for peaks.

Viewed this way, encounter group leadership becomes little more than a structuring of behavior to provide the arena within which groupers fulfill their own prophecies. Once leadership of a group has been established, manipulative steps only rarely need repeating—since conformity, group pressure, and the newly established norms have a momentum of their own. If such steps are needed, the leader can easily reestablish control by telling the errant group member that he's free not to respond. In most cases, the other members of the group will then tease, cajole, or challenge him to try it.

In addition to this basic hypnotic technique, leaders have borrowed a variety of techniques from psychotherapy and psychoanalysis. One favorite at the T-group or sensitivity-training end of the encounter spectrum, for example, is silence: the leader refuses to respond to questions, demands, or bids for direction. Many leaders have learned to fall back on silence at difficult times, but to maintain nearly total withdrawal from the group requires training.

Most leaders are far more intrusive; they encourage participants to share their feelings, to speak out and not hold back their thoughts. Sometimes a leader will pick up on what one person says, ask another what he or she feels about it, ask a third if he believed the second, then ask a fourth if he liked the way the third responded, and finally go back to challenge the first speaker, saying that he once felt that way too and it led to some horrifying emotional upheaval which was finally worked out with the help of his own group. Since people almost automatically take cues on how to perform from their leaders, the leaders intentionally act as a model for the members to imitate. There are special procedures for the quiet ones found in every group, most notably getting others to express their feelings about them. After a few such techniques have been presented, it doesn't take long before the whole group is actively interacting.

The techniques for getting a group of people to encounter are easy to copy; success depends largely on a display of self-assurance on the part of the leader. Leaders can also count on the expectations of the groupers, the presence of at least a few who've been to groups before, the absence of an explicit structure for the allotted time, and the effects of the encounter culture propaganda.

Interestingly enough, even those who have copied the techniques of encounter leadership are seldom aware of their origins or the reasons for their use. I've often heard encounterists attack psychoanalysis while using techniques and strategies derived from it, or criticize classical group psychotherapy while unknowingly using the techniques of group therapists.

I have asked several highly committed encounterists to name the top five contributors to encounter methodology. The list always includes Bill Schutz, Fritz Perls, and Carl Rogers, but after that the answers tend to sidetrack toward body manipulators, fringe leaders like Dan Casriel, or the leading light at some local growth center. Few encounterists can say which leader made what contributions (except in the case of Fritz Perls), and even fewer are aware that techniques being used in the encounter game were covered in psychiatric literature twenty to forty years ago.

If during an encounter game inning you are asked to localize and talk to a pain in your body; to act out parts of a dream, including taking the role of inanimate objects; to talk to an empty chair, or place your parent or another significant person in it and tell him what you've always wanted to tell him—you are participating in the twenty-year-old grand tradition of Gestalt therapy, whose most important practitioner was Fritz Perls.

Frederick S. Perls, who held both an M.D. and a Ph.D. degree, is considered by many to have been one of the primary contributors to the mental-health movement in America. At least as many others thought he was a nut, and even his friends have described him as a self-righteous iconoclast. Puckish, usually smiling, bald, with a flowing gray beard, Fritz Perls generally dressed in old turquoise wide-wale corduroy pants, sandals, a guru shirt, and love beads. At times jumpsuits or a foreign sports car would round out the picture of a crazy, jolly old man having fun with life.

Right up until his death in March 1970, Perls was the grand California guru. He always had a following, often of young people; but many senior members of the mental-health profession and interested public could also be found both figuratively and literally sitting at his feet while he accused one person of "mindfucking," then helped another through one of the complicated emotional sequences of Gestalt therapy.

"Mind-fucking," incidentally, is a term Perls reputedly coined, and in so doing he defined one of the central ground rules of the encounter game. He would use that term, or others even more pungent, whenever he felt that someone was being too intellectual or too "intellectualized." The latter word comes from the psychoanalysts' term "intellectualization," and refers to thought processes devoid of feeling. It is an important concept, since it is one of the most common ways to avoid the emotional impact of something being said. Most psychotherapists view such defense mechanisms as necessary protections learned in childhood, though their overuse in adult life may cause complications.

Perls, and other Gestaltists and encounterists, seemed to view such ego protections as personal enemies to be slain on sight. As a result, one of the most widespread characteristics of encounter groups is a tendency to attack a member whenever the emotional content of what he's saying is not immediately apparent.

In *Turning On,* an account of her personal trip through the encounter game, Rasa Gustaitis noted, "According to Perls, verbiage comes in three varieties: chickenshit, bullshit, and elephantshit. Day-to-day chatter is chickenshit. Bullshit is role-playing. Elephantshit deals with life and death, meanings, ideals and theories."

Perls was an absolute tyrant, always putting down psychoanalysis, schools of encounter other than his—anyone, in fact, who would not do things his way. But he usually did so with such skill, and communicated so much readiness to help the victim he had just devastated, that he got away with treatment that others could not hope to imitate. In at least one instance he slapped a girl "hot-seater" whose bitchiness gave him trouble—perhaps this was "therapy"; perhaps a continuation of his "I please myself" philosophy. Some would even say both, since by such displays he could be presumed to be teaching his victims how to please themselves through the joy of directly expressing anger.

My most vivid memories of Fritz Perls feature him playing his guru number in front of large audiences. He would usually pull up a chair next to a small table and sit quietly for a while. Then he'd begin with a quip that all he needed was his ashtray, his cigarettes, and an empty chair—"the tools of my trade." Usually somewhere in his opening he'd find a way to include his famous line, "I please myself first," especially if one of the young people on the floor near him would ask if he was ready to begin. The audiences loved it.

"So who vants to vork?" he'd ask, traces of a German accent coming through. Dozens of hands in the front rows would be raised; people would start to move forward immediately, eager to take the famous "hot seat," or empty chair.

"Working" meant getting into one of the rituals of Gestalt therapy, through a dream, a fantasy, or the expression of some concern from the person's life. Usually Perls would keep working until some reconciliation occurred between diverse aspects of the volunteer's personality, or until he got disgusted with the volunteer's "mind-fucking." Occasionally he would comment on some theoretical point or explain to the audience that what he did was greater than Freud's revolution.

Gestalt therapy is rather loosely derived from Gestalt psychology, a school that flourished in Germany and in the United States just before World War II. "Gestalt" is the German word for configuration or pattern. The basic notion was that the human brain goes through organizing activity to integrate diverse stimuli. Thus, if we see several coins randomly on a table top, we automatically group them into "change" rather than see them as discrete, different-colored, round objects of varying sizes. This mental organizing activity, whether done on the basis of similarity (they are all coins) or because of some geographical or contextual arrangement, is called "closure."

Gestalt psychology focused mainly on the brain's activity in integrating diverse stimuli. Reasoning from this—though the reasoning is not quite clear, even to the pros—Gestalt therapists try to bring together the contradictory aspects of a personality into one totality, or Gestalt. The technique for doing so usually involves placing the person on the hot seat and making two sides of him conflict vividly through acting. It was never merely acting, though, as Perls would allow no artificiality—at the first sign of hollowness or conformity, he'd pounce on the hot-seater with anything from wry humor to scathing insults in an attempt to provoke an emotional response that he considered authentic.

For example, I remember a young man who told of a dream about a Nazi raping a young Jewish girl. "Be the Storm Trooper," he was told, and with a little encouragement he quickly got into the role—stomping his feet, marching about the platform, even shouting pseudo obscenities in pseudo German. Next he was told to play the helpless girl. It was tougher for him to get into that role, but as he played it out we could see that passivity, helplessness, and the need to be victimized were as much a part of his personality as the Storm Trooper's aggressiveness.

Assuming that the player has not reached an emotional impasse, cried, become confused or enraged, or somehow tapped some unexpected and hitherto unknown part of himself by this point, the customary next step in such Gestalt therapy is to arrange a dialogue between the diverse personality traits brought out by the drama. Accordingly, the young man was asked to stage a conversation between the Storm Trooper and his victim—to have them talk, interact, and discuss their attitudes toward each other. Should they reach an impasse, Perls might ask a question like "What do you *admire* about each other?" When the resolution of such an impasse works, it seems to lead to some sudden rapprochement between the opposing parts of the person, at least momentarily. Too often Perls's imitators stop at that point, though Fritz often said that hundreds of such impasses need to be worked out before a neurosis may be cured.

Many of the Gestalt techniques developed by Fritz Perls have been adopted by players of the encounter game. But he objected to the superficiality of most encounter groups:

"It took us a long time to debunk the whole Freudian crap, and now we are entering a new and more dangerous phase, the phase of the turner-onners: turn on to instant cure, instant joy, instant sensory awareness. We are entering the phase of the quacks and the con men, who think if you get some breakthrough, you are cured—disregarding any growth requirements, disregarding any of the real potential, the inborn genius in all of you. If this becomes a fad, it is as dangerous to psychology as the year-decade-century-long lying on the couch. At least the damage we suffered under psychoanalysis does little to the patient except to make him deader and deader."

Nonetheless, Perls's affiliation with Esalen made him one of the main contributors to the superficial, quickie-therapy ideology. The emphasis on technique is clear in his work and in his writings, partly because of his refusal to work out a thorough theoretical structure, and partly because of the essentially autocratic, work-with-one-person-at-a-time-with-the-group-watching technology that he developed.

A common criticism of Perls's work is that he sacrificed pains-taking thinking for quick, flashy insight, of which he was admit-tedly capable. And there's the rub. Perls was a remarkably gifted clinician, though few of his imitators fall into that category. Whatever his therapy style, any sort of encounter with Perls was likely to be a significant event in a person's life, if only because his was such a forceful and thoroughly self-directed personality.

After Perls, we go increasingly downhill in terms of the skill, learning, clinical insight, training, and emotional capacity of the word manipulators. Next on the list of movers and shapers is a man who, despite his professional credentials, or perhaps because of them, is considered by many professionals to be a public menace.

Dan Casriel, M.D., is probably the most successful private practitioner of the encounter game in the country, at least finan-cially. Members of his groups are taught to grab hold of a feeling—any feeling—and express it in a series of yells, screams, and moans which increase in volume to almost unbearable intensity.

Casriel, who recently purchased a half-million-dollar townhouse near New York's Waldorf-Astoria, claims to treat as many as eight hundred clients each week. The fee, following an initial thirty-five-dollar interview, is fifteen dollars for an evening group session conducted by one of Casriel's ex-patients, or twenty dollars for a session led by the doctor himself. He usually suggests that a new grouper begin with two or three sessions per week. Casriel's mimeographed information handout says it takes "about 100 to 150 group meetings and three to four 'marathons' [thirty-hour sessions at $100 per shot] during the course of a year to solidify [these] new, healthy feelings." The exact arithmetic is not clear, but it would appear that Casriel is grossing as much as twelve thousand dollars each week.

At the New York City Council's hearings on encounter groups, Casriel was asked whether he knew of any other psychiatrist in the nation who grossed better than six hundred thousand dollars per year. Casriel replied that he thought perhaps the Menninger Clinic did as well! Casriel now bills himself as "the Casriel Institute for Group Dynamics," but it seems clear that he is really more an entrepreneur than an institute. When he made the point about being "an institute" with "a staff of thirty and expenses of six thousand dollars per week," he was asked if the "institute" was nonprofit. Casriel's answer was no.

To handle the hundreds of people nominally under his supervision, Casriel must rely on many group leaders with little or no professional training. He is, however, one of the few M.D.'s in the encounter field, and with his medical credentials he assumes the right to train new leaders, generally selecting the most promising members of the groups he leads himself. Casriel points with pride to his organization's forty-thousand-a-year senior group leader, an ex-patient whom he once called a "formerly psychotic lawyer." While maintaining a program to train his own men, he does acknowledge the danger of untrained group leaders entering his field.

Casriel is short and quite bald; he makes his baldness even more pronounced by shaving what would be the fringe around his ears. He wears heavy black glasses which he has a tendency to push up on his forehead when distracted, concerned, or about to give forth a theory of human behavior. He dresses conservatively and better fits the image of an accountant than of a world-saving doctor. Of course, Casriel is one of our more capitalistic encounterists, inasmuch as he has an army of paraprofessionals who get two dollars per session for each participant, enriching Casriel to the tune of thirteen dollars per participant without his even being there.

Name any psychiatric symptom, and Casriel will tell you how long it will take him to eradicate it—to the horror of most mental-health professionals as well as those encounterists who seem unwilling to accept him. The encounter world makes for strange bedfellows, and while many players of the encounter game don't really accept Casriel, he seems quite willing to cast his lot with them. He often appears at conferences and other encounter-world activities, and he was at the City Council's hearings. His rejection by almost all encounter game superstars is not hard to understand, considering his tendency to act as though he invented the whole movement and has now gone well past it.

Casriel's trek through the forest of new techniques seems to have begun with a two-month grant from the National Institute of Mental Health to study drug addiction during July and August of 1962. He dates his consulting work with Synanon from August of that year. He had also begun work with a court-operated "halfway house" for addicts, Daytop Lodge, in June 1962. Several years later—April 1965—he became "Co-founder and Medical Psychiatric Superintendent" at Daytop Village, Inc., a therapeutic community run along the lines of Synanon attack-and-humiliation therapy.

Casriel's groups reflect the kind of individual therapy, where one person at a time is jumped on by the group, that is common in the Synanon and Gestalt worlds. Fritz Perls and Casriel may best typify the extension of individual therapeutic authority into the encounter game, despite its nonauthoritarian ideology.

Casriel, like Perls, starts with the question, "Who wants to work?" In a new group he may begin by having a volunteer go tell each member of the group, "Fuck you! I'm angry," regardless of how he's actually feeling. If a hot-seater says, "But I'm not angry," Casriel replies, "Say it anyway, and try to get in touch with your anger." For some this is an impossible task; for others, a few tries make it at least *seem* possible.

Casriel encourages increasingly intense expression as the volunteer proceeds from one person to the next, each time saying, "Fuck you! I'm angry." Casriel and others in the group will say, "Louder, I don't believe you. More feelings! Go on! Out with it," and other exhortations designed to increase the amount of anger expressed. Under this sort of pressure most people will scream louder and louder. After a few minutes of this, Casriel tries to get the person to scream without words and then escalate the nonverbal screams to greater and greater intensity. As the volunteer crosses the threshold into painful screaming, Casriel's voice becomes increasingly soft and comforting.

Once the volunteer has screamed to Casriel's or the group's approval—and it may take a half hour or more—Casriel encourages him to go from person to person for his reward—the ritual encounter hug. People sitting close to somebody who has gone through such a loud, gut-wrenching experience develop an immediate sense of empathy, so the hugs become a blend of compassion and reward.

I remember watching a thin young man who, responding to Casriel's "Who has a feeling?" quickly announced that he had a feeling of pain and loss. Casriel varied his usual technique, and stood up in the middle of the group, holding the man in his arms. The man began to cry and moan, his body heaving with sobs, though there was no apparent reason for his pain. Casriel held him tighter and tighter, stroking his back and encouraging him to "get it all out, scream it all out, cry it all out." The man's pain and sobbing increased to a nerve-wracking pitch. Many of the spectators also began to cry. The whole process rapidly took on aspects of a religious revival meeting, a wake, or a cry-in, with the greatest effect being experienced by those who were seated nearest Casriel and the sobbing man in his arms. After a while the man seemed to be all cried out, and Casriel encouraged him to go around the circle and collect his hugs. He received strokes and gestures of compassion from the others, especially the women; then Casriel moved on to the next person. All of this, of course, was allowed to settle without any discussion or attempt to fit those painful feelings into the context of the man's life.

Casriel sees himself as nothing short of an evolutionary step. His mimeographed handout informs new patients that "an overwhelming percentage" of those who have entered his groups have found education, therapy, excitement, and enjoyment:

> *WHAT ARE MY GROUPS?* Evolutionary in their historical formation (since 1963), these groups are revolutionary when encountered for the first time. My groups are based on a fundamentally *new* theory and technique of psychotherapy, better understood as an ACCELERATED RE-EDUCATION of your "A.B.C.'s." A = affect - feelings - emotions. B = behavior = act = actions. C = cognition = attitudes = thoughts. Here, you can change self-defeating patterns of feeling, actions, and thinking, by discovering and exercising your basic emotions through interaction with your peers.

Casriel's group leaders evidently find it simple to just imitate his style, and sometimes they don't even bother with the attack. In some of the groups, patients may just moan and rock quietly and expressionlessly, saying, "I'm angry," over and over until they or someone else gets sick of it.

Most of his patients are pretty sick and hence especially ill equipped to walk away from these promises and seek individualized treatment. The skill of Casriel's aides is limited to what their leader has taught them. If a patient complains that his progress is too slow, he is told to work harder.

Casriel's brochure offers several types of groups: children's groups, prepuberty and postpuberty groups, a special group for parents of children in groups in addition to their own adult groups, groups for those over forty, beginners' groups, married couples' groups, and postmarathon groups. In addition, Casriel offers special groups for people interested in problems such as "prejudice, influence of subcultural attitudes of race, religion, or sex . . . symptom groups for smoking, obesity, homosexuality, drugs, impotence, and frigidity." Casriel's Community Room, as his brochure states, is open to all group members at any time and as often as they wish, from 9:30 A.M. until midnight, six days a week. Complimentary coffee is always available; food, beverages, and cigarettes may be purchased; and babysitters are there for mothers who want to bring their children along.

Casriel runs a full-time residential program that he claims can cure anybody—especially drug addicts—in nine months to a year. In addition to extensive participation in Casriel's many groups, resident members also serve as assistants, and as housekeepers in his building. All of this attention is available at fifteen thousand dollars a year. Casriel claims a 100 percent success rate with this program, and says he is still waiting for the first failure that will prove the rule of the efficiency of his techniques.

During the New York City Council hearings on encounter groups, Councilman Theodore Weiss began to question Casriel, who had begun to train addiction counselors in city-funded programs, about his criteria for cure. Casriel admitted that only one class had ever graduated from his program, and that his criterion for cure was that none of the graduates had gone back on drugs a few months later. When Councilman Weiss pointed out that the critical problem in drug addiction is recidivism after a longer period, Casriel said, "I can't guarantee that they'll never go back on drugs, but I know they're cured." Weiss asked, "How do you know?" And Casriel replied that, "I know by my judgment. I was medical director of Daytop Village, have been involved in Synanon, I've worked with addicts for years, and I'm a psychiatrist; and as a result, my judgment is sufficient."

Continuing downhill, we can easily find a wide range of local word manipulators who, with few qualifications other than chutz-pah, offer encounter to the public complete with sex, dating services—whatever there's a market for. In many places encounter groups are listed in the phone book or advertised in local news-papers. A study in Palo Alto, California, turned up two hundred different groups operating at one time—in a city of sixty thousand, figuring an average of ten people per group, that's at least 3 percent of the people in town involved in encounter groups. In a recent recheck the number of groups had dropped to one hundred, as the crest of the encounter wave continues to move eastward.

As the American Psychiatric Association's Task Force Report, "Encounter Groups and Psychiatry," put it:

> Many of the encounter groups have no institutional back-ing and recruit participants by word of mouth or written advertisement. Some teachers lead encounter groups in the classroom, housewives lead groups at home for their friends or the friends of their adolescent offspring. Some have loose institution affiliations; for example, one small free university offers approximately fifty encounter groups of various as-sortments every quarter; one highly structured institution, Synanon, offers an astonishing number of groups for non-addicts (square games): the Oakland, California, branch alone has 1,500 individuals participating weekly in groups and another 1,000 on a waiting list.

A woman I interviewed described a reasonably typical first experience with this sort of encounter group:

> Joe Ben David does his thing at the Ansonia Hotel. . . . At one of his groups, a six-hour feel-in, the subject was some-thing like, how to have more trust in interpersonal relation-ships. He charged three dollars; there were about thirty people. He started by saying, "How many of you would put your pocketbooks on the table and walk away?" Quite a few people said yes, but I said no. Of course I was disturbing the whole feel-in, I wasn't feeling, wasn't trusting. Somebody said something about faith in God; he said, "We do not talk about God, we do not believe in God. Humanists do not

believe in God." I took exception—he had not advertised that this was for humanists only, therefore could not inflict his standards upon us. Several others started agreeing with me. He got very angry, said I was an emasculating bitch suffering from a tremendous case of penis envy. I said that I would like to believe I was enjoying a case of penis appreciation. . . .

He was giving a lecture that day on techniques to improve problems of impotence. There were three or four women there. He told all the guys that he thought it was important that they tell all the women they knew to learn to do what prostitutes do, to contract their vaginal muscles. I said Bullshit.

He said he was going to have me arrested if I appeared there again because he thought I pulled the audience away from him.

This woman, who had once considered writing about the encounter game, visited a variety of groups and later testified at the New York City Council hearings on encounter groups. When I interviewed her shortly afterward, it seemed to me that her motivation for going to so many groups was largely social. Her comments are fairly typical of the reactions of the encounter game's "disappointed customers":

I attended two encounter groups with Ed Mentken, a commercial artist, in his filthy, vermin-infested room. His three children were sleeping in the back room. I understand they were the children of various mothers; Sara Dawson is the lady of the house. Ed believes in venting your hostility, so as soon as you walk in the door he's ready to give you the business. Sara and Ed do their thing, fighting, calling each other every name in the book. . . .

One guy told me he'd met Sara and Ed through an ad that said, "Attractive swinging couple seeks partners, young girls or boys, boys with long hair especially wanted. Write." He did, and they called and told him they were having an encounter that evening which would end up in a swap session. . . . Sara tried to get me to come testify for the movement [at the City Council hearings]. I told her I thought she was eminently unqualified to be a leader of a group, that she was pulling people in, running her own thing and taking money for it. . . . She said I just didn't understand.

Then there's Bob Simberg, a former patient of Casriel's. He's just crazy enough to be brilliant. He had encounter groups going day and night, getting ten dollars a head, five telephones going at once. You can always spot his ads, he uses "in depth," and now he's with the primal scream. He had told me that anything I'd wanted—drugs, boys, girls— he'd get me. He was charmed, I guess, by the way I attacked him. He does have this record of three stays at Bellevue. He comes out and he's so shaky, disoriented . . . and then in a few weeks he's got another place.

Professionals in the encounter game admit the existence of leaders like those described above, but tend to minimize their number or play down their importance. In their own work, of course, they are unlikely to see many of these absurdities.

But the issue here is not simply the training or integrity of the leader. The whole encounter framework encourages superficial mockeries of therapy, primarily because no one feels any responsibility for the process. One woman described such a leadership failure at Aureon, which most observers place at the high-quality end of the encounter spectrum:

The first evening, after dinner, the group got together and went to Streitfeld to ask him to take over or get another leader, as our original leader was incompetent and self-absorbed and not at all interested in the group. Some of the techniques were very anxiety-provoking—closing your eyes and touching people. . . . At one point when the leader was criticized by one of the women in the group who had had experience dealing with disturbed people, the leader got down on his knees and banged the ground like a kid of three. It was very frightening. He's a psychologist, teacher at N.Y.U. and State University, author of a book on encounter. I thought, My God, what are the rules around here?

Professional credentials—in or out of the encounter game— obviously are not sufficient to eliminate unethical or destructive behavior. But the credentials at least provide some minimal control over the training and practices of individual leaders, and those who have credentials at least can be held accountable to state and local societies or to government agencies. For those without such credentials, suit for damages—if provable—may be the only kind of control.

After a television appearance I got a call from a young lady who said that she agreed with my view of encounter and was pleased to hear me state it publicly. She went on to say that she had developed a new "visual therapy," which she would like to tell me about. She sent me some written materials in which she introduced herself as a visual therapist, including a statement which she thought of as the basis for a book to be called *The Visual Feeling:*

> People cover their faces with masks . . . or should I say cover their feelings. . . . When you start to look, and think of the shape of a subway car ceiling (curved-arc) or the outline of a crumpled bag of bread, you start to think differently, about the world. You start seeing all these crazy things, you never looked at before, and you react to them, you have feelings about them. . . .

She summed up her therapy in the following lines:

> If I could only teach the world to see . . . I think that psychotherapists would be out of work. And Visual Therapists, would replace them . . . Perhaps I should explain exactly what I mean by "fogged-up" . . . One may have bad childhood experiences, which led to an overload of "masking feelings" such as guilt. Which make it difficult for a person to see. If you're constantly worring about your problems, you forget to look at the world. When a "neurotic" is in this situation, more often than not, he does not see the world. Instead—his head is filled with all of him, the guilt over childhood, or whatever! That he simply is an entity unto himself, and could not possibly see, and feel clearly . . . I might add, that the same goes for "normals"; for as I stated: normal, into neurotic, into normal, it all doesn't exhist. What does exhist is not a psychologist's fancy work-termonology game. But PEOPLE, IT'S PEOPLE!

From this conceptual framework, Jean-Ann developed a series of exercises which would help people eliminate their fogs and really see the world. The first exercise, called "Catsup Soup," was designed to help with "outline seeing," which in some unspecified way was connected with artist Claes Oldenburg's method of seeing. Basically the exercise consisted of drawing things like bottles of catsup, a whole or partially eaten loaf of bread, several assorted jelly jars or mustard jars.

After reading this document I suspected Jean-Ann to be seriously disturbed. Certainly I didn't think she had "a therapy." She did have persistence, and I finally agreed to meet her at the upcoming second Esalen weekend ("I'll be wearing purple hot pants"). When I did, I learned that she was sixteen years old and just about to start college.

Having dismissed "visual therapy" as laughable, I had not heard the end of it. One of the people Jean-Ann met at the Esalen weekend had suggested that she "take it around to her local growth center." She did, and Aureon became her first sponsor. After participating in a workshop there and trying out her therapy, she phoned me to report she now had "a credential," and had already told several people that she was on the staff of Aureon. Since that institution is respected in the encounter world, several other growth centers were inviting her to do her thing with their people, among them, she said, Anthos and a place called "I Feel."

I recently received a letter from her describing her subsequent activities:

> the workshop i did with hal streitfeld was Fantastic. What went on was basicly the old time bio-energetics.
>
> i loved it, i felt completely Free. hal demonstrated the exercises on me, most i had previous experience with; one in particular—'the jelly Fish' was a panic. because i Freely let myself go. When i opened my eyes i Felt vibrations going completely through me. Streitfeld said he could see the vibes. practically see my AURA, and said i have a 'vibrant personality' he also said i have a very 'supple body'
>
> i might add. he told everyone to wear bathing suits—girls came in leotards—he failed to tell me and one other guy. i did the workshop in these obscene shocking pink print pants with a zipper up the front, and a nude bra. while the guy vibrated in a pair of dilapidated white cotton jockeys.
>
> i loved every minute of it . . . afterwards hal held out his arms to me and gave me a big hug—it felt good. i invited him

to come to one of my groups. i now have my office at the above address [a prestigious New York office building].

Jean-Ann now has several private patients, uses a live monkey as an assistant, and advertises in underground New York papers. I have very little doubt that her approach will take its place among the ranks of the new "therapies" finding a home in the encounter world.

6

Caution: Encounter Groups May Be Hazardous to Your Health

Is encounter a beneficial new form of mass therapy, or just a lot of possibly dangerous fun and games? Are there lasting results, or is there just a fast-disappearing illusion of change? If you "grow," what's the most likely direction? Will others know it, or will you simply have a different sense of yourself? What are the odds on coming away with a few days of insomnia, a six-month depression, a broken arm, or an enduring psychosis—or with the determination to tell off all your friends, break up your marriage, or forget your career and drop out?

Nothing approaching comprehensive statistics on these and other vital questions has been kept by the growth centers, most of which operate more like theaters or resorts than institutions offering intensive therapy. People come to workshops or weekend marathons, go through the games and emotional sweatbaths, and then disappear. Their leaders will probably never see them again, and if a later attempt is made to follow up on the workshop, it's to send them an announcement of the next session and urge them to bring friends. No investigations are made to determine the effects of encounter, nor do encounterists feel responsible for the effects. Most encounterists are wary of any formal evaluation of their work.

Professionals are increasingly aware that a significant number of people get hurt by encounter experiences. Many groupers have become concerned enough to seek out professional help, turning to mental-health clinics and private practitioners.

As a result, an increasing number of articles in professional journals and the press has begun to reflect the negative side of the encounter movement. Concern is being voiced about the number of new patients who have told their therapists that participation in an encounter group precipitated serious emotional disturbance. Arnold Lazarus, an innovator in behavior therapy techniques, pointed out in 1970 that the number of new patients who are "victims of encounter groups is becoming so large as to constitute a new 'clinical entity.' " While it is important to recognize that clinicians base their judgment on a highly selective sample—patients who've had an unfavorable encounter experience *and* seek help—their reports must be taken seriously. Even a single instance of avoidable human stress—or worse—requires us to identify the cause of the problem and protect others from it.

In the mental-health field there is no organization analogous to the Food and Drug Administration and the role it takes in protecting citizens from dangerous substances, like botulism in soup or mercury in tunafish. If encounterists were licensed professionals, their behavior would be subject to the control of state licensing agencies and professional peer groups. But most encounter leaders are beyond the range of professional control. Hence individual clinicians must research the issues, then make their views known to their colleagues and the public.

It is now clearly necessary to warn potential encounter game players that encounter groups may indeed be hazardous to their health. Besides the possible benefits, citizens must be helped to understand the risk involved in order to make an informed judgment about participation in such groups. In fact, at this writing there has been more scientific evidence of the hazards of encounter than of its reputed value.

Until recently, very few studies could meet scientific criteria and hence offer a reliable estimate of the risk factor. There is no question that there is risk; even the staunchest encounter advocates acknowledge it. However, we still do not know how the risks of encounter compare with the risks of everyday living or the rate with which the problems occur in the total population.

Data on the incidence of physical injuries is scant, but it is now apparent that injuries do occur regularly. In one of the first comprehensive critiques of small encounter groups, Morris Parloff noted in 1970 the "increasing instance of physical injury—contusions, strains, sprains, and broken limbs—as a consequence of uninhibited expressions of feelings." The American Psychiatric Association's Task Force Report on Encounter Groups says: "There have been many instances of participants suffering physical injuries; some encounter groups focus on the mobilization and expression of rage, and physical fights between participants who have long suppressed rage are encouraged. Severe bruising and broken limbs have been reported."

In a 1971 article on professional liability insurance, John Brownfain warned psychologists that "the number of physical injury claims growing out of group therapy has increased," and the American Psychological Association's insurance carrier has asked whether "modification of the definition of psychological practice . . . will place some realistic limitation on what psychologists may or may not do?" Among other instances, Brownfain noted:

> A patient participating in a marathon group was hit in the ear by another patient who was allegedly encouraged to express his hostility. The first patient's eardrum was punctured with resulting loss of hearing.
> A patient participating in group therapy alleges that he was lifted up, dropped, and beaten by other participants. He alleges injuries to the lumbosacral area, neck and shoulders, both sides of the mandibles, and various internal organs. Damages being sought by the claimant exceed $1,000,000.

The December 4, 1970, New York *Post* carried the story of Constance Grant, a young woman whose employer, the Department of Health, Education, and Welfare, recommended encounter to her. She attended a twelve-day sensitivity-training group lab sponsored by the National Training Laboratories. Toward the end of the session she and one of her groupmates "were encouraged to physically demonstrate aggression and hostility." What resulted was a judo hold that threw Miss Grant flat on the hardwood floor. She filed suit for half a million dollars against the sponsors of the course for injuries sustained. A critical point in her charges was that the group leader "made no attempt to prevent injuries to Miss Grant."

This case was believed to have been the first legal action for civil damages against the sensitivity-training movement. Many other cases have not come to trial but were handled directly by insurance carriers. Vin Rosenthal, a leader in the psychotherapy field, recently warned clinicians that group leaders who direct members into physical encounters do so at their own risk, as professional liability insurance now covers talking only.

An important aspect of these cases is that there was someone to sue. A mental-health professional with malpractice insurance can be held responsible for his activities, but most encounter leaders are not licensed or trained professionals and so can't get insurance. To proceed against them requires a civil suit and the establishment of legal responsibility in this uncharted area. Without the protections of professional treatment, individuals physically or emotionally hurt have no other recourse than general public liability.

Milton Berger, former president of the American Group Psychotherapy Association and a strong critic of wanton encountering, recently discussed encounter group conditions that can lead to physical injury:

> In a recent book by John Mann [1970] which could serve as a textbook for encounter techniques, the author describes an episode early in the group life in which he gives permission to a male and a female member to confront each other physically. She, much in anger, struck him with her fist on the arm, although stating a moment later she really wanted to kick him in the balls. I do believe that Mann, the group leader, had the right to give her permission to kick himself in the balls, but I cannot see on what basis, human, legal, ethical, professional or moral, he had the right to give her permission to kick another group member in the balls.

Evidence shows that participants in encounter groups experience problems of social interaction on returning to their homes and jobs. Various explanations for these "reentry problems" have been offered, but for the most part they can be summed up, as Morris Parloff says, as

> a nondiscriminating, single-minded adherence to the redis-covered ideal of directness and openness in interpersonal relationships, [which] may be greeted by one's employer and co-workers with more restrained joy than by the encounter group leader and one's fellow participants.

All observers have noted that reentry problems are a serious issue. Carl Rogers warns that the sexual component of the warm and loving feelings cultivated in encounter group members may constitute "a profound threat to their spouses if these feelings are not worked through satisfactorily in the workshops." In many cases an individual's dissatisfaction with his life pattern and spouse seem to surface as a result of the encounter group. This can lead to tragic results.

Mrs. Anita L., an attractive redhead in her early forties, reported:

> My husband was very intrigued with bio-energetics and encounter so he went to a marathon last spring. He decided he needed more of it and spent the summer at Esalen. He came back to say he was going to enroll in their leadership-training program. That was going to be his new career.
>
> We'd been married twenty years, our kids are eighteen and fourteen. He was fifty at the time, a music teacher. He found people there who agreed with the way he thinks; who find life right now stifling, who are feeling the effects of their age and the fear of getting older.
>
> He definitely went out there with the idea that it was a kind of therapy. He never came back.

Mrs. L.'s story is not an uncommon one. Certainly, divorces do occur; the L.'s were having difficulty, and their problems might well have ended in divorce or separation even if Mr. L. had never heard of encounter. But Mr. L.'s refusal to discuss their problems with his wife or to give her a chance to fit into his new-found "emotional freedom" showed little of the relatedness, caring, and concern that are the goals of the human-potential movement.

On the subject of reentry problems, the American Psychiatric Association report states:

> Some have responded by using the group not as an agent to aid them in their lives but as a substitute for life. The encounter group culture thus becomes the "real" world and a new clinical entity, labeled by Carl Rogers the "group addict," is created.

The case of Julia discussed in Chapter I is an example of a suicide precipitated by mishandled encounter experiences. In my research for this book, I discovered six other cases of suicide where, either in my judgment or in that of another clinician, the encounter experience was clearly the precipitating factor. The existence of such cases does not prove that the suicide risk for encounter group participants is higher than the rate for nonparticipants. Nevertheless, I have little doubt that encounter has caused suicides that would not have occurred had the victim not suffered a devastating encounter experience.

Many people have dismissed the case of Julia on the basis that suicides also occur among patients in psychotherapy. That is certainly true, and in fact confirms my argument: that *it is reprehensible to expose people unscreened for psychiatric illness or suicidal tendencies to an intense and disruptive psychological process without protecting them with all possible skilled care and observation.* In conventional treatment, Julia's therapist would have been able to spot the signs of emotional overload; he could have varied her treatment if it proved too intense; he probably wouldn't have exposed her to such violent psychological stress; and in all likelihood, he would have followed up after the treatment to make sure of its effects.

Individual cases of long-term bad reactions to encounter began to appear to professional literature in the early 1960's, and countless informal reports have since been presented at conferences. Many clinicians have contacted me to describe the reactions of their patients. Dr. Robert Yufit of Chicago wrote:

> I have had two patients who had serious reactions to encounter groups. One had a severe anxiety episode following an encounter group, requiring immediate therapeutic intervention ... a second became severely depressed immediately following a weekend encounter group and sought help when she was unable to function.

Case reports alone do not indicate whether the apparent increase in casualties reflects more extensive reporting by clinicians, or an actual increase in the number of groupers hurt. Even if the rate were fixed, there would be an increase of reported casualties, since the number of people playing the encounter game has increased.

While case reports may be useful to suggest trends, somewhat more reliable data can be obtained when a clinician or researcher examines the participants in his group and, either by himself or with the help of an independent observer, attempts to determine how many of his subjects suffered harmful consequences. Several such studies have been carried out, but findings cannot be generalized. Their principal drawback is that without a control group (a group of people similar to those in the encounter group who have not been exposed to the group process) their conclusions are unreliable. Further, since participants choose their own groups, it is difficult to sort out the effect of the group leader from the participants' self-selection factors. A reliable study would have to examine many groups with subjects randomly assigned for a length of time sufficient to determine whether the ill effects were short-term or lasting.

Perhaps the most serious limitation on the evidence presented so far is that each researcher (often the group leader himself) uses his own definition of "ill effect" or "psychosis." In fact, many encounterists believe that psychosis is not undesirable in the process of human growth. The May 12, 1969, issue of *Newsweek* quoted Frederick Stoller, a pioneer in the development of marathons: "Everyone has the strength to deal with the encounter experience." Admitting that psychotic breakdowns occurred in his groups, Stoller said, "If the leader doesn't become frightened, people will often go through the experience and come well out of it."

The consensus among mental-health professionals is just the opposite. The American Psychiatric Association's Encounter Group Task Force reported that almost all consider psychosis harmful, since

> experience has shown that the common effect of a disorganizing psychotic episode on an individual is to leave his self-confidence and sense of mastery badly shaken. A psychotic experience is a manifestation of illness, not a way toward health and maturity.

And Morris Parloff of the National Institute of Mental Health has said:

> Our back wards are filled with patients who have failed to attain maximum benefit from their psychoses.

Such differences of opinion exist on nearly every psychiatric symptom. Many encounterists consider new symptoms in group members to be proof of the change process, hence positive. Most clinicians agree that new symptoms indicate change, but feel that its value depends on how well the grouper integrates his experience. For example, a depression may be a necessary and important step in dealing with a feeling of loss and may ultimately lead to a new sense of self-confidence. But it can also be a terrifying period which the patient cannot bear to think about, lest the black clouds recur.

Carl Rogers, a well known encounter advocate whose "client-centered therapy" is often studied in psychology, personality theory, counseling, and child-development courses, followed up on 587 subjects from some forty of his groups. On the basis of the 481 responses to his questionnaire, Rogers determined that two participants had had psychotic reactions during or immediately following the group experience. Rogers' analysis included only those cases of psychosis which he did not consider transitory, since he believes "individuals have also lived through clearly psychotic episodes very constructively in the context of a basic encounter group." Rogers' data suggests that the rate of enduring psychotic reactions is 0.3 percent, but does not show the frequency of other kinds of emotional stress. Rogers' study had no control group, no basic definitions of psychiatric states, and no indication of the length of time these people were exposed to encounter. No dropout rate from the original groups is reported, and we cannot even guess the fate of the more than one hundred participants who did not respond to the questionnaire.

Other researchers, however, have found considerably higher rates of serious disturbance. In 1966 Dr. Louis Gottschalk observed thirty-two subjects in laboratory groups; he reported psychotic reactions in two participants (6.5 percent) and severe disruptions of performance in four others (12.5 percent). Thus Gottschalk's figures indicate that 19 percent of the participants he observed were seriously disturbed by their group experience. When mild and moderate disturbance has been included, the figures have gone as high as 47 percent of group members suffering ill effects. Even NTL-sponsored studies, with their casual methodology, have revealed psychotic reactions in 1 percent of participants.

A broad-scale research program started in 1968 at Stanford University probably offers the most compelling evidence on the effects of encounter groups. The authors, Irvin D. Yalom, Morton A. Lieberman, and Matthew Miles, are well known in the field of group therapy and T-group research. Their project compared ten different approaches to personal change in eighteen groups of Stanford undergraduates during the 1969 winter quarter. Two groups each represented (1) sensitivity training following the NTL model, (2) NTL West ("personal growth," with a black-white encounter focus), (3) Synanon orientation, (4) transactional analysis, (5) Gestalt therapy (Esalen-Fritz Perls derivative), (6) psychodrama orientation, (7) marathon groups (Rogerian; eclectic personal growth), and (8) leaderless tape groups. One additional group used the sensory-awareness approach of Esalen groups and one had a psychoanalytic orientation. The final study population consisted of 209 participants assigned to eighteen groups, and sixty-nine control subjects.

Participating students were randomly assigned to various groups balanced for sex, academic year, and previous encounter group experience. In order to approximate the usual encounter group situation, there were no preliminary screenings, and during the course of the study the research staff never intervened in the sessions or gave feedback to the leaders or group members.

The sixteen leaders in the study either had national reputations or were considered among the most prominent West Coast group leaders in their fields. Some of them used highly aggressive, confrontive techniques. While the authors express some concern about placing their subjects in high risk situations, they point out that "encounter groups of all types are so common that approximately 50 percent of the student population had been in at least one group," and that the aggressive leadership styles were already very much in evidence on the Stanford campus.

Before the subjects were assigned to groups they were warned that "participation in encounter groups sometimes results in considerable emotional upset." They were also told about the university health facilities and given the names of the principal investigators, should they need to consult them. When one of the group members committed suicide during the project, the investigators requested all leaders to remind their groups of the mental-health facilities on the campus. This was the one intervention by the research staff during the experiment.

The investigators point out that the overall effects of the research conditions were to *reduce* risk. The leaders knew that they were being observed, that they would be evaluated and compared with the other leaders, and that the results would eventually be published. The investigators note that such conditions could only serve to put leaders "on their best behavior."

Several different research reports came out of this study. The report on encounter group casualties was published by Yalom and Lieberman in 1971. They defined a casualty as

> an individual who, as a direct result of his experience in the encounter group, became more psychologically distressed and/or employed more maladaptive mechanisms of defense; furthermore this negative change is not a transient but an enduring one, as judged eight months after the group experience.

Since they did not interview all 209 subjects in depth, they used seven criteria to identify a sample for more intensive study: requests for psychiatric aid; dropouts from groups; peer evaluations; reports of a drop in self-esteem; the subject's evaluation of his group; psychotherapy begun while participating in the group; and the leaders' ratings of the students' progress. Several miscellaneous sources of information were also used, such as expressions of concern by observers or participants.

Once a list of 104 suspected casualties was compiled by these methods, the authors attempted a fifteen- to twenty-minute telephone interview. If they suspected the subject had had a psychologically destructive experience, they held an in-depth interview. As an example of a subject *not* considered a casualty, the authors note the case of D.A.:

> D.A. was the major tragedy of the study. A few days after his second meeting he took sleeping pills and committed suicide. It would have been easy to impugn the group as responsible. However, upon careful study, we learned that he had a long history of psychiatric disturbance and had, during the course of the group and over the preceding three

years, sought help from a number of sources. . . . Six months before his death, he had begun both individual and group therapy in two university health facilities and was, concurrently, in another group in a nearby growth institute.

It is impossible to conclude with certainty that the encounter group did not in some way contribute to his suicide. However, after considering all the evidence, we decided that his participation in the encounter group was more a manifestation than a cause of his despair and did not, therefore, consider him a "casualty."

Yalom and Lieberman included his suicide note in their report:

I felt great pain that I could not stop any other way. It would have been helpful if there had been anyone to understand and care about my pain, but there wasn't. People did not believe me when I told them about my problems or pain or else said that it was just self-pity; or if there had been someone to share my feelings with, but all they said was that I was hiding myself, not showing my true feelings, talking to myself. They kept saying this no matter how hard I tried to reach them. . . .

Through their screening process Yalom and Lieberman identified 104 suspected casualties. Of these they managed to contact 79 by telephone; the additional 25 could not be reached. Further examination of the casualty suspects left 16 students designated as casualties—7.5 percent of the 209 subjects who had begun the study, or 9.4 percent of the 170 who completed it. Yalom and Lieberman state:

The severity and type of psychological injury varied considerably. Three students during or immediately following the group had a psychotic decomposition—one a manic psychosis, one an acute paranoid schizophrenic episode, and the third an acute undifferentiated schizophrenic-LSD episode. Several students had depressive and/or anxiety symptoms ranging from low-grade tension or discouragement to severe crippling anxiety attacks to a major six-month depression with a forty-pound weight loss and suicidal ideation. Others suffered some disruption of their self-system: they felt empty, self-negating, inadequate, shameful, unacceptable, more discouraged about ever growing or changing. Several subjects noted a deterioration of their interpersonal life; they withdrew or avoided others; experienced more distrust, were less willing to reach out or to take risks with others.

These authors point out that leaders' ratings prove to be a highly inaccurate means of identifying casualties. One other common method of identifying casualties, that is, by noting the number who seek help, also proved to be an insensitive index. True casualties were, in fact, likely to be identified by more than one method. Of the casualties, 62 percent were identified by three or four different modes. Yalom and Lieberman noted: "If a group member is cited by more than one member of his group or cites himself as having been hurt by the experience, it is highly probable that he represents a casualty of the group. . . . All of the more severe casualties were identified by this method."

It seems clear from this study that leader behavior is the critical factor in psychological injuries. Yalom and Lieberman point out that the casualties were not evenly distributed among the eighteen experimental groups. Six groups had no casualties at all, while other groups generated several casualties. The ideological "school" with which the leader identified had no relation to his actual behavior, so that two leaders with the same stylistic designation were no more likely to resemble one another than they were to resemble leaders of any other schools.

One particular leadership style, which they called Type A or "aggressive stimulators," accounted for 44 percent of the total casualties in the study. Five leaders were identified in this type, including two Gestalt leaders, one psychodrama leader, and the two Synanon leaders. In their groups the average risk factor was 17 percent. Their behavior was intrusive, confronting, challenging; at the same time they demonstrated "high positive caring . . . and revealed a great deal of themselves. They were the most charismatic of the leaders." These leaders tended to have an authoritarian manner and to focus on individuals one at a time rather than encourage group interaction. Their style was the familiar "hot-seat" style characteristic of Fritz Perls' and Dan Casriel's work. The investigators state: "Not only were there more casualties in Type A groups, but there were more severe casualties."

The follow-up interviews revealed several common group events which the individuals blamed for their adverse reactions: attack by the leader or by the group; rejection by the leader or by the group; failure to attain unrealistic goals, "in-put overload," and group pressure. Attack by the leader was cited only in the case of Type A leaders and was associated with some of the more severe casualties. Yalom and Lieberman cite an illustration:

> N.N. was unequivocal in her evaluation of her group as a destructive experience. Following the suggestions of the leader, her group was an intensely aggressive one which undertook to help N.N., a passive, gentle individual, to "get in touch with" her anger. Although the group attacked her in many ways, including a physical assault by one of the female members, most of all she remembers the leader's remark that she "was on the verge of schizophrenia."
>
> He would not elaborate on this statement and it echoed ominously within her for months. She remained extremely uncomfortable, withdrew markedly from her family and friends, was depressed and insomniac; she was so obsessed by her leader's remark that she dreaded going to bed because she knew her mind would focus on it. Often she lapsed into daydreams in which she relived, with a more satisfying ending, some event in the group. The only benefit of the experience, she said, was to help her appreciate how lonely she was. We consider N.N. a severe and long-term casualty.

Attack by the group was another mode of injury that occurred, either in conjunction with attack by a Type A leader or where leaders tended to be distant and offered little supportive behavior. Yalom and Lieberman cite the case of E.D.:

> "I didn't want to come, and came out of responsibility. I was not in the mood for encountering and was almost forced to. I don't trust anyone in the group and felt threatened by it. I came away having many self-doubts without being able to resolve them within the group."
>
> The last meeting was particularly bitter for him since he was vigorously attacked for his uninvolvement. He recalls nervously picking at the carpet during the onslaught; he was criticized for that and when he stopped he was criticized for his passivity and suggestibility.
>
> After the group he felt deeply depressed for about a week. Following this he left with a residue of deflation,

helplessness, self-disgust, and discouragement. Even months later he continued to feel anxious, depressed, and less trustful of others. . . .

We consider E.D. a moderately severe casualty of long duration.

Rejection was a significant factor in at least six of the casualties in the Yalom and Lieberman report. They describe the example of a woman who had planned to reveal a great deal about herself in the group, mainly details about "sexual liaisons with black men and her deeply held racist feelings." However, she failed to make an accurate judgment of the receptivity of the group. "Self-disclosure by one group member places implicit demands on the others for reciprocal disclosure," say these authors, and evidently the group was not ready for the degree of intimacy demanded by her revelations. As a result the group withdrew from her, regarding her as a "sex maniac." Her high expectations led to an even greater disappointment, and for many months after the group was over she felt great shame and self-contempt.

Unrealistically high expectations seem to have caused negative results for several of the casualties in the Yalom and Lieberman studies. They had entered the group with great expectations "to learn to relate, to break through their restrictive schizoid straitjacket, to get in touch with their emotions."

> Despite their vigorous personal resolutions to do things differently (resolutions which were abetted by the current optimistic mystique surrounding encounter groups) they found, to their great dismay, that their behavior was more locked, rigid, and repetitive than they had known. They soon re-created and reexperienced in their encounter group the same interpersonal environment from which they had fled in the outside world. All of them left the group more discouraged and more pessimistic than ever.

Another source of casualties identified is described as "group pressure effects." Two of the casualties of the study reported that they were unable to accommodate to the group pressure "to experience and express feelings," and ended their group with a sense of hollowness and failure. Research has established that opposing group pressure is difficult and anxiety-provoking. Studies by Solomon Asch (1958) and Muzafer Sherif (1958) pointed out that individuals will misperceive or intentionally misrepresent their perceptions in order to conform to pressures by the rest of the group. Stanley Milgram (1963) has shown that response to authority will lead a majority of subjects into acts where they believe they're inflicting severe pain on others simply to conform to "scientific authority."

Such influences are easily engendered in the encounter group, and when the norms call for vigorous displays of emotion, it becomes difficult for individuals to resist. Further, having conformed with such expectancies, and having ended the group on a high positive note, participants are highly likely to evaluate the experience as positive—still in keeping with the group norms.

Lieberman, Yalom, and Miles were not only concerned with the risks of encounter. In addition, their data indicated:

> It is three times more likely that the subject who is in an encounter group will seek psychotherapy during the time he is in the group or in the eight-month follow-up period than a control subject.

This is not necessarily a negative finding. True, about a third of those who entered psychotherapy did so in an attempt to repair the damage done to them in the groups. But the remaining two thirds entered treatment for the same reason they had joined the groups, in search of help, or because they wanted to continue work started in the group.

Just as the casualty rate varied greatly from group to group, the incidence of positive results also depended on the group in which a participant found himself. "Some groups had almost no impact, others affected nearly every participant," say the authors, who cite as an example one group in which 100% of the participants rose on a test of self-esteem, while in another group only 15% showed a similar improvement. The conditions in groups with maximum benefits included a non-aggressive climate in which feedback was closely related to participants' life experiences, and where members had the opportunity to try out new solutions to interpersonal situations. On the whole, about 8% of participants showed positive changes.

Lieberman notes:

> The picture at the end of the groups was that of a highly satisfied clientele: 75 percent of the participants reported that the group had changed them in a positive direction; of these, three quarters expected the change to be lasting.

But when the investigators returned to question subjects six to eight months later, more than half of those who had thought the experience very valuable no longer thought so.

The investigators also surveyed friends of the groupers and the control subjects. Regardless of the measure of change used, *the controls came off better than the encounter groupers.* Lieberman says: "78 percent of the participants (compared to 86 percent of the controls) were perceived by their social network as having at least one change in a positive direction." For negative changes the proportions were reversed: 25 percent of the participants were described as having at least one negative change, while only 17 percent of the controls were so described.

If there were solid evidence of positive change resulting from encounter groups, and if a player knew what kind of group he was getting into, he could sensibly evaluate whether the process could benefit him. But when research indicates that most of the positive effects reported are transitory and illusory, it seems clear that the degree of psychological risk makes encounter a costly gamble. Who would take a ride in the family car if he knew that almost one out of every ten rides would result in serious personal damage?

CERTIFICATE OF DEATH

STATE FILE NUMBER

STATE OF CALIFORNIA—DEPARTMENT OF PUBLIC HEALTH

LOCAL REGISTRATION DISTRICT AND CERTIFICATE NUMBER

DECEDENT PERSONAL DATA	1a NAME OF DECEASED—FIRST NAME	1b MIDDLE NAME	1c LAST NAME	2a DATE OF DEATH—MONTH, DAY, YEAR FEBRUARY 9, 1971	2b HOUR 2:30 PM
	3 SEX Male	4 COLOR OR RACE White	5 BIRTHPLACE (STATE OR FOREIGN COUNTRY) New York	6 DATE OF BIRTH	7 AGE (LAST BIRTHDAY) 24 YEARS
	8 NAME AND BIRTHPLACE OF FATHER		9 MAIDEN NAME AND BIRTHPLACE OF MOTHER		
	10 CITIZEN OF WHAT COUNTRY United States	11 SOCIAL SECURITY NUMBER no Record	12 MARRIED NEVER MARRIED WIDOWED DIVORCED (SPECIFY) Never Married	13 NAME OF SURVIVING SPOUSE (IF WIFE, ENTER MAIDEN NAME) None	
	14 LAST OCCUPATION Teacher	15 NUMBER OF YEARS IN THIS OCCUPATION 2	16 NAME OF LAST EMPLOYING COMPANY OR FIRM (IF SELF EMPLOYED SO STATE) no Record	17 KIND OF INDUSTRY OR BUSINESS Education	

| PLACE OF DEATH | 18a PLACE OF DEATH—NAME OF HOSPITAL OR OTHER IN-PATIENT FACILITY Coast Ridge Route Big Sur | 18b STREET ADDRESS—(STREET AND NUMBER OR LOCATION) Coast Route Highway # 1 South | 18c INSIDE CITY CORPORATE LIMITS (SPECIFY YES OR NO) No |
| | 18c CITY OR TOWN Carmel | 18d COUNTY Monterey | 18f LENGTH OF STAY IN COUNTY OF DEATH 1 | 18g LENGTH OF STAY IN CALIFORNIA 1 YEARS |

| USUAL RESIDENCE (IF DEATH OCCURRED IN INSTITUTION ENTER RESIDENCE BEFORE ADMISSION) | 19a USUAL RESIDENCE—STREET ADDRESS (STREET AND NUMBER OR LOCATION) | 19b INSIDE CITY CORPORATE LIMITS (SPECIFY YES OR NO) No | 20 NAME AND MAILING ADDRESS OF INFORMANT |
| | 19c CITY OR TOWN Big Sur | 19d COUNTY Monterey | 19e STATE California |

| PHYSICIAN'S OR CORONER'S CERTIFICATION | 21a CORONER INVESTIGATION | 21b PHYSICIAN | 21c | C. H. Hill, CORONER | 21d DATE SIGNED 2/16/71 |
| | | | 21e ADDRESS SALINAS, CALIFORNIA | | 21f PHYSICIAN'S CALIFORNIA LICENSE NUMBER |

| FUNERAL DIRECTOR AND LOCAL REGISTRAR | 22a SPECIFY BURIAL ENTOMBMENT OR CREMATION BURIAL—Removal | 22b DATE 2-10-71 | 23 NAME OF CEMETERY OR CREMATORY Brooklyn, New York | 24 EMBALMER—SIGNATURE (IF BODY EMBALMED) LICENSE NUMBER 2676 |
| | 25 NAME OF FUNERAL DIRECTOR (OR PERSON ACTING AS SUCH) MISSION MORTUARY, MONTEREY | 26 | 27 LOCAL REGISTRAR—SIGNATURE M.D.K | 28 Feb. 10,1971 |

MEDICAL AND HEALTH DATA	CAUSE OF DEATH	29 PART I DEATH WAS CAUSED BY IMMEDIATE CAUSE (A)	ENTER ONLY ONE CAUSE PER LINE FOR A, B, AND C Massive brain damage	Mins.	APPROXIMATE INTERVAL BETWEEN ONSET AND DEATH
		CONDITIONS IF ANY WHICH GAVE RISE TO THE IMMEDIATE CAUSE (A) STATING THE UNDERLYING CAUSE LAST	DUE TO OR AS A CONSEQUENCE OF (B) Gunshot wound of head	Mins.	
			DUE TO OR AS A CONSEQUENCE OF (C)		
		30 PART II OTHER SIGNIFICANT CONDITIONS—CONTRIBUTING TO DEATH BUT NOT RELATED TO THE IMMEDIATE CAUSE GIVEN IN PART I	31 WAS OPERATION OR BIOPSY PERFORMED FOR ANY CONDITION IN ITEM 29 OR 30? (SPECIFY) NO	32a AUTOPSY (SPECIFY YES OR NO) YES	32b IF YES WERE FINDINGS CONSIDERED IN DETERMINING CAUSE OF DEATH (SPECIFY YES OR NO) YES
	INJURY INFORMATION	33 SPECIFY ACCIDENT SUICIDE OR HOMICIDE Probable Suicide	34 PLACE OF INJURY (SPECIFY HOME FARM FACTORY OFFICE BUILDING ETC.) Near barn	35 INJURY AT WORK (SPECIFY YES OR NO) No	36a DATE OF INJURY—MONTH DAY YEAR 2/9/71	36b HOUR 2:30 P
		37a PLACE OF INJURY (STREET AND NUMBER OR LOCATION AND CITY OR TOWN) Route 1, Hot Springs Creek	37b DISTANCE FROM PLACE OF INJURY TO USUAL RESIDENCE ITEM 19 5 MILES	38 WERE LABORATORY TESTS DONE FOR DRUGS OR TOXIC CHEMICALS (SPECIFY YES OR NO) No	39 WERE LABORATORY TESTS DONE FOR ALCOHOL (SPECIFY YES OR NO) Yes
		40 DESCRIBE HOW INJURY OCCURRED (ENTER SEQUENCE OF EVENTS WHICH RESULTED IN INJURY NATURE OF INJURY SHOULD BE ENTERED IN ITEM 29) Self inflicted. gunshot wound of head.			

| STATE REGISTRAR | A | B | C | D | E | F |

REV 1-1-66 Form VS-11

CERTIFICATION STATEMENT

This is to certify, that the attached is a true and correct copy of the vital record which is on file in this office and of which I am the legal custodian.

Richard St Eraser MD Registrar

SIGNATURE OF CERTIFYING OFFICIAL   OFFICIAL TITLE

P. O. Box 2137
Salinas, California   Feb.18,1971

PLACE OF CERTIFICATION   DATE OF CERTIFICATION

1270 Natividad Rd. Salinas, California

STATE OF CALIFORNIA
DEPARTMENT OF PUBLIC HEALTH

6-1-90
Form VS-199

7

Death at Big Sur

The existence of psychological and physical dangers in the encounter game is acknowledged, in varying degrees, by most observers. Many growth centers now issue a fine-print warning to prospective players not to view their programs as psychotherapy and try to discourage players who consider themselves mentally ill. But a fine-print warning is as far as they go. The centers operate under the you-are-responsible-for-yourself ethic and accept no responsibility for the psychological pressures created in the name of growth. Few make any effort to screen out people with histories of emotional disturbance.

Barring a professional psychological evaluation, a player's own report of prior emotional disturbance is probably the best means of identifying persons for whom encounter is a high-risk game. But there is an important fallacy here: we cannot expect all vulnerable people to have already acknowledged their psychological difficulties or sought help before knocking at a growth center's door. For many, that knock is the first attempt to deal with a psychological fire alarm ringing within.

In our culture most people are ashamed of any sort of mental illness—only crazy people seek professional aid. Because of the stigma, those most in need of psychological help are often the least likely to seek it. Most mental-health professionals agree that once a person has taken the step of actively reaching for help, he is well on the way to change and is healthier than the person with similar problems who refuses help, feels that asking for help shows weakness, or tries to ignore his emotional difficulties.

In its repeated promises to increase human potential and emo-

tional growth for "normal, healthy people," the encounter movement seems to deny the existence of psychopathology, as though
there were something other than illness that prevents health. The
would-be player is encouraged to believe that he holds within all
the strength he needs to cope with psychological stress, and—with
a little help from his encounter friends—to use that stress for
personality growth. Further, he is promised that, having grown, he
will have most of the tools needed to help others grow, should he
wish to do so.

Group leadership, encounterists hold, requires no special responsibility or emotional maturity, since any time a leader is in
trouble the group can be relied upon to help. The writings of Carl
Rogers and Bill Schutz suggest that they believe that a group is
magical. Its wisdom is presumed to be infinite, its judgment
unerring—certainly more reliable than that of a single person
whose natural capacities have been dulled by professional training—and its natural, life-supporting, health-generating resources are
believed capable of dispelling any emotional pathogens that might
attack its members. They fail to recognize that groups are often
bad judges; that the health-generating capacity of a group may be
insufficient to cope with the disease; that, in fact, the intense
whock of the change processes may inhibit natural recuperative
powers or even halt them entirely.

In March 1971 I was contacted by an attorney for the estate of
a young man who, a few weeks before, had shot himself through
the head at Esalen. The attorney and the young man's parents
were trying to understand the psychological changes he had undergone during his exposure to encounter, and wanted to know
whether the people with whom he had been involved at Esalen
could be considered legally or morally responsible for his death. I
interviewed his parents and his best friend, and examined all the
relevant documents that could be gathered, including a journal in
which he had made irregular entries during the year he was
involved with Esalen. (I have changed his name here, but have left
unchanged the names of those at Esalen and in the encounter
movement who influenced him.)

A psychological autopsy is never easy to make, especially when,
as in Steve D.'s case, no mental-health professional had examined

him while he was alive. Even if Esalen *had* used any screening procedures, Steve had no history of psychiatric contact to disqualify him. By almost any standard Steve would have been viewed—and viewed himself—as psychologically fit. Mrs. D. was too upset to discuss her son at any length, so I'll let Mr. D. describe Steve before his Esalen experiences:

> Steve was a very square, conservative type at that time—Republican with a big R, pro-Buckley, anti-Social Security, etc. He was an extrovert all his life, excellent student, big man on campus, had tremendous energy, could be involved with fifty different things at the same time.
>
> Steve was an economics major. He started looking for a job while still in college and got one with a very young, very aggressive financial company for twenty-five dollars a week. In a very short time he made a lot of money—into five figures, without blinking an eye. He spent a lot of money, had to have the best of things, spent three hundred dollars for a suit. I don't think he thought in terms of money per se—money was just something to be used.

Steve won approval from his parents and friends in various ways, usually through financial success or leadership. At ages thirteen through fifteen, he imported toys from Japan and sold them at Christmas time. What he couldn't get rid of one year, he sold to a children's project. He never lacked schemes and ideas, and it was important to him to be master of his fraternity, a judo specialist, and an Eagle Scout.

Steve's friend Tom, describing Steve in college, said, "He had so much magnetism—we used to kid him in college, saying that if we had enough money we could make him President, we could market him, sell him like cigarettes."

In the summer of 1969 Steve and Tom decided to travel, camp out, and see America—California in particular. Tom said:

> We first went to Esalen in October of 1969, when we were camping out at Big Sur. Prior to going to Esalen we were arrested for possession of marijuana and chemicals for LSD, and spent a few days in jail before the sentence was suspended.... Steve developed Bell's palsey—his face was half paralyzed for two weeks. Being in jail had an effect on him, "being in a cage." This added to his disillusionment

with establishment practices, authority, police picking on kids with long hair.

At Esalen Steve and Tom first participated in a Gestalt-oriented encounter group. It was Tom's first encounter group, and he was quiet and somewhat intimidated. Not Steve. Tom said:

> Jack Downing was the leader of that first group—about twenty people in it. The group was very impressed with Steve. Steve was changing his behavior and personality. He wanted to get away from Steve, called himself Rainbow, changed his appearance and living style.
>
> He explained to the group why he wanted to change. Jack had him take two chairs and have a conversation between Steve and Rainbow. It was noticeable that when he was Steve he was very loud, aggressive; as Rainbow he was quieter, more passive, softer. Steve didn't realize this difference in his voice. He was very impressed with that group—it was light, not intensive.
>
> Steve became enchanted with Big Sur. He had met Bonnie, who was working at Esalen—I think that had a lot to do with it. He went into a group for rich people—the Millionaires' Group—they didn't resolve anything but had a good time. They gave parties and threw money around, burned fifty-dollar bills—it was all part of the therapy.

It is difficult to determine whether changes Steve was going through were the result of his group experiences before and during his first two weeks at Esalen, or whether they would have occurred without his fairly heavy encountering. Mr. D. did not view Steve's group experiences prior to his full-time absorption in Esalen as particularly important, but he did notice clear personality changes. Mr. D.'s description is, not surprisingly, somewhat money-oriented. Tall and handsome, Mr. D. is a successful businessman, and Steve clearly tried to follow his example—though not without conflict. The changes in Steve's attitudes toward money can be considered clinical evidence of profound personality changes.

Mr. D. said:

> He changed in manner and style, started giving away all his possessions. One reason for the change was a parting of the ways with Tom, who'd been his friend all his life—

through schools, fraternity, etc. . . . It was while they were separated that Steve changed. Dressed like a hippie, he'd take the company limousine to meetings with successful financiers. Many big names in finance were astonished that a boy his age with one year's experience could come up with great ideas.

I don't know when he started on drugs. . . . He never used hard drugs, but must have taken LSD. I don't know when or how often. I saw or talked to him frequently—at least once a week. . . . He seemed no different, except for his manner and clothes. His change was against society, and it wasn't important for him to have money. When he went to California he said he had set things up so that he wouldn't have to earn any money for a year or more—took twenty-five to thirty thousand in ready money. I don't think Steve could have been conscious in the last months of how much money he went through—must have been fifty to sixty thousand in fifteen months.

When he left California for the second time he was a functioning person—had it all planned, financially. . . .

During that first two-week stay at Esalen, Steve was in groups almost constantly, but Tom only took on a little of the encountering. He told me that he hadn't had Steve's prior exposure to the game—Steve had been in several groups while in college—and that he was pretty scared by the whole process, although Steve was enthusiastic.

"He was at Esalen about ten days," said Tom, "and then we started home. He talked about wanting to minimize the baloney, the bullshit in his life. . . . He had a breakfast interview with Bill Schutz about joining the residence program, and also spoke to Downing about it. Schutz told him they had eight or ten openings and about eight million people applying, but Steve felt pretty confident he'd get in."

Shortly after the two-weeks of encounter at Esalen Steve was invited to go through the four-month leader-training program starting in February 1970. Phone conversations between Steve and his parents while he was at Esalen were regular. Mr. D. described Steve's excitement:

He was thrilled—it was a big game to him, he thoroughly enjoyed it—he was in his glory, could dress and do as he pleased, act as he pleased, perfect freedom. But he was anxious to go out and prove himself by building his own home, living on his own land, building his own road. . . .

Steve made the following entry in his journal:

ESALEN INSTITUTE RESIDENCE PROGRAM began Feb. 1, 1970. Today is ~~Apr~~ March 23. Spring & full moon— also Rainbow became drizzle & lost his voice for a while. Generally feeling very high & centered—eating well loosing weight (15-20 lbs. since N. Y. (approx. 8 weeks)). Less & less dope more & more meditation. Breathing & chanting exercises every morning @ 7-7.30 for ½-1 hr. usually evenings too—find I can concentrate easily—seem to need less stimulation in order to feel good. Feel good solid friendships growing, if too slowly. Must be patient—am aware that time is the answer. I'm told I must learn to think in seasons— learning to play the drums, congas & feel that this Fills a previously missing gap. Have very little unresolved anger or resentments. Usually find that I can be up front about everything.

Steve's earlier pattern of being more successful than those around him seems to have carried over to Esalen. But the old values that he learned at home—success, money, academic achievement—were no good in the encounter culture, and at several points we can see Steve looking to his friends for new standards. His search for a philosophy to live by was evidently influenced by the most recent esoteric religion to become a part of the Esalen potpourri: Sufism.

The next entry in Steve's journal consisted of several pages of notes on "Sufi Mentations" and exercises:

The sufis are not a sect, being bound by no religious dogma & using no regular place of worship. "We friends" or "people like us" is how they refer to themselves, they recognize one another by certain natural gifts, habits, qualities of thought.

What makes them so difficult to discuss is that their mutual recognition cannot be explained in ordinary moral or psychological terms—whoever understands it is himself a Sufi.

A Sufi may come dressed as a general, a peasant, a merchant, a lawyer, school teacher, anything. To be "in the world, but not of it," free from ambition, greed, intellectual pride, blind obedience to custom, or awe of persons higher in rank—That is the Sufi's ideal. . . .

Sufism develops a line of communication with ultimate knowledge no theorizing at all!

Sufism is known by means of itself.

The number of Sufi followers today is unknown. There is a Sufi monastery in Chile, where several Esalen people have gone to carry their knowledge back to California. In fact, Steve D. loaned a thousand dollars to one Esalen resident to make that pilgrimage.

Steve was not only learning a new religion—he was experiencing intense psychological pressures daily. Full-time encountering, alternating with periods of reflection and silent meditation designed to "unfreeze" his old emotional props, left Steve at times feeling unsure, lost, and lonely. At 1 A.M. several days after the Sufi entry, he made the following notes in his journal:

> Today seemed mellow—its as if I know what I'm doing here. For the first month I felt here but not here. Getting used to a new environment & new friends without the comfort of old ones to turn to for understanding was (is?) hard. I cry occasionally when I flash on [old friends]. I feel so beautiful here & I want to share this place, my new insights, new friends, with my old pals. . . .
>
> Tomorrow I cook breakfast for 100 @ esalen—I'm *really* looking forward to it. I'm digging the fact that they trust me to do it. . . .
>
> Next week I plan to give up all drugs (dope, grass etc.). (its lent)
>
> Kathy blewout during massage today—so did Alicia—As these experiences get more common, I see new depths of myself & others—a closer tie with the beyond, an experiential dive into the unknown & *Back*—easier each time—I feel more in control.

A few days later Steve wrote:

> Synanon Game began today—I'm told it will be a heavy trip—looking forward to it—willing to experience anything. . . .

Steve wrote little about his actual encounter experiences. During this period entry dates become vague—perhaps because he was confused, or perhaps because dates were less important:

Today is Sunday early April—Bonnie left Friday morning & I really miss her. I'm grooving on all sorts of things & yet I fell as though I'm spinning—actually for a change its jazy to be on my own & yet its as if a piece of me were missing.

Fri. night went to *Nepenthe* [the local cabaret hangout frequented by Esalen people] & got it on with a few people, met some locals who I never would have rapped with if I weren't alone—Got into a strange sexual encounter—Sue was with David yet she slept with me David slept next to us & was really pissed Sue was cool & I was semi-up tight—I felt bad for David also I Kept thinking about Bonnie Anyway we all talked about our feelings in the morning & I feel real good about those people now. I see Bonnie and Sue as so much alike—Very Centered & digging their existance. I love Bonnie so much—its an experience like that that clarifies my feelings.

I finally am getting to like John Lilly. It took so long because I was afraid of him—Now I can separate the wheat from the chaff when he speaks to me. I know that his feelings are good, he's just mind fucking most of the time.

Mr. and Mrs. D. had little understanding of the experiences their son was having; they could only judge his behavior. Mr. D. again:

Some people he met, casually, at Esalen encounter sessions invested with Steve in the purchase of some land (it proved to be a sound investment, he used good judgment). . . .

He thought of himself as buying his own mountain, his own island, his own escape. . . . Hard property physically for anyone except young, fit people, to get to. But when you reached it, you could see fifty to seventy-five miles out into the Pacific. I'm sure one's mental outlook would change up there, knowing it was yours—"my own world that I'm in." . . .

At this period Steve's whole personality and manner had changed completely; he was far out, with a heavy beard, eccentric dress (he had to make his own pants and shirt; everything had to be done by himself for himself), but at the same time he bought a ninety-five-hundred-dollar sports car, paying cash for it—completely at odds with his attitude that material things didn't mean anything to him. . . .

All his money was gone by June of that year. As fast as his commissions would come in he'd spend them, he paid no attention to how his money went.

The first Esalen extravaganza in New York provides us with different views of Steve. About the benefit itself Steve said only, "Esalen benefit sort of fun but too many hassles with Suki and Claire to suit me." And of New York: "Good to see friends ...N.Y. ugly and fucked...went to lunch with guys from office." Then in a list of friends and relatives, each of whom he noted that he loved, Steve said of his parents: "Mom and Dad are groovy. We're communicating beautifully. These months since last summer have really changed all our attitudes."

But the changes that Steve saw in his parents were evidently changes in his own perception and style of communication. His parents did not see these changes so positively:

> He had come east for Esalen's first weekend. This was the first time I felt a real change in him, and teased him about this slow way of talking, question-and-answer "how do you feel about this" stuff, the typical clichés of pseudo-psychology.
>
> One night we had dinner at the Elysee (Steve, his girl, Tom, my wife and me), and had a little to-do. I asked how it was at Esalen. His conversation was stilted; there would be aside comments to his girl to such an extent that I told him that we'd all enjoy having a conversation with him but we'd all have to talk the same language. He took it very well and apologized.... There was general discussion then about what he was doing in the encounter groups. He was very serious, explained it was hard to do; they really worked at it.
>
> He gave us a format of a day's activity: they'd go into a heavy twenty-hour discussion group, nonstop. There was no prescribed ritual they went through. My wife and I thought it was all fun and games. That's when he told me that one of the girls there who'd worked in the kitchen had hung herself. He couldn't understand how, with all the great minds present, this could happen....

Tom's view of Steve was a bit different at that point, but he too sensed that Steve felt something was wrong at Esalen:

> When he came back in April for the first big Esalen shindig he was changed, but still caught in the paradox of New York-buying-things, etc. vs. Esalen's "quiet" life-style. Said that at Esalen one time he wanted to quit—felt that he was being exploited, didn't like working at menial jobs. In fact he had organized a work stoppage out there, a

strike. . . . I think there was a conflict between people who really dug Steve and some who thought he was disruptive and on his own ego trip. He spoke highly of John Heider and of John Lilly. He felt this strike didn't endear him because the hierarchy thought he might be getting people to follow him (instead of them).

My girl said Steve appeared to be a very sensitive person who threw up defenses because he didn't want others to know he could be hurt. I had never looked at him as being defensive before. . . .

Evidently Mr. D. noticed this change in Steve at about the same time:

A couple of months later we got a letter from him from Esalen. Other friends and I got the feeling he was a bit lonely, that he missed closer relationships, people out there sort of stood back, didn't really warm up to him. He said the training was demanding and taxed all his energy.

A couple of months after the residency program, and even at the end of the program, I sensed his disenchantment with Esalen. How it came about, I don't know. It was something that Steve felt was not right. I never doubted he'd come to that understanding himself, because in discussions with him you'd have to believe that he was laughing at himself as well as laughing at Esalen.

I felt he'd gone through a stage in his development as a person. I had no idea that it was during this time [August] he had thought of and talked of suicide. He made no specific comments about it; he said that life in itself was such a pleasure to him—the small things were tremendous—the only fear I had was that the pleasures were a little bit infantile, when so much joy would be generated from just playing (playing at building a house, making his own clothes). Yet I couldn't fault it—there was no harm in it.

The conversation about people, too, was artificial; there were too many *grand* guys, *marvelous* people. The over-enthusiasm about individuals—he had never been like this before. He might have had to prove to himself that he could do things, but it was never important to show others.

We had a good time that August, teasing. He had a great swimming place, a natural hundred-foot waterfall, very hard to get to, back in the woods. Steve, my other son, and I went there, it was too hard for my wife to get to—the place was rocky, hard to climb, isolated. We had a great time, when all of a sudden someone started throwing rocks down from the top of the waterfall. Three kids had hiked in from the back end of the property, saw three nude bodies in the water, and threw stones down at them. We teased Steve that his Nirvana—that's what he said he'd come to Esalen to find—was like the East River. He took it well.

Steve's journal entries for this period show that he was on an emotional merry-go-round:

Co led workshop with Stanley last month—he got sick so I took over—smashing success—Really Far out—I got so high!!! Want to do more—John Heider invited me to co-lead month long [group] after Residential program is over—quite an honor! ... ups & Downs with Bonnie as usual but we're still together.... Thinking about going to Japan to see Worlds Fair.... feeling very into my head & anxious to let go for a while—stop this Esalen microscope trip for a while—

Nine Rolfings & Im not sure what thats all about—can't feel specific changes—But Im sure it all fits together somehow—

Went off all Dope & alcohol for 2 weeks—including trip to N.Y. Cant say exactly what happened—Temptation to have a Beer or glass of wine was great—dident touch a thing though—Smoked grass first day off—Felt a loss of energy with grass all day—decided no dope Before dark—cant get any work done—expect ill try abstance again soon ...

June 2: Bonnie isn't here & I'm really wishing She was. If I knew where she was I'd go find her. I'm lonely & time seems to drag—Fucking another chic or 2 isn't worth It—Being apart shows me how much a part of my life Bonnie really is—Being alone really is a trip—I've never been in quite this space before—I've got so much time on my hands—Ive been reading—drawing house plans—writing etc.—time seems slower—

Went to ford ord this weekend—led encounter groups (3 days) for 10 army officers—very high group. I was superb & really dug it!!! Met some new types of people. Mormons ("would you rather watch 100% of your $ or have you & God watch 90% of it?")....

Residents acid trip last week was very heavy ...

dearest Bonnie I love you. Come home soon

Spent last night with Kathy. I was only ½ there—Kathy is sweet & good but I dont love her & don't need to. I feel sort of guilty now that I've used Kathy and Joan as parts in an experiment....

Im most confused by my relationship with Esalen. This is such a wierd place. I came with all my energy directed

towards taking and giving energy with this place—Yet somehow now I really want to leave. but not completely.

Something's wrong here. lots' is Right, but lots is wrong.
I guess a ? is where I'm at with Camp Esalen Now.

When Steve finished the resident's program he began leading
Esalen workshops periodically, while finishing his house in the
mountains. Tom visited him there:

When I visited Steve in the hills where he'd built his cabin
he mentioned that Dick Price had taken a trip on this
mysterious drug. These trips could last anywhere from three
days to three months. He said Price really flipped out, had a
psychotic episode, almost tried to kill someone, thought he
was all different people—a bullfighter. Price went to Agnew
State Hospital. Steve said he wanted to try this drug but it
would be foolish at that time—he had too much to do on his
house. I imagine he probably took it toward the end.

Evidently changes were occurring in Esalen as well during this
period. Tom said that when they first went there in October
everything was free and open, but the next time there was a gate, a
pass was required, and "it was like a military compound." A friend
gave Tom a pass:

I went up to see Steve at his camping place. He was very
busy chopping wood, etc. He didn't want to leave the
campsite and was becoming a kind of recluse; I felt he was
sincere because it was really a sacrifice to live that way, very
primitive, unless you honestly wanted to. At that point he
showed me the diary he was keeping. He said he wasn't
going to return to Esalen because at the conclusion of the
residential program they had made him an offer to be a
co-leader, but he would have to restrict his behavior in the
group and follow the dictates of someone else. He felt his
freedom was being curtailed. I think he felt they didn't trust
him, and he couldn't work like that.

Steve and I had taken drugs prior to going to Esalen—
took our first acid trip the summer of 1969, tried LSD,
mescaline, but not heavy. When we were there the first time
they said drugs were not allowed, but drugs were everywhere—like everyplace else. There was a rumor that there
had been a death from an overdose of heroin, but that the
body had been taken off the grounds so it wouldn't be

found at Esalen. I was inclined to believe it. But all I saw when we were there was just smoking grass, nothing heavy.

This strange drug Steve mentioned frightened me, though the only reason I could see to take it was to see what would happen to me if I did—but Steve wanted to try it. That scared me because he was always more rational than that.

During this period Steve's diary entries reflect his involvement with his land, and his almost total absorption in the drug culture surrounding Esalen:

> Property owners meeting 2 weeks ago really like an old town meeting—BIG SUR IS SO GREAT!! . . .
> Mountain Nellie has been coming up & hanging around which creats a hassle. She dosent have an old man. I really dig her & she turns me on. Bonnie & Nellie & I tripped one night & slept together. I want them both but of course thats heavy. So that Karma is in the air. . . .
> GREAT (FABULOUS)! party on sycamore Ridge at M.'s (from Nepenthe) house. A couple of hundred stoned people—ALL NIGHT (we stayed from 7-3 AM) & it was still going strong. Music Food Dope—Very Very *high!*. . .

Mr. and Mrs. D. visited Steve that summer:

> We saw him again in August, and there was never anything in any of our conversations that was disquieting to me. When he came back here in September or October he stayed with his old girl friend in the city for a few days. We saw him a few times; my wife and I agreed that he'd had enough of whatever he was involved in, and was going to make a change, was mentally preparing himself—but we had no idea what direction this change would take, how it would come about.

From that summer on Steve became increasingly depressed and self-absorbed. He made several suicide attempts and signaled his need for help to those around him. They either didn't get the signals, or didn't believe them.

Steve's diary skips from July 4th to December:

> Aug—Sept—Oct & November have gone by & so have many many trips I'll try & put them in order & make some comment or other as best I can remember. . . .

Somewhere along the line 2 major turning points in my life came up.

I had my first heavy (Bad?) acid trip—after always being the joy boy, Rainbow, etc. I decided I didn't want to live anymore—So I acted out suicide—Drove my truck off the road into our campsite & was going to put gas line into the tent & go to sleep—Bonnie somehow played along with me (the whole thing started at a party in Sycamore Canyon. . . .

after leaving the party & driving home etc etc the trip wore off & somehow I'm still not dead, although for the first time in my life I've begun to look carefully at the possibility—

I went thru 2 more similar trips (once with Alan & Barbie on the land when I decided I'd have to get rid of Bonnie & once at The Renaissance Pleasure Faire in Marin County when I decided that everybody & everything, including me, was fucked up. . . .

The Second major turn was a trip I took to New York—

My business affairs have been quickly disintergrating ever since I left the scene 1½ years ago as was to be expected But I always figured there would be plenty of $ for the next several years. . . .

The Hypocrisy of the money games was astounding!

I'm now (for the first time In my life) getting close to having more than I need. I don't fear the future & in fact am looking forward to being the same as everyone else—

So now I'm getting Into another world—Goodbye Amerika Goodbye N.Y., Goodbye Wall Street

> Hello God
> Now Sufiism   Meditation
> Gurdjieff   Yoga
> Zen   etc . . .

I seek myself & will not be stopped.

Mr. D. learned much of the following from interviews with Steve's acquaintances when he visited Esalen shortly after Steve's death:

His house was finished, the weather getting bad. He needed money and gravitated back to Esalen, where they paid him for some of his group work. His girl friend told me that generally it was felt Steve was "too heavy in his leading"—that he came on personally too strong but that the groups he led were so sensational, everybody found them so interesting. He spent some time in and out of a residential group run by John Heider during late 1970.

Each of the individuals was aware that Steve had problems. But it was an accumulation of problems that were being expressed through his wish to commit suicide.

Steve was seriously involved with two girls—God knows how many others. He enrolled, with the two girls, in Betty Fuller's and Janet Lederman's couples groups—supposedly the top in this.

Steve acted as a co-leader with John Heider in his last residential program. He and Heider were very close, and Heider knew all about him. Heider and many of the individuals at Esalen who knew him all said the same thing—they had listened to Steve talk about suicide but his life force—they all used that phrase—was such that he could never do it.

His girl friend told me that she would never take an acid trip with him; his trips got so heavy that someone well enough to bring him down again had to be in the room. Yet it was common for them all to trip together. In fact, shortly after noon on the day he killed himself, he had taken psylocibin with a girl, Mary Lou, who was "out" for about twelve hours. Mary Lou said that without question Steve was high on psylocibin at the time he killed himself. She told me he couldn't wait that morning to get the psylocibin; he was afraid it would all be gone by the time he got there. She said Steve was obsessed with having to do it right then and there.

My feeling in general from her, Heider, and the rest of the group close to him that last month was that they were fully aware he was in serious trouble. A couple of the girls said that Heider had gone away—he had some marital problems of his own, and that if Heider were there this wouldn't have happened.

Tom also could see the signs of Steve's deterioration during the months from the summer of 1970 until his death:

The next six months he really experimented—went into religion, philosophy, morality. When he came in that October for a not-too-friendly business meeting, he said that "any philosopher, like Socrates, who is true to himself and his values, seeing that he couldn't live in a corrupt world, would remove himself from it." I didn't pick up on this because I didn't feel he was talking about himself. He had everything to live for. . . .

I got a letter from him in January indicating his depression: "You can only go as high as you can go low."

The last entries in Steve's journal sum up his final weeks:

I've really gotten close with Mary Lou and Pat. Both individually & the three of us as a group a very novel & rewarding experience I love you both & am so glad we have entered each others lives.

My inner struggle has lead me to allow & follow my fantasys. I have once again sent Bonnie away this time for a month—

After a few days of anguish, followed by a few of the most joyous days of my life, we parted very lovingly—she went to Mexico & I to my destiny—

I am afraid of being alone—So I am going Into It—I am now In the cabin, its pouring out & has been for 6 days—The road is *very* closed—I've got plenty of fire wood & plenty of food. . . .

Yesterday morning I left the sycamore house (had been there 2 days, after returning from AGNEWS [State Hospital]—BLOW OUT, ward where I played with the psychotics & did a group for 2 days—actually I played with the residents & Dick Price) & drove up the hill. . . .

The first afternoon was very long, I kept looking for someone to come down the road—talked to myself for hours on end! Really felt that I'd never be able to stay nore than 1 or 2 days without going down—what could I possibly find to occupy my time?

Sleep solid—wouldn't get out of bed for a long time—
Finally the day is happening & wow!!!
WOW!!!
I'm busy, all sorts of things to do—clean the house
very clean
attend to all little details
Fix everything
Go outside
& start to clean up so much to do!
Cut Kindling
Bring in firewood
Organize tools
oil tools
Build Nail Box
Do every little thing no matter how small—pick up nails from ground—economize write list of things to do as Ideas come—
practice Banjo
Get washed

Its now very dark out, I've been writing this for a long time—Hand hurts- -I haven't eaten anything since tea & toast (7:30 a.m. listened to radio).

Its now time for dinner then more Banjo & then read
I'm looking forward to tomorrow. . . .

On Tuesday, February 9, 1971, at 2:30 P.M., Steve walked into a craft shop at the edge of Esalen, picked up a Hawes .357 magnum pistol that he knew was kept there, pointed it at his right temple, and fired.

Mr. and Mrs. D. were notified by telephone at 10 A.M. the following day, and Mr. D. went to Big Sur to arrange Steve's burial.

About a month later Mr. and Mrs. D. went to Esalen again. At this time Mr. D. interviewed Steve's friends, and met with the Esalen administrators.

My meeting with Mike Murphy, Dick Price, and Ken Price was held in Fritz Perls' round room. Heider, Mary Lou, and Bonnie were also there. Everybody sat around and tried to look wise; nobody would talk until I finally said something—I told them I had waited a month before coming in the hope that I could think a little clearer; that I wasn't there to blame them or myself or any individual, but I wasn't there to purge myself either. I just wanted to get some feeling from them about whether they felt they had some responsibility.

Dick Price immediately picked up a pamphlet and said he'd like to read something from it. I told him I'd kick him in the balls if he didn't have enough sense to talk from how he felt, not from what somebody carefully wrote out. He got very indignant. I told him he had to talk about the fact that Steve died, killed himself within their premises when everybody in the room except for his family knew that Steve had had problems for a long time, and nobody did anything about it.

Price then said, "Let me put myself in your shoes, and I am the father, and I am here to talk, and this is what I hear you saying." I interrupted him again, and told him I was not there to listen to explanations of what he heard. I wanted to hear what *he* had to say, not what he heard me saying. I was not interested in how I came across to him—only in what he thought his responsibility as the director of Esalen was— nothing more.

Murphy started asking me questions then—did I know about Steve's preoccupation with suicide, did I do anything about it. I finally got through to Murphy that the first I knew about it was after he died; that everyone else in the room knew about it. Murphy asked everyone else in the room whether they'd known. Price never answered, the girls laughed in his face.

Ken Price [the business manager of Esalen] finally said to Dick Price and to Mike Murphy, "Look, why don't you listen to this man? He told you the same things that I've been telling you for months—something is radically wrong, we have no control, we don't pay attention to the problems when we have them, and we're leaving ourselves open for bigger problems."

At this point Dick Price wanted to adjourn the meeting, and I was ready also. I told him that what I was looking for was some statement about what they intended to do in the future. There was nothing more they could do for me, or for my son.

At that meeting I felt a total detachment on the part of the Esalen officials, an absolute refusal of responsibility. They said things like, Well, I didn't know him very well, or I tried, or I held out my hand to him. But nobody said, Well, I talked to X or Y or Z and the two of us went to talk to Steve, or all of us got together.

During that meeting the prior suicides were mentioned. In ten years they had only had two others, they claimed. Price said, "Well, that's not a bad record."

After the confrontation, the Esalen hierarchy wrote Mr. D. to assure him that steps would be taken to prevent future such occurrences. The letter—signed by Esalen directors Mike Murphy, Richard Price, and John G. Clancy—acknowledged responsibility for Steve's death, expressed regrets, and outlined the steps they planned to take to minimize the risk of further tragedy. The steps included: more training for leaders and "back-up" by professionals; improved screening for participants; and clarification of Esalen's definition "as a school and place of exploration rather than as a psychiatric clinic." The letter stresses Esalen's intention to "develop more supportive tools for such persons as do manifest troubles at Esalen and to establish a better liaison with institutions to which we could quickly refer those who need clinical help."

In short, Esalen acknowledges the need to provide psychotherapy-like protections, at the same time claiming not to offer psycho-therapy. To date, there is no indication that the steps outlined in the letter have been implemented, or that Steve's death has made any appreciable impact on Esalen's operations.

Perhaps Tom summed it all up best:

> At first I thought Esalen was doing good things—so many happy people there, people with credentials; I viewed them as professionals, they seemed to know what they were doing. But after Steve's suicide I changed my ideas about them. There were certainly great influences on his life out there that made him change. Maybe hostilities surfaced—he changed too quickly, or tried to take on a new culture, way of life, and environment too quickly. Or maybe he just took his problems three thousand miles west.

8

Encounter *v.* Psychotherapy

Psychotherapy is painstaking work. The therapist must not only empathize with, control, and understand what happens to his patient, he must also simultaneously cope with his own feelings. He must be able to know, for example, whether his responses to the patient result from his therapy plan or from feelings of his own which he has not adequately examined. The latter possibility, known as countertransference, is an important issue. Contrary to the dehumanized stereotype of psychotherapists held by many encounterists, the voluminous literature on countertransference clearly indicates that therapy is a human process for all parties involved. Therapy is geared to helping one person, namely the patient; and it is the therapist's responsibility to make sure that the patient's needs come first.

Maintaining such a stance imposes profound burdens on the therapist. Circumspection, delaying his impulses, planning his steps, not responding to certain of a patient's demands, are some of the ordinary procedures designed to keep the patient's needs primary. At the same time the therapist must be emotionally accessible if the therapy is to hit its mark.

Encounter offers many more immediate rewards for the therapist. Once a therapist takes the stance that he need behave no differently from his patients, any of his own impulses may become primary. And since he is the most powerful person in the group, gratification of his own personal, social, sexual, and interactive needs soon becomes a legitimate activity for the group. A central tenet of the encounter ideology is that with regard to "working" on himself, the leader is no different from any other person present. Encounterists hold that this provides a model for other group members, lessens the distance between member and leader, and by alerting group members to the leader's problems diminishes the likelihood that leaders will abuse their authority.

The notion that the therapist is also a patient is considered by many critics a hallmark of nonrational therapies. In group work this style has been called "status denial" leadership; while it attained some popularity during the 1950's, it was largely rejected by therapists in favor of recognizing the natural authority that comes with training and experience. In fact, most therapists find that one of the aspects of therapy most valuable to their patients is learning to deal with therapists as authority figures. Most patients begin therapy with irrational fears and expectations of authority, derived from relationships with their parents. To ignore the distinctions between therapist and patient is to render authority problems inaccessible for therapeutic work.

The psychotherapists who have adopted encounter as their principal therapeutic method tend to be marginally trained professionals. In many cases they have dropped out of graduate programs, or have earned master's degrees but were not admitted to Ph.D. programs in psychology. Only rarely are therapists with the highest level of training and professional status involved in encounter, though by this writing almost all mental-health professionals have had the opportunity for some exposure to encounter techniques.

The unfortunate reality is that less than 5 percent of all psychotherapists treating patients in this country today have received specialized psychotherapy training. The consensus among leaders in the mental-health field has long been that basic professional training—M.D. and psychiatric residency, Ph.D. and psychological internship, and M.S.W. (master of social work) and field work for social workers—is insufficient training for a psychotherapist. The common test of therapy competence is graduation from an advanced training institute or program, which usually requires about four years' training and includes intensive personal analysis. The public, however, is grossly ill informed on training standards for psychotherapists. Most people cannot differentiate between psychologists, psychiatrists, psychotherapists, and psychoanalysts, and incorrectly assume that every psychiatrist and psychologist has undergone analysis as part of his training, and is qualified as a psychotherapist.

Stringent requirements, the scarcity of places in advanced training institutes, the economic burdens of an additional four years of training, and the hunger to get out and "do it" have led to a grossly uneven pyramid of trained professionals. The public demand for therapy has made it possible for significant numbers of professionals to become successful private practitioners without specific psychotherapy training.

While many "credentialed" encounterists come from this minimally qualified professional group, an even larger number come to the encounter game with none of the legal and professional qualifications for independent practice. Again because of economics, most hospitals, clinics, school systems, and social and governmental agencies tend to employ such people as "staff psychologists" or "staff therapists." In the public eye, though, any affiliation with a hospital or clinic is often confused with advanced therapy training. Much hospital experience is actually irrelevant to the sort of problems customarily dealt with in private practice.

It's easy to see why professionals and state licensing boards take a dim view of unregulated practitioners; it's less easy to understand why encounterists should be opposed to professional training. To my knowledge, not one of the current encounter game stars holds a certificate from a program specializing in conventional psychotherapy. Dan Casriel has explained that he was dismissed from his analytic institute because he couldn't handle the authority. Martin Shepard came closest, but was dismissed a week before graduation.* Shepard and other encounterists argue that institute training leads to rigidity and dehumanization. Counter to that argument is a far more simple truth: that training builds the individual's capacity to make fine distinctions in details of theory and technique.

If training in individual therapy is hard to come by, training in work with groups is even more rare, and therapists with such training form a rarefied elite. Many individual therapists (including

---

*At first, Shepard suggested that he was the victim of doctrinaire conservatives who disagreed with his modern views. More recently, he has admitted that he was called on the carpet for having sexual relations with his patients. "What do you mean patients?" said Shepard at a recent Anthos lecture. "One patient I fucked."

the few with institute training) have simply undertaken group therapy without training, or having attended two-day training institutes and workshops sponsored by professional organizations in a desperate attempt to make up for the training deficit. With the general training level so low, it's little wonder that so much shoddy therapy is available, and that so many undertrained professionals should gravitate to encounter.

There are, of course, a few highly trained and skilled psychotherapists who have become very interested in encounter. For some, encounter offers a revitalization of their own careers, the opportunity to innovate and reexamine treatment techniques and principles. For such therapists, involvement with encounter is selective, and for the most part they exercise good clinical judgment in experimenting with the new techniques.

The principal organization in the encounter movement is the Association for Humanistic Psychology. Though it started out as an assemblage of philosophers and thinkers, now its meetings are more like an encounter Mardi Gras than a psychology convention. Its programs are like those of the growth centers, complete with yoga, reincarnation hypnosis, Zoroastrianism, astrology, psychedelic psychology, and sensory bombardment. Since a 1969 blowout at Silver Spring, Maryland, the appearance of the police has been an expected part of their annual event—the convention usually shares a hotel with other guests who are unable to ignore the sexuality of the scenes they witness in the pools and hallways.

The A.H.P. leadership has recently become concerned about some of the wild things happening under its banner, and there are indications that some members miss the early days when serious debate on humanistic issues was possible. Many of those who started the group have resigned, though, and efforts to uphold the tradition of scholarship have recently met considerable flak.

The spread of encounter through the mental-health professions has also led several hundred encounterists to form a new Division of Humanistic Psychology of the American Psychological Association, and to meetings of local professional societies devoted entirely to encounter. The New York Society of Clinical Psychologists, with a thousand members, devoted its 1972 annual conference to two days of "personal participation" in the "newer developments in psychotherapeutic practice," a program that mirrored a growth center catalog down to the last encounter game. Several members were involved in the G.R.O.W. scandal of 1972, and the society's current president, Carmi Harari, Ed.D., owns a small growth center and claims the dubious distinction of leading the first encounter group in Egypt.

For many therapists, the appeal of encounter seems to stem from its heightened sense of involvement and stimulation; professionals who participate in T-groups are not immune to the "postencounter high." Mental-health professionals are basically givers and feeders of other people's emotional needs; they have been taught to approach patients with emotional reserve, and to keep a separation between therapy and their own lives. As a result, their own emotional reservoirs are drained regularly. They hunger for increased intimacy with their patients, and for many the new encounter behavior styles offer legitimatization for such conduct. Many therapists are delighted with the opportunity to move from voyeuristic to active participation in their patients' lives.

The aggressive, manipulative, and physical needs of the therapist are also given considerable room for expression as encounter thinking moves into the psychotherapy realm. A good fight is satisfying to sedentary people; and therapists have few ways to drain off their tension. Teachers of psychotherapy commonly recognize the degree to which therapists inject their own needs into their treatment methods. These needs are studiously downplayed by most therapists, but given license by encounter thinking.

There is much truth in the notion that encounter may be most valuable as a way of emotionally replenishing therapists; affiliation with the new method seems to make some middle-aged therapists feel younger. In fact, some of the largest and most enthusiastic demonstrations of encounter that I have observed have been those staged for the mental-health profession. At the East Coast Esalen shindigs, for example, many of those present were either therapists, guidance counselors, probation officers, or teachers. Esalen leaders have indicated that mental-health professionals make up the biggest single occupational group that has participated, with teachers and clergymen following.

The same yearning for emotional involvement and magic cures found in the general population is especially present among mental-health workers. It is widely accepted in the field that the degree of neuroticism is higher in mental-health professionals than in the overall population, since most people are originally attracted to the field in order to work out their own problems. In addition, mental-health professionals are often frustrated with the slow progress of their efforts. The painstaking and often tedious nature of psychotherapeutic work can lead therapists to disappointed expectations of themselves and a desire for results even more intense than those manifested by patients. Big displays of emotion seem to provide both therapist and patient with evidence that something is at least happening, and encounter clearly makes that result possible.

In the last twenty years there has been a marked shift within the mental-health field in the direction of groups and group therapy. Practitioners have discovered that in many cases, treatment can be expedited when patients evaluate themselves in the presence of others similarly trying to improve aspects of their lives. Originally, groups were viewed as a supplement to individual psychotherapy, but more recently they have been used as a treatment method in their own right. Increasingly, therapists are treating patients only in groups, after individual assessment and treatment planning. In almost all cases, though, the therapists are available for individual sessions with their patients to deal with matters the patient cannot bring up in the group, or that, because they are particular to an individual, may interfere with the progress of the rest of the group.

The only sensible comparison between the effects of encounter and psychotherapy is the comparison of group psychotherapy with encounter groups, not of individual psychotherapy with encounter. W. Brendan Reddy, a psychologist at the University of Cincinnati, attempted such a comparison in 1970, studying four groups: two sensitivity groups led by NTL-trained leaders; one psychotherapy group led by a clinical psychologist; and one control group, an introductory psych class. All subjects were tested before and after the study for self-perception and pathological disturbance.

Before the group experiences, the four groups did not differ significantly on most of the tests, except for the Number of Deviant Signs scale, where the psychotherapy group showed much greater pathology. Each group met one evening a week for twelve weeks. At the end of the experience, the pathology indicators had been exactly reversed: the psychotherapy group had dropped markedly in the number of deviant signs, while the two T-groups showed a marked increase in disturbance. The control group showed no significant change.

While this study used a relatively small sample (fifty-eight students), it clearly showed that something quite different was happening in the psychotherapy group and in the two encounter groups.

Let's look at some of the differences in the ways encounterists and psychotherapists operate in general. While each field displays an almost infinite range of variations, nevertheless certain common features appear in each, reflecting two fundamentally different views of man and two fundamentally different technologies of change. Of course, the technologies overlap—many psychotherapists have integrated encounter techniques into their work, and most encounter game processes have been borrowed or adapted from psychotherapy.

Historically, psychotherapists have accepted and acknowledged certain treatment responsibilities. Basically, these center around the assumption of offering professional care, which includes: that care implies not doing harm; that the treatment will last as long as the patient's needs require; that treatment will be suited to the problems of the patient; and that any negative effects of the treatment are the therapist's responsibility.

Based on these principles, therapy strategies are built on a historical view of the individual. His development, case history, and life patterns become critical in understanding not only his needs but the causes of his pathology. Almost all professional therapists agree on the need for diagnosis, at least in the sense of an accurate understanding of the individual's personality. Most therapists also agree on the need to set specific treatment goals, and on the concept that certain parameters of the therapy process are repeatable and must in all cases be well managed.

Encounterists differ on all of these points. They hold that they are not responsible for the change process, that every individual is entirely responsible for himself. For the most part they deny any special status, or even authority, contrary to their actual behavior in the group sessions. They avoid the "caring" position in the professional sense just outlined, making diagnosis, technical skills, and follow-up unnecessary in their view.

One example of the chaos that can result from encounter techniques was presented in a journal article by two psychologists, based on their observations of an encounter weekend. George Goldman and Helen Brody wrote:

> Group member, Paul, complained about feeling ignored by the group and said that this was characteristic of his interactions with people. He felt people looked down at him and said that he thought that people considered him an ass-hole. Whereupon one leader asked him to lie on his stomach and repeated to him over and over, "You're an ass-hole." Paul made minimal sounds and gestures of objection, lying on the floor, occasionally raising himself. At each objection the leader repeated more forcefully, "You're an ass-hole." This continued for about five minutes. Paul got up and sat on a couch then, while the co-leader followed him and sat on his lap. A group member jumped at the leader to push him off Paul but did not succeed. A second member then sat on the leader and wrestled with him. This exchange ending with the leader apparently reflecting this member's aggressiveness by mimicking an apelike jumping up and down, knees flexed and arms upright.

It is to avoid such random and apparently absurd interactions that psychotherapists concern themselves with a patient's life history. One pattern they look for is *transference,* defined as the way in which an individual carries childhood emotional solutions into adult relationships. Much of the work that is done in psychotherapy is geared to analyzing and understanding these childhood projections, and nearly all professional therapists see the analysis of transference as one of the most potent therapy strategies. Encounterists for the most part deny or ignore the existence of transference as a human dimension. Their emphasis on the "here and now" leads to a view of man rootless in time and devoid of history.

The encounter leaders cited in the excerpt above made no attempt to ground Paul's feeling of being ignored in his childhood experiences, nor did they try to help him see how he was perpetuating that pattern in his current behavior, as most psychotherapists would have done. While it is true that overconcern with history can lead to interminable psychoanalysis, the absence of history leads to a "therapy" unconnected with the person's total life pattern. One of the most serious limitations of encounter is that while great emotional reactions do occur in encounter groups, they tend to be unrelated to an individual's basic problems, and hence there is little curative effect.

Another critical difference between those who practice psychotherapy and encounter lies in their attitudes toward *resistance*, best understood as the ways in which personality distortions protect themselves from change. Once a therapist has identified and understood a patient's resistance, half the battle is won, and therapy takes on the strategy of confronting and reconfronting the patient with his maladaptive behavior. Psychotherapy has been defined as the "acquisition of flexibility," precisely because neurosis is a rigid display of past emotional reactions that don't fit current circumstances. Encounterists ignore the phenomenon of resistance; they assume any change, however momentary, will be integrated into the personality.

Encounterists almost never speak of neurosis or psychosis, only of growth and the enhancement of human potential. Most encounterists hold that to view man as having pathology of the psyche is to denigrate him, to see him as an object, and hence to make it impossible to relate honestly and openly as equals. That a therapist could understand a patient's neurosis *and* relate as an equal is an alternative that most encounterists fail to consider.

Aside from a simple-minded humanism, most encounterists have no theory of behavior to guide their activities. In its absence, encounterists are left with no standard to judge and set goals for beginning players, no means of determining a player's progress, no model for the finished player, and no rationale against which group interactions may be tested. Each of these is a significant factor in professional psychotherapy, and each is substantially ignored in the encounter game.

A case in point is the encounterists' view that the expression of emotion is in itself curative. The fact is that emotional expression alone—called catharsis if it's big enough—was long ago shown to have no lasting effects on the personality. The important distinction lies not so much in the expression of feelings at a given time, but in the capacity to express, control, and differentiate feelings.

One of the most important distinctions between encounter and psychotherapy centers around the use of games and gimmicks. Most psychotherapists try to intervene in the patient's communications as little as possible; when they do, their interventions are a part of their treatment plan. Thus a game or technique is not an end in itself, but a means to an end. Most encounterists, on the other hand, see a game as an end in itself, valuable for the sake of experience. In short, their position is that experience equals growth.

In the small-group context, where there is an expectancy of continued work, the emotional confrontation games may be more useful than in one-shot encounters. Group members may reconfront a participant with his behavior pattern again and again, but without a focused therapeutic plan, the odds are that he will learn nothing.

Because learning does not happen all at once, psychotherapy tends to be a difficult, complex, and lengthy endeavor. The American Psychiatric Association's Task Force Report states:

> The overly simplistic approach to behavior changes espoused by many encounter group leaders [has led to the situation where] in the public eye these practices are equated with psychotherapy. Many encounter group leaders have adopted a crash program approach, successful in industry, advertising, and some scientific ventures, but resulting in a *reductio ad absurdum* in their attempts to change behavior. The part has been equated with the whole; the naïve assumption has been made that if involvement is good, then prolonged continuous marathon involvement is better; if expression of feelings is good, then total expression—hitting, touching, feeling, kissing, and fornication—must be better; if self-disclosure is good, then immediate, prolonged exposure in the nude must be better.
>
> Untrained encounter leaders have little concept of the specificity of psychological needs. Generally they appear to assume that everyone needs the same type of learning experience—to express greater affect, display more spontaneity,

chuck inhibitions, etc. Little consideration is given to the fact that some impulse-ridden individuals need the opposite: to learn to delay and control expression.

Patients constantly barrage therapists with the demand to fill a void in their lives: be my friend, be the good parent I never had, be my lover, be the authority I can undermine, seduce, or control. If the therapist accedes to these demands he usually fails to bring about significant change in the patient, since the presence of the need remains unchanged. It is difficult and trying for the therapist to deny such demands; it's far easier to give patients what they think they need. It is on this point that the major and most fundamental difference between the ideology of psychotherapy and that of encounter occurs.

Most encounterists hold that the principal value of an encounter experience resides in its warmth, human contact, and need-fulfillment. They reason that, for example, if someone's emotional life is devoid of intimacy, then the best thing one can do for him is to provide him with some intimacy: simply fill the void, and growth will follow. Noting that the void is most often insatiable, most psychotherapists take a directly opposite view and try to help a person examine why he has geared his life to create the absence of intimacy. Most psychotherapists believe that character is established in childhood and maintained in adulthood to serve a variety of needs, both healthy and otherwise. Thus the person lacking in intimacy has an investment in staying that way—to provide gratification for his masochistic needs, or to give him the opportunity to fantasize about relationships without putting the fantasies to the test, or to avoid the anxieties of an intimate relationship. Therapists are alert to the regularity with which isolated people fail to act on opportunities for change; when faced with a chance to form intimate relationships, they usually find a way out.

For the most part, encounterists ignore the patterns in people's lives and force the player to do the very thing he's most frightened of, regardless of the cost in terms of anxiety. They assume that once a person realizes he can behave differently without risk to himself, that recognition will allow him to change his behavior pattern.

There is some evidence that such sudden growth spurts do occur, both spontaneously and in encounter groups, and people often use such experiences as a sort of mental reference point to remind themselves that a certain type of behavior is within their capacity. By and large, though, most people in such a situation experience the brief sense of exhilaration that comes from mastering a fear, but close up again soon afterward. A man who usually avoids competition, for example, may arm-wrestle in an encounter group and momentarily overcome his feelings about competition. This will not lead him to change his behavior outside the group if his fear of competition is rooted in a more basic and unacknowledged fear, say, that he will be destroyed should he lose.

Encounter advocates frequently attack verbal methods of psychotherapy as "mind-fucking"—unemotional and verbose. Yet anyone who has had a good psychoanalytic experience knows that psychotherapy can be an intensely emotional experience. In my judgment, though, much of the encounterists' criticism on this point is, in fact, warranted, primarily because so few professionals who consider themselves Freudians are actually trained in that method and can create the intense emotional experiences it requires. Many ill-trained therapists, as well as some Freudians, have adopted a remote and excessively passive therapeutic stance which results in minimal involvement on the part of their patients.

The traditional psychoanalyst would agree that talk may be a cover-up, and his efforts are devoted to bringing out his patient's significant emotional experiences. But he also knows that just expressing or "acting out" feelings can be a cover-up as well. Even while putting down all talk as useless, most encounterists do encourage certain kinds of talk, couched in emotional words. To say "I think" is seldom well received, but any statement preceded by "I feel" tends to be listened to. This often reaches the point of absurdity, as in "I feel it's eleven o'clock."

Most psychotherapists try to bring the patient's adult capacities to bear on the emotional situations that were not well handled in childhood. They try to help their patients talk about things first and explore what motives might be behind an anticipated action, because in simply reenacting a childhood situation, the real motivation gets lost in the action, and the cycle continues. In effect, the original childhood *shtick* causing the undesirable, even painful, behavior patterns remains hidden as long as the defensive pattern continues. The encounter leader takes just the opposite tack, believing that if you talk about your feelings before expressing them, you won't experience their full power. Act out your impulses, he says, and you'll feel what's inhibiting you and be able to change your character and behavior.

Most therapists, on the contrary, believe that ego development includes the development of impulse control, particularly the control of anger and violence. Not all people are overcontrolled. One therapist reported the case of a man with whom he had worked for two years, building the patient's capacity to control his rage. The man got a new job and as part of it was expected to be a member of an ongoing encounter group. Since his therapist voiced some demurrer, the man concealed the fact that he participated in the group five or six times, until it became obvious that he was becoming increasingly disturbed and violent. The group had perceived his suppressed rage and insisted that the man shout and beat mattresses. When he really did express his intense rage in the group, his superiors decided that he had a problem with authority and should not continue to work there.

Too often in encounter groups, to fail to respond to another person's feelings is *verboten*. To be openly bored or uninterested results in the group's criticism of "defensiveness" or "unrelatedness." The idea that a bland exterior can be a way of hiding or controlling powerful feelings was originated by psychoanalysts, but in analysis such behavior would lead to an exploration of the causes of the defensiveness, rather than a frontal assault on the defenses.

Too often, though, the response of an encounter group when confronted with such a defense is a litany of: "Don't sit there like a dummy!" "Get involved!" "You're silent because you're scared!" "Get out of here if you don't want to be part of the group!" The only way to stop such an onslaught is to say with anger (an emotion the group respects): "Let me alone! I'll stay silent if I want to." Few players have the strength to stand up against the group's pressure and realize that they cannot remain aloof for long if the group is to like them. Jane Howard, noting this demand for emotional expression, said: "An unspoken Esalen motto seemed to be, 'I hurt, therefore I am.' "

Professional psychotherapists strive for exactly the opposite emotional climate in their group practices. Emotional conformity is frowned upon; after all, isn't being remote and aloof as much a human quality as being "warm and open"? Suppose a grouper decides to conceal his hostility toward another player: why is that not as acceptable as punching the other guy in the mouth?

Encounterists and psychotherapists agree on a lot of things; emotional integrity, openness, and authenticity are goals that both camps share. The divergence occurs in the methods each group uses to achieve those goals. Against the encounter culture's promises of instant growth, most therapists see that position as magical thinking, holding out a cruel and false promise of psychological nirvana.

An esteemed teacher of psychoanalysis in groups, Emmanuel K. Schwartz, commented on this mystical quality in a critique of writings of the encounterists. Of a Martin Shepard group, Schwartz said:

> From the beginning there was a mystical overexpectation among the members that something special would happen. An air hung over the group that is remindful of the Hassidic *Verbrengung,* a gathering of the mystic disciples before the Wonder-rabbi for a prolonged contact when a miracle, a confirming miracle, is awaited.

All concerned therapists wish they had a magic cure for their patients. But unlike the encounterists, therapists know that they do patients a disservice when they take the short cut offered by the magic cures.

9

Sex in the Encounter Game

ENCOUNTER GROUP
By Eric Bentley*

Come together with strangers
Everyone takes his clothes off
Run your hands over strangers
Everyone run his hands over everyone
Hope for the miracle
Tristan and Isolde
Antony and Cleopatra
Lady Chatterley's Lover
Or a replay of those first orgasms at age twelve
Surprises of the swimming pool
Soft sweet ecstatic

Hope for a lesser miracle
Evergreen Review
Oh Calcutta
Screw Magazine
Sex is beautiful
Filth is clean

Hope for no miracle
Boys and girls
Front and back
Top and bottom
Hand and lip
Tongue and tooth
Cock and cunt

*Reprinted by permission of Eric Bentley

And so on and so forth
Only don't expect the number of variations to be infinite

Hope for no miracle
You wanted sex
This
    is
        sex

Contrary to the widespread rumors about frequent way-out sexual experiences in sensitivity groups, sex in the encounter game is generally pretty dull—self-conscious, antiseptic, and overly full of verbal "relating." For the most part, sex stays on the level of talking and teasing. That's not to say that people don't have sex in groups, or that the sexual talk and openness in groups doesn't lead to a number of couplings, triplings, and other sexual encounters that probably would not have occurred had the participants not gone through a ritual seduction in the encounter group.

One technique that many encounterists use to warm up a group and prepare it to deal with tabu subjects is to introduce verbal games of sexual ranking or seduction. Shortly after a group has begun, the leader will pick up and focus on the first hint of sexual attraction, and ask the object of the attention if he or she is similarly inclined. To provide a model for openness, he's likely to quip about his own immediate attractions, and then ask other groupers who they find most attractive in the room.

Most people have difficulty publicly stating their sexual preferences so early in the game, and their discomfort facilitates the progress of the group, which can now begin to work on "sexual uptightness." In a situation like this, it doesn't take long before everybody knows who is attracted to whom. These flirtatious interchanges often become the basis for subsequent pairings and alliances among group members, and in poorly run groups such developments are often encouraged, since they seem to conform with the encounter ideology of creating greater "intimacy."

George Goldman and Helen Brody have reported an incident which illustrates the casual acceptance of sexual contacts between leaders and participants:

The setting was rural, and the "blind walk" was designed to be both a trust experience and an exercise in developing sensory awareness. Each person, with his eyes closed, was to experience as many sensual things as possible, and the walker who led the "blind" person was to facilitate this.

The senior author, on his "blind walk," walked into a barn to give an anticipated olfactory sense experience and saw on a pile of hay a naked man and woman, apparently just parting from having sexual relations. It was the co-therapist and one of the female group members, who looked up but did not seem either shocked or surprised. The author waved and walked out, leading his "blind" companion.

Rustum Roy, a Pennsylvania encounter participant, commented that one of the main reasons middle-class WASP's go to encounter groups is

> The possibility of an expansion of legitimized sexual experience at all levels, from the mildest touching to regular intercourse following candlelit, warm, nude baths. I am at a loss to explain the gross dishonesty of the "movement" in not openly affirming that they are providing, in our highly eroticized culture, one of the few channels of legitimized "co-marital" sex. The percentage of participants becoming sexually involved with each other or with the leaders is so high that anyone who avoids dealing with this aspect of the movement is covering up something.

From my observations Mr. Roy is right; and the reason encounter leaders cover up the sexual aspect of the movement is that by and large they are downright puritanical about sex. One often gets the feeling that—as with most emotions—encounterists would like to be much more open and free about sex than they are. In fact, though it's inconsistent with their overall act-out-your-feelings philosophy, many encounter leaders hasten to warn groupers that active sexual contacts are forbidden while the group is in session. What happens after the session, of course, is another story.

Dreams, thoughts, and interactions that occur between sessions frequently become subjects for group discussion. Often this is so with sexual experiences that occur privately between groupers, and morning-after confessions to the group—spurred by the desire for honesty and openness—occur with great frequency. There is, of course, no punishment or condemnation, only interest and concern, so that the bonds among group members are solidified, and such actions and revelations are encouraged.

Given this permissive environment, and the overall *zeitgeist* in encounter groups opposing the prevailing culture's standards, it is interesting that sexual behavior in the encounter world is still subject to the usual constraints, except as regards sexy talk.

Public criticism of encounter points to the inadequacy of a social movement that tries to apply one set of standards to a wide range of people. In the well-known but scientifically careless study sponsored by the YMCA after a large number of their employees participated in some mild, primarily verbal sensitivity training, the authors note the concern with "sexual overtones" or "homosexual overtones" voiced by the YMCA officials. Their comments seemed to imply that the voicing of sexual feelings was the same as engaging in sexual acts. The study was clearly a defensive reaction on the part of the YMCA officials who'd engineered the sensitivity training. Naturally, the result was an affirmation that no one was hurt and that nothing sexual really occurred.

I have no doubt that many of the criticisms of encounter and sensitivity training are similar reactions to a perceived sexual threat. It is at this point, in fact, that right-wing criticism of encounter fuses with criticism of sex education in the schools: both are seen as eating away the foundations of our society, or at least the society of middle-aged, middle-class, Middle Americans.

A case in point is the Darien, Connecticut, sexy sensitivity scandal. In May 1969, as part of a pilot program to prepare them to teach courses in family life and sex education, thirty-six teachers participated in a round-the-clock sensitivity session held in a local motel. The program was 80 percent funded by the federal government through a local HEW agency which had conducted twenty-four similar programs in the area.

One teacher, forty-seven-year-old Mrs. George Dasher, took offense at the encounter style of learning, which included "communicating by stroking each other." Mrs. Dasher detailed her experiences in an article for the *Darien Review:*

> Friday night and Saturday afternoon, sexual arousal was the technique. It began with foot rubbing, arm stroking. It progressed to arms around each other, permitting breast

stroking. The trainers were actively participating. "Dry fucking" . . . is not a pleasant term. Nonetheless it very accurately describes the activities in my group. When my trainer attempted to French-kiss me—and wouldn't stop trying—I walked out in shock.

Mrs. Dasher contrasted the enjoyment derived from hugging, kissing, and "feeling up the girls," with the eternal values, "sanctity of marriage, self-discipline, emotional control, the Golden Rule," and noted that, in the culture of the workshop, "faculty who were exhilarated and set free by their twenty-four hours were the real people," while those who were not turned on were characterized as uptight.

Mrs. Dasher's article opened up a hornet's nest of public controversy, which included countercharges by the majority of participants that Mrs. Dasher had grossly misrepresented the events, and defensive statements by Peter Caffentzis, who with some assistants had conducted the workshop. Though Mr. and Mrs. Dasher denied membership in the John Birch Society when interviewed by Lacey Fosburgh of the *New York Times,* their statements added fuel to the Birchers' fight against sex education that had been raging in the area. Right-wing criticism is so widespread and so undifferentiated in its choice of enemies that any group training endeavor—particularly those that occur in motels or have no written curriculum—may face charges of brainwashing, Communist takeover, and sexual excesses.

As I see it, that kind of criticism, with its fear of sexual openness, is a reflection of the more general American inability to separate sexuality from intimacy. Most Americans, unable to feel comfortable about touch as a friendly or affectionate statement, see physical contact between adults almost exclusively as a prelude to sex, and hence subject to the usual range of sexual taboos.

In his recent book, *Touching,* Ashley Montagu pointed out the variety of ways in which Americans hinder child development, sexuality, and physical health with their institutionalized taboos against touching. Frequent cases of parents unwilling to touch or fondle children, lest the boys become effeminate and girls seduced, are well known to students of child development, and it is this trend that the encounter game hopes to reverse. Bill Schutz, for example, has recommended that parents not avoid touching their children's genitalia, because that attitude teaches that sex is a no-no. Schutz also feels that parents should massage their children, so that they will know that they are loved right down to the viscera and can grow up without body hangups.

Besides our cultural confusion of sexuality and intimacy, there are several other reasons why sexual experiences tend to become a part of the encounter group experience. Many participants react to the promised "intimacy" and "peak experiences" of encounter groups as a sexual promise, remaining alert for sexual cues throughout their group experience, and often attempting to turn the public expression of feelings into a personal sexual experience.

Sexual contacts had been used as an antidote to loneliness long before encounter hit the scene. Rather than providing a new sort of promiscuity for lonely people, as some observers have stated, encounter groups may in this regard merely offer an easier and faster means of fulfilling a basic human urge. In my judgment, most of the people who use encounter groups as a sexual happy hunting ground would follow the same behavior pattern under any circumstances, and the groups simply make sexual solutions to neurotic problems easier.

Because of the feeling of uniqueness encouraged in encounter groups, it's often hard for participants to see that relating to a person of the opposite sex in a new way may allow a change in their view of the other sex in general, rather than to the individual member of the encounter group who made him feel so different. Thus to John it may seem that Mary, who has responded to his revelations of shameful weakness with a touch of warmth, is demonstrating her unique goodness. It may not occur to him that other women might respond that way, or that to be able to respond warmly is one of the capacities of womankind. Since John is not about to foul up his relationship with his wife and kids back home, and Mary is equally concerned about her relationship with her husband, they may turn to a brief sexual liaison to seal the bond of their intimacy.

From Mary's side, let's imagine she's always viewed men as strong, powerful creatures against whom she had to defend herself. As a woman she could offer very little in return except sub-mission. In the group she gets an inkling that John, the tough guy, has within him the little boy who needs help and protection. She may enjoy the feeling that she has offered him warmth at a critical moment, and relish the opportunity to have sex on a basis different from her ordinary submissiveness to men.

In all the varieties of sexual experience that can be generated by encounter, what we most often see is people following their usual neurotic patterns. In his autobiographical *Hot Springs,* Stu Miller makes it perfectly clear that he went to Esalen with the intention of having as much sex as he could with as many girls as possible. It's also clear that his style was that of an adolescent obsessed with the sex act itself, and his seductions were devoid of any attempts at intimacy, loving, or emotional involvement.

Occasionally sudden flashes of insight or intense emotional pressures lead participants to a sudden reversal of their usual sexual games. For example, a man who avoids commitment by being involved only with hostile, aggressive women may now go through a round of involvement with affectionate, passive women. In the long run, such mirror-image patterns leave players as unfulfilled as they were when they began.

A majority of the people I interviewed made it perfectly clear that, like Miller, they came to encounter groups for new sexual contacts. Some (usually the men) have acknowledged that sex is their immediate goal, while others (especially women) placed their sexual needs in the broader emotional context of "developing a meaningful relationship." One man, a thirty-one-year-old psychologist, said:

> I know that in a microlab I can single out the prettiest chick in the room, get into a minigroup with her, start staring intensely into her eyes, and, if she doesn't turn on to me, really give her a hard time about it. If she does, so much the better.

Another said:

> I'm very easily turned on by a lot of different people, and as soon as I hug a girl I tend to get sexually excited. Somehow I'm bolder when there are other people around, especially if they're into their own thing. I very quickly start to neck. It's surprising how many girls turn on that way. Maybe it's the excitement of being in a group where not

much seems like it can happen. Of course, once you get that feeling going, the rest falls pretty much into line.

One woman, a divorced thirty-five-year-old writer and theatrical agent, discussing her experiences at Group Labs in New York, said:

> So many of these guys are just out for free feels. Every time you like a guy and just want to hug him to express affection, he gets a hardon and tries to sexualize the thing. It's a real drag.

This woman was not phobic about men's erections; in fact, she described several sexual experiences she'd had with group leaders, and though they didn't prove terribly satisfactory, she treated them as a matter of course. She did take offense, however, when one of the leaders tried to convince her to make it with a sexually frustrated man in her group for "therapeutic purposes." She quit the group at that point.

I've come across several cases of men in their forties, never before seriously tempted by extramarital affairs, who have been hard hit by the emotional and sexual pull of women they met in encounter groups. In most of these cases the women were unmarried, in their thirties, sexually more liberated than the wives of the men in question, and hence more "glamorous." Most of the women had had one affair after another in what they saw as a constant search for Mr. Right. In most cases, it seemed to me that these affairs proved far less disastrous for the women than for the men, who were usually more idealistic, believed in romantic love, and had settled into long and fairly rewarding marriages.

While the occasional encounter game player may get emotionally stirred up enough to fall suddenly and profoundly in love during his group experience and want to affirm his or her love sexually, in the vast majority of cases the affairs are as short-lived as the group. For most people, a brief taste of intimacy is enough to add the requisite dash of spice to their relationships beyond the allotted group time. Often it seems as though the relationships can't go on without the group magic that permitted them to develop in the first place.

There is a definable subgroup of highly committed encounter game players whose sexual behavior takes on a somewhat different pattern. In a sense they are the best encounter game customers. For the most part in their mid-twenties to mid-thirties, they are mostly graduate students and young professionals in the fields of teaching, guidance, social work, psychology, nursing, and communications, who have adopted and try to live by the rules of the encounter game. It is this group, usually bright and well educated, which tends to carry encounter thinking into the schools, clinics, poverty programs, and social organizations where they work.

The ideology of this group includes heavy commitment to sexual liberation and positive, or at least tolerant, attitudes toward marijuana and other aspects of the youth culture. In most such cases, their involvement with the "affective revolution" has made them more than casual encounter game players but less than full-time group leaders. Most have had various forms of traditional psychotherapy until it came out their ears. This group, by occupational choice, lack of religious identification, liberal political ideology, and a Consciousness III social orientation, has become the true proselytizing force for the encounter movement.

The sexual mores in this group are considerably more liberal than those of the more typical players of the encounter game. They consider immediate response to sexual feelings healthy, indeed desirable, as an index of freedom and personal maturity. By the very frequency with which they engage in encountering, they tend to develop an increasing need for new stimulation, which in many cases leads to an increasing spiral of promiscuity. Some of the nude marathons that have experimented with sex, much of the sexuality in the baths at Esalen, and several of the wilder group sexual encounters at conferences like those of the Association for Humanistic Psychology have been populated by this young professional crowd. At the 1970 AHP shindig in Miami, one young woman told me she'd "balled six different guys in the pool" one night.

Martin Shepard recently illustrated the standards of this group to an approving audience at Anthos. As an example of the therapeutic value of sexual openness, he cited an incident he'd witnessed between Suki Miller and an encounter group member who expressed his wish to suckle at Suki's more than ample breasts.

Suki promptly exposed her top and encouraged him to go ahead. He spent the next twenty minutes joyfully sucking, while the group went on with its encountering. Shepard's third book, *The Love Treatment* (1971), documents a number of cases of sexual contacts between therapists and patients, and takes the position that the experiences were beneficial to about half of the patients. His fourth book, just published, is an autobiographical account of how, under the encounter banner, he has experienced every one of his sexual fantasies, from performing fellatio to watching his wife copulate with another man to group sex. Shepard believes that everyone has the same fantasies, and that anyone who has not acted them out is "hung-up."

Any number of encounter groups organized for the uninitiated public have turned into straightforward group sex experiences. For the most part these have been California endeavors, although I know of a few such happenings in the East. While they are clearly at a statistical minimum, the fact is that, especially when nudity is involved, a leader determined to create an orgy can do so without much difficulty. Several experienced group members determined to create an orgy can also usually pull it off easily if the leader doesn't take a firm negative stand. In most cases, though, leaders have decided to uphold the common public morality, or have felt that nude encounter was a sufficiently antiestablishment stance in itself.

Paul Bindrim, the founder of nude marathons, says very explicitly that the contact which groupers will have with each other while encountering nude in the pool is to remain absolutely asexual. Bindrim has a set of rules for everyone who signs up for his nude marathons, and among them is that there shall be no sexual intercourse or touching of the genitals.

Bindrim and others who have picked up on his crotch-eye-balling technique aim to reduce people's "neurotic" shame and guilt about the genitalia. Members of nude groups are encouraged to inspect each other's genitalia in order to overcome fears of looking and being looked at. In one variation, participants stand spreadeagled with a large mirror at their feet to see their own bottoms as the other group members have. Bill Schutz, not to be outdone, once provided men with gynecologist's speculums so they could get a good look at their wives' vaginas. Bindrim frequently claims that this sort of peak experience, especially in the context of his nude marathons, generates profound personality changes.

Bindrim stresses the asexual nature of his work. He relates that fears expressed by the typical male participant are involuntary erections (which he says rarely if ever occur) and that his penis will be smaller than that of the next guy. The women, says Bindrim, are concerned about breast size and flabby figures. Most therapists find Bindrim's statements of asexuality absurdly naïve, and many participants report that his marathons are not so asexual as he'd have us believe. One man in his mid-thirties, a writer, said:

> Bindrim asked us to sign statements at the beginning of the session, saying we would not engage in overt sexuality any more than we would in the street. It was very hard to live up to that, and in fact I succumbed to the sexual lure. When you go into a heated pool and you're being touched and passed around, fondled and then hugged with genitals rubbing, you get turned on. Bindrim noticed what was happening with me and a girl in the group, and suddenly said, "Everybody out of the pool." I had to take a few laps around the pool before I could get out. After the session, we had another nude swim, everybody did an exercise, embracing. You could see who was going to call the other up by the way they embraced.

While this man regretfully indicated that a waiting wife made it impossible for him to carry out what had been started in the pool, one young woman, an attractive thirty-year-old medical social worker, said:

> Most of the guys were sort of creeps, and there were very few erections. In fact, toward the end one man said that, and the guy I'd turned on to laughed and said he hadn't looked very hard. I laughed too. We'd been so turned on to each other that we could hardly wait to get home. In fact we started to make love in the car, but that was too clumsy so we waited.

Bindrim takes considerable offense at any suggestion of such goings-on; in fact, he made an enemy of a man who helped make him famous, largely as a result of that issue. Stephen Banker is a free-lance TV journalist who, as an outgrowth of a story on California extremists, shot a lengthy documentary film of one of Bindrim's nude marathons for the Canadian Broadcasting Company. Banker described Bindrim as "wearing a Hawaiian shirt and looking very much like an out-of-place construction worker," and explained that the camera, lighting, and sound crews were all crowded into the bathroom in order to record the proceedings from the door of the john.

> In a final interview with Bindrim, I asked about overt sexuality. He blew his stack, became very upset. After we turned off the camera he yelled at me a little bit. Back in L.A. Bindrim called the Canadian consulate and my boss in Toronto. He frightened the people in Toronto into thinking he was going to exercise the veto power which they had already signed over to him.

Banker had to sneak out of the country with the film. He was told by his bosses at CBC to stay away until the film was aired on nationwide Canadian TV. Said Banker:

> Bindrim, within his rights, is now using the film for his own aggrandizement, but he is lying about the source of the film. He is advertising the film as a Production of Paul Bindrim and the CBC. He lists himself as producer. The only way to describe that is "a lie." I am the producer of the film. I am the director of the film, the co-editor of the film. His role was that of a subject or source. He's been distributing it through N.Y.U. library and charging something like three dollars a head.

From the encounter point of view, Bindrim's written rules of behavior for nude encounter participants are a sellout to the prevailing society's morality. After all, if one is aiming to shed neurotic hangups about the body, why stop short of the freedom to enjoy sex publicly?

Bill Schutz has made this paradox a public issue, at least in professional circles. He once said that the only thing preventing him from encouraging all forms of sexual activity was fear that he couldn't stand up under public scrutiny. At the 1971 meeting of the American Group Psychotherapy Association in Los Angeles, after Schutz presented his view of the impact of encounter on group psychotherapy, one psychiatrist, determined to embarrass Schutz, stood up and asked, "Is it true, Dr. Schutz, that you have advocated sexual intercourse in your encounter groups? And if so, what do you do when homosexual members make advances to you?" Schutz said yes, he had advocated that sexual acts become part of encounter groups, in order to "explore" that dimension of human experience. He went on to say he felt a distinction should be made between what one can publicly advocate in the light of administrative and social constraints, and what one thinks is best therapeutically. Schutz acknowledged that he was not anxious for any more public censure and advised his followers not to get into "administrative hassles" over this issue. He did say though, that in his view there ought to be no limitations on what kinds of experiences people engage in in encounter groups, since all experiences are grist for the encounter mill.

Schutz responded to the question about homosexual advances toward him without embarrassment, explaining that at Esalen he and some of the other leaders had tried to conquer their fear of homosexuality by "exploring" it, but that he personally had had great difficulty in doing so and didn't venture very far in that direction. The way he explained it, the audience ended up regretting that Schutz's timorousness had kept him from expanding his potential in these directions.

Today sex acts in the theater and on film are far more open than what goes on in most encounter groups. At the same A.G.P.A. conference mentioned above, therapists were given a different look at the problem of sexual limits in group experiences. In a talk on "group responses to simulated erotic experiences," Jacques Levy, director of *Oh! Calcutta!* and a psychologist with several years of postdoctoral training at the Menninger Foundation, came down pretty hard on encounter. In his words, encounter was "being packaged like a TV dinner," and he suggested that the trend toward sexuality in groups will one day lead to a combined convention of the A.G.P.A. and the Swingers Association. Levy pointed out that the sexual stopping points in encounter groups are as ritualized and arbitrary as sex and dating behavior in the rest of the country.

At the first rehearsal of *Oh! Calcutta!*, Levy's problem lay in the difference between individual exposure and group exposure. He tried to create a team spirit, a feeling of the cast against the world, without sexual arousal. The problem was to create real theater work without the group's getting into continual orgies. He also was concerned lest they be too turned off and perform with a "so what" attitude. A fine line between being turned on and turned off had to be maintained.

Using his knowledge of therapy, Levy set two rules for the cast, but without any penalties or enforcement: first, no outside socializing; second, no sex. During fourteen weeks of rehearsal only two instances of breakage of rules occurred. There was considerable group pressure to get down to straightforward sexuality, which Levy pointed out was parallel to the tendency at Esalen. The major difference, however, was that Levy's group had an outside referent or goal, namely, that there was a theatrical performance to be accomplished.

In order to help the cast cope with the sexual encounters in the performance with the proper measure of workmanlike stage reality, Levy created an experiment in sensuality designed to stop short of actual intercourse. One day he let this experiment go on longer than usual and had the participants move from one person to another for over two hours, practicing sensual contact. It was excruciating for him to watch. He had defined it for the group as an acting exercise, and clearly it was only this conceptual structure that kept it from turning into an orgy. After this experience, most of the cast felt very depressed; one or two felt relief; and several shared the feeling that their conduct was justified by the knowledge that defined limits existed, and that this was part of their job.

Levy noted that had this become an orgy, he couldn't imagine how the cast could have gone on with its work; once the line is crossed, he said, "even a snake won't buy back the apple." This is, as I see it, the fundamental problem with sexuality in the group or even in the individual therapy context. Once the line is crossed into sexual activity, then pleasure—not personality change—becomes the primary goal. Every therapist knows that once there's been sexual contact, there can be no objectivity about behavior. This is the reason therapists don't treat their wives or lovers, any more than surgeons will operate on their wives, and why good therapists explore a patient's efforts at seduction to determine whether they constitute an attempt to sabotage the treatment.

Here again, a distinction has to be made between encounter, psychotherapy, and a stage production. Levy noted that in the encounter group the ultimate goal is to relate, to get more pleasure, to overcome conventions, and to experience more joy and human contact. His task was to turn a group of actors into a working ensemble. The psychotherapist's task, as I see it, is more like Levy's than like the encounterist's—to turn the group into a working therapy situation. In all three situations too much immediate pleasure may make remote goals unachievable. Sooner or later every therapist, theatrical director, and encounter leader must face the same question: Where should the limit be placed on expression of feeling?

An example of encounter's quest for pleasure reduced to absurdity is the X-rated film by Alex DeRezney called *Group Encounter,* which recently played New York's off-Broadway skin-flick houses. In this film a group of young people, clearly not professional actors, gather for an unrehearsed encounter experies in a California hillside house. An innocuous and flaccid young man named George announces himself as the leader of this encounter group. People introduce themselves with their first names and signs of the zodiac only. Next comes a series of evidently uncomfortable disrobings, graded in sexual intensity to include a variety of touchings and turnings on. One girl after another, standing with her eyes closed, has her pants taken off and her legs felt by two people, and is then asked to guess which was the male and which the female. "Sensitivity" is taken quite literally, as each girl is asked, "Which way do you like it better, firm or gentle?"

This was the only attempt at anything remotely akin to self-perception, and at all subsequent points there was almost no talk—simply dumb, ritualized conformity to the leader's "suggestions."

Once fully nude, participants arranged themselves in an inner circle of girls facing an outer circle of boys. George told the participants that they'd have a few minutes to turn on the person facing them before the circles would move in opposite directions, exposing each person to another member of the opposite sex. The game lasted only one or two rounds before couples dropped to the floor to complete what they'd started. A testimony to the lack of relatedness and the dehumanized sexuality of this encounter was the almost total absence of verbal communication, while the facial expressions of the participants ranged from amazement to pained embarrassment.

Most real group sex participants, or "swingers," make no attempt to cloak their activities under the goals of "sensitivity." One exception is *Sandstone,* a swinging resort in the Los Angeles area, which has put out a brochure that essentially expresses the encounter ethic on sexuality.

> The concepts underlying SANDSTONE include the idea that the human body is good, that open expressions of affection and sexuality are good. Members at SANDSTONE may do anything they like as long as they are not offensive or force their desires on other people.
> The strength and lasting significance of the SANDSTONE experience lies in human contact divorced from the cocktail party context with all its games and dodges and places to hide. Contact at SANDSTONE includes the basic level of literal, physical nakedness and open sexuality. In these terms, the experience goes far beyond any attempt to intellectualize it.

Membership is one hundred dollars a year and dues are fifteen dollars a month; members can bring guests, and I'm told that Sandstone makes Esalen look tepid in comparison.

I suspect that the recent upsurge of swinging, documented in the *New York Times* and in several recent books, may be an indication our culture's changing sexual mores. Group sex may be the natural result of the increased group experiences among strangers and the simultaneous lessening of group contact within the structure of the family. My concern is with the tendency to obscure what may be new and healthy cultural sexual developments with terms like increased human potential and deeper intimacy.

Raymond J. Corsini, one of the earliest leaders in the group therapy field and more recently an (essentially verbal) encounter group leader himself, has drawn some interesting parallels between encounter groups and swinging:

> Encounter groups are a kind of refined orgy. Where else can a respectable man put his hands on a strange woman's bosom, cavort in the nude, and speak out his most lascivious thoughts? One encounter leader asks members of his groups to pair off and go into a separate room for fifteen minutes, during which time the two are to seek a deeper relationship. Shades of playing "post office"!
>
> There is a need for sensuous gratification, for deeper and closer intimacy with strangers, for orgies. We should admit that this is precisely what group encounters are all about: an emotional, intellectual, and physical encounter. Parallel to this "open" movement is a covert one—and there are probably more covert groups than open groups. These groups are known as "swinging parties." Men and women, single and in pairs, come to these groups. There is low music, dim lights. Strangers group, pair, regroup. A woman may have sexual relations with one, two three . . . a dozen men, all strangers. They talk, open up, feel each other's bodies openly, in a languid sense of nothingness.
>
> I contend that the encounter groups and the swinging parties are essentially the same, and I also contend that their emergence is a sociological phenomenon, possibly a function of factors we don't perceive too well, including the Bomb, the wars, the decline of public morality, the decline of honesty in government, overcrowding . . . and all the rest of it. . . . The timid ones go to encounter groups; the bold ones to the swinging parties.

10

Playing for Money

The amount of money involved in the encounter game is hard to estimate. The price of encountering depends on who is selling it, where the shop is, and what size package you buy. If our average includes three-hour microlabs and two-week workshops, most people buy about two full days' worth. Nationwide fees average about twenty-five dollars per day. If we take Carl Rogers' estimate that 750,000 people bought some form of encounter in 1971, the encounter game amounts to a thirty-five-million-dollar-a-year industry. That's a very rough estimate of the sums involved, but until a formal market survey is carried out, it may be the best approximation we can make.

The distribution of economic rewards in the game reflect our society's overall economic structure. It's the familiar pyramid: few at the pinnacle, more at successively lower levels. At the very top are the superstars of the game and the businessmen who have found ways to market encounter or its by-products. In them we find the achievement-oriented traits of top dogs in any game. They may be a bit more gutsy, brighter, more innovative, or more hard-working than those lower on the scale, and most have had the social, educational, and financial advantages that make success possible.

Most growth center operators don't get to the top of the pyramid, and a few have admitted they wish the sale of encounter were more lucrative. Bill Swartley of Philadelphia's "Center for the Whole Person" recently complained that he'd lost $8000 in the past year and was driving a wreck of a car. Most growth centers provide a living for their key people without becoming enormously successful.

The qualified mental-health professionals involved with encounter are probably the largest group that consistently make money from it. While there are few leaders in the category of Bill Schutz (a thousand dollars a day) and Dan Casriel (five hundred thousand a year), numerous others make the rounds of workshops and growth centers, sometimes billed as "trainers" for the paraprofessional group leaders. M.D.'s and Ph.D.'s, as well as detailed hospital, university, and clinic affiliations, serve as advertising for the professionals and legitimization for the growth centers. Without the status associated with a professional degree, it would be hard for visiting circuit riders to command their three hundred to a thousand dollars per day.

It is among professional practitioners that quality is most variable. Some therapists, highly skilled and trained, can integrate encounter techniques with treatment practices that are ethically and technically sound. For others, encounter represents the path of least resistance to financial success. Perhaps one of the most unfortunate problems of the encounter game is the same difficulty which the public faces in selecting a good professional in any field: it's hard for the public to evaluate an institution or an independent practitioner's standing in the professional community. The best-known encounterists seem to have all the right credentials, but few laymen recognize that teaching freshman psychology at a university (which almost every Ph.D. in psychology has done) has little to do with the competent practice of psychotherapy.

The local professional who pops into a growth center for a microlab or an evening demonstration may be paid anything up to two hundred dollars. The rare ones who undertake running an ongoing group may get a few dollars a head from registration fees or twenty to fifty dollars a session but these are almost by definition the marginal professionals. If a therapist has a successful private practice, he needs no additional source of revenue. Often the growth center performer is not conducting an ongoing practice, is unlicensed or untrained, or needs a new source of patients.

A step down the pyramid are the group leaders trained in the encounter world, who don't get very much for their endeavors but can earn a living at it. They rarely work on a regular salary basis—most growth centers can't afford that—but often get a few dollars a head from attendance fees. This system encourages innovation, since newness is a key factor in bringing players back. Because the staff group leader can't count on his growth center for a living, he is often forced to develop a "private practice," or to generate more and more offbeat ideas to enliven the center's brochures.

One group of encounter leaders attempted to overcome these economic limitations in a plan of nationwide proportions. The 1972 investigaton of G.R.O.W. revealed that under the organization's multimillion-dollar scheme, groups of ten "counselors" with degrees from such unaccredited colleges as Indiana Northern University would form Neighborhood Centers for Human Development, setting up rent-free offices in church basements. Each of the 100 planned centers would be able to treat up to 1500 clients per week at fees ranging from fifty cents to ten dollars per session. Group leaders were promised three dollars per head and were told they could expect an annual income of around twenty thousand dollars. The organization's forty-page prospectus estimated income of over a million dollars a year in fees.

Many of the leaders at this level have a decidedly Consciousness III value system; they consider themselves outside the economic rat race, and can easily rationalize their subsistence-level earnings. They have many fringe benefits as well—they don't have to work regular hours, they meet lots of vulnerable neurotics of the opposite (or same) sex for brief affairs, and since they are usually paid in cash, they often yield to the temptation to consider their income tax-free. Sometimes they even deduct the costs of their apartments—where their "private practice" takes place.

Near the bottom of the pyramid is a much larger body of untrained (by *any* standard) encounter group leaders, usually part-timers, who simply operate on their own. Few have met even the flimsy standards of the local growth center. After a brief exposure as workshop participants they copy their leaders, sure that they can offer the same thing for a few dollars less.

At this level we also find members of a group who become so sure of their curative power that they feel their fees to the growth center are wasted. They split off to form a satellite growth center or become "private practitioners," placing ads in local newspapers, on billboards, in university dorms, and in coffeehouses. These self-led groups are usually harmless, and seldom make much money. Most of their clients recognize them as encounter freaks trying to carry good experience to the masses and rarely show up a second time.

At the very bottom of the heap are the leaders who offer the least in the way of competence, training, or experience. As a result, their economic potential is usually lowest, and only personal motivations keep them going. They use street-vending sales techniques like "bring a friend, free," "silent trial sessions," and periodic bonuses such as free sessions. Sometimes these bonuses are offered to participants who, because they're attractive, have lots of friends, or are "up front" players, are especially valuable group members.

At this bottom rung of the encounter ladder, coffee and cookies or a weak punch are often served, and the fee is ostensibly to cover their cost. Some leaders have participants stand up and announce how much they've decided to pay for the night. While that's a bit chancy, social pressure usually nets the leader as much as or more than he might otherwise collect. Most of these entrepreneurs manage to clear twenty-five to fifty dollars per evening, probably tax-free, and enjoy themselves as well. The real prize, of course, is an ongoing group or a few "private patients," usually paying five to twenty dollars per session, with the average around ten dollars.

The bargain-priced leaders are clearly attracting lonely party seekers, and their encountering is usually heavily mixed with social games and icebreakers. Held in lofts or living rooms, such groups rarely offer more than the Friday-night singles party so common in big cities. I went to a singles "house party" not long ago and soon headed for the door. As I did, someone else asked the host when he'd be having another such gathering. He replied, "Oh, I'm not going to do this any more—I'm starting to run encounter groups."

Encounterists ply their trade in various ways, and most have not failed to recognize the advantages of operating as a corporation. Some growth centers are incorporated as nonprofit organizations, others as profit-making businesses.

In terms of dollar volume, the National Training Laboratories* leads the nonprofit field. Before the 1971 recession, NTL was a multimillion-dollar business, showing gross receipts of $2,056,000 for the period from June 1, 1969, to December 31, 1969. Of this, over $1,256,000 came from fees paid by participants in its laboratories; over $700,000 came from consulting and training contracts with business, government, and private organizations; and almost $100,000 came from sales of publications. For this period NTL's gross profit was $557,000.

NTL's expenditures have kept a lot of people going. During that same seven-month period, for example, they spent $183,690 for regular payroll salaries; paid $646,742 to members of the "NTL Network" (the group leaders); and claimed travel, living, and other expenses of $668,434; for a total of $1,498,866 in "operating expenses."

The only other growth center whose finances compare to NTL's is Esalen, where gross income for 1968 and 1969 (before the Broadway spectaculars) was approaching a million dollars a year. Esalen's salaries are nowhere near as handsome as NTL's; but while NTL has run into financial difficulties, Esalen has so far been able to remain solvent. Stu Miller tries to give the impression that the whole place is run on a shoestring, is not really profitable, and reflects a massive altruistic endeavor on the part of all concerned—particularly Mike Murphy: "Mike has been very unselfish in virtually giving the property to Esalen—it could be rented for sixty thousand a year or sold for a million."

According to Miller, Murphy leased the property to Esalen for forty-five years at four hundred dollars a month. Miller explained that besides its salaried employees, Esalen hires leaders to run workshops. Except for Schutz and a few other big shots, people who run the workshops get forty-five dollars per registrant for a five-day workshop, or fifteen dollars for each person who signs up for a weekend workshop. The amount is the same for psychiatrists, psychologists, and people with a high school education.

Participants at Esalen now pay about thirty-five dollars a day for room, board, and tuition; no tipping (it used to be a resort). Miller said that he makes fifteen thousand dollars a year. Michael

*More fully, the National Training Laboratories Institute for Applied Behavioral Sciences, Inc.

Murphy draws fifteen thousand and the few other salaried people are paid between twelve and fifteen thousand a year.

I decided to check the information that Stu Miller had given me. Since the growth centers were unwilling to show me their books, I contacted the Internal Revenue Service.*

Esalen's tax returns for 1968 and 1969 shed a different light on Miller's story. In 1968, for example, Esalen's total gross income was $724,025, and they claimed costs of $671,875. Income included about $475,000 from services, fees, and tuition. According to their 1969 tax form, gross income was at the same level ($754,000), but costs had gone up to $847,587; their operating expenses exceeded income by $93,452 for that year.

With officers' salaries accounting for only $45,000 and rent also low, why do the tax returns indicate that Esalen is losing money? In 1967 Esalen invested over $300,000 in the property, and added another $100,000 in 1968 and again in 1969. Such "leasehold improvements" in the long run benefit the property owner. Murphy does seem to be an altruist, but he's no fool.

Usually untrained as businessmen, characteristically renegades from the middle class who scorn the business world, most growth center operators find it difficult to make their businesses successful. Seed money comes largely out of their personal savings or small amounts of pooled capital. They keep overhead low and operate on a pay-as-you-go basis; most price their own time at zero or close to it.

Harold Streitfeld, the founder, principal, trustee, director, and president of Aureon Institute, is a prime example. Aureon is a nonprofit tax-exempt operation, and its tax forms reveal that under its grand brochures it is a small-potatoes operation. Streitfeld incorporated Aureon in January 1968; the gross receipts from seminars that year were $71,800, and direct costs were $70,182. Aureon ended its first year with $1618 in accumulated income. Streitfeld had paid himself $2200 for "expenses," and $200 as a seminar leader; he paid his wife Virginia another $200.

---

*It is every citizen's right to inspect the financial and tax records of nonprofit tax-exempt corporations or foundations.

Jerry Gillies, who had a brief sojourn at Aureon, described Streitfeld as a man of unpredictable moods. Their relationship ended badly, with Streitfeld filing one suit and threatening several others against Gillies and Carole Altman, another leader and business consultant. Gillies told me that Aureon had been running at a loss. Carole had been earning $150 per month; she offered to drop the salary and work for a percentage of profits that she could generate. Since there had been no recent profits, Streitfeld couldn't lose much by the deal; but evidently the whole thing upset him enormously. He refused to pay Carole her last $150, she withheld a newly printed Aureon brochure she'd worked on, and mutual nastiness escalated.

Gillies and Altman branched off into an operation called Together Circle. Streitfeld was furious, but his suit against them lost. Gillies and Altman have since moved on to the field of brainwave feedback at the Bio-Feedback Institute. Combining growth center ideology with some new and highly suspect scientific theories, they give lectures and train people to overcome anxiety, alter their states of consciousness, and "reach new states of awareness, creativity, and efficiency" by controlling their alpha brainwaves. Although she is not licensed for the independent practice of anything, Altman is described by their brochure as "a psychotherapist* with a private practice," and "a pioneer in the use of biofeedback."

The evolution of brainwave therapy illustrates a basic economic problem in the encounter movement: the continual need to create variety. Once you've seen a few rolfing demonstrations, you've seen them all. And unless you go through the ten-hour sequence, that's it for rolfing. The same is true of almost everything else in the encounter world. The techniques spread like wildfire, get swallowed up, and then very quickly become passé. The very motivations that drive people into the encounter game—boredom,

---

*Under current New York law, only falsely representing oneself to the public as a physician, psychologist or social worker, or performing services that are clearly governed by statute, is punishable. "Psychotherapy," "counseling," "growth," and "education" are all rubrics under which unlicensed persons may operate with impunity. Efforts are under way to close this loophole by legislation, but at this writing anyone can call himself an encounter group leader or a psychotherapist.

alienation, saturation, or stimulus deprivation—are the factors that make them easily dissatisfied with the game itself. Hence encounter has a built-in declining market, not the built-in expanding market that its superstars so often speak of.

Streitfeld was concerned about his brochure not only because of its expense, but because attractive brochures are critical to the encounter business. They serve as credentials, programs, and information indexes, and give encounter its unique selling edge over more traditional forms of therapy: advertising.

This is an advantage that mental-health professionals can get in no other way: direct advertising is considered unethical and illegal. Advertising of a professional service by an unlicensed person is a criminal offense. If one is licensed, failure to desist usually leads to revocation of the license. Continued violations after the loss of license can also lead to criminal charges, but most professionals cease after the first warning.

Accordingly it is impossible for most professionals to make their names known to the public without holding a major office or writing successfully. Professionals have long sought ways to become well known without violating ethical standards; in the past that usually meant some form of public speaking, but they may not "treat" in newspaper columns, on TV, or through lectures, give free demonstrations, or do anything that amounts to advertising. Violations of advertising constraints account for a significant percentage of cases brought to the attention of the ethics committees of professional societies. Their decisions are usually quite clear: professionals simply may not send announcements through the mails to strangers, print colorful brochures, or advertise in newspapers, magazines, or playbills, or on the radio. But if they call themselves a growth center, advertising becomes possible.

How does it work? Simple. In addition to glowing descriptions of the growth centers' workshops, each brochure includes biographical blurbs about its key people. Usually these mention professional positions held, degrees and affiliations—just the sort of thing prohibited under customary ethical constraints. The growth center brochure is mailed to ten or twenty thousand people. After the workshop or microlab, the emotions the leader has generated make it almost certain that several people will be shaken enough to approach him. "Call me at the office tomorrow," he says. "We'll see what we can do." And even if they don't, they may call another time, or recommend him to a friend.

At the New York City Council's hearings on encounter groups, Lloyd Merrill, the legal counsel to the chairman of the hearings, asked encounter game stars Casriel and Shepard about their experiences with advertising. Shepard denied ever having a patient come to him as a result of his work at Anthos. Casriel emphasized that he was very cautious with his brochures, but still the local medical society's ethics committee had raised a question about one of his mailings. Casriel indicated that until that question was settled he would not distribute his brochure. The next day I had my secretary call his office and ask for that brochure. It arrived in the mail two days later.

Advertisements for encounter groups to be held at the Flamboyan Hotel overlooking the Caribbean in San Juan prominently featured the name of a well-known psychologist. For $245, participants received air fare, a deluxe room, two meals a day, and three group encounter sessions. The sessions were held from four to eight each day, so the groupers could spend most of the day at the beach and end with an encounter session leading to a cocktail party and dinner. The advertising made it clear that what they were offering was a vacation, and timid souls who ordinarily have a hard time hooking up for an evening's entertainment recognized that the encounter groups would give them a head start.

The mixture is clearly a travel agent's dream. A few airlines have offered in-flight encounter groups, but without much success. Encounterists have to be presold, and springing an encounter group on a captive group of passengers may not have been the best idea the airlines have come up with. Movies are safer—and besides, you can turn them off.

Many businessmen have invested in the green fields of encounter; Warren Avis of car rental fame is a well-known example. But perhaps the top entrepreneur of the encounter movement is Leonard Blank, a psychologist and psychoanalyst who took the unusual step of going public on encounter. Short, fast-talking, and intense, Blank incorporated the Princeton Associates for Human

Resources in September 1968 under New Jersey law. Six months later he reorganized it under Delaware corporate law—notably more relaxed than that of New Jersey. In 1969, Blank netted $65,000 from the sale of 60,000 shares of his stock to a small group of private investors. By 1970, after two unsuccessful underwriting attempts, he succeeded in going public.

While the prospectus of any small company going public is traditionally understated, Blank's recitation of risks probably outweighed any other in recent times. His company had incurred losses of $23,000, and "development costs" of $33,000 (questionably listed as "assets"), at the time of the new offering. It did not manufacture any product, nor did it have a regular sales organization. It had fifteen employees, most of whom were not being paid and were not full-time. It was faced with massive competition, had paid no dividends, and was unlikely to pay any in the foreseeable future. Quoting from the prospectus:

> The company performs its services on a per-task and/or long-term contractual basis. Its behavioral training involves the use of techniques in group interactional processes, including "encounter," and "skill" groups, microlabs and simulated work situations, including psychodrama and varied applications of role playing.

In fact, the company had done almost none of these. It had only one significant contract—purchased from another company—to serve as a "track record," and had to go through any number of technically permissible but rather misleading financial gyrations in order to show a few hundred thousand dollars on its balance sheet.

In November 1970, 29 percent of the company's stock was offered to the public for $5.50 a share. By late January of 1972, it had moved up to $21.

As president, treasurer, and chairman of the board of directors, Blank pays himself $40,000 a year and owns 229,000 shares. As of 1972, Blank's holdings were worth $4,709,000, on paper. He had acquired several smaller companies, including a travel agency, a management consulting firm, and four old age homes. Naturally, the travel agency is now booking encounter vacations in places like Haiti.

Some of the encounter products on the market have been books, tapes, records, films, toys, sensitivity kits, and plastic bats for working out aggression.* Several companies are now marketing taped lectures and discussions of encounter groups by Carl Rogers and other stars.

One company sold several thousand "sensitivity kits" at twenty-five dollars each. Essentially they consisted of a manual of instructions to help industrial supervisors to understand the "perceptual world" of a hard-core unemployed black when he first gets into the white job world, and a pair of plastic and cardboard multiple-image eyeglasses. When the foreman put on the glasses, everything in his field of vision was split into dozens of images. He was supposed to conclude that this was how his plant would look to a newly hired black on his first workday. The glasses and manual were treated as a joke by most of the employees who were given the kit, yet many firms, including American Airlines, bought them.

By the following year American Airlines had learned its lesson about the kits, but tried out another money-saving approach to sensitivity. They requested bids from twenty or thirty consulting firms which specialized in designing training programs, for a program to train eight hundred supervisors across the country in one day to become "more competent at human relations" (a euphemism for working with blacks). Once the consulting firms had submitted their detailed proposals and plans, they were informed that American had decided to do the job "in the house," and no contract would be let. This move probably saved American thousands of dollars—now all they had to do was take the best parts of each plan to take advantage of some of the country's best training talent.

One of the most financially successful corporations in the encounter game is the Human Development Institute (HDI) of At-

---

*A company called Uniquity, based in California, is now marketing plastic bats called Batacas for the "safe and satisfying release for anger, hostility, frustration and excess energy!" They come in two models: The Olympic model ("best for heavy use") is twenty-two inches long, comes in red with white trim, and can be yours for $15.95 plus postage and handling. For those with a smaller anger, they also sell an "economy model for light use" at $9.95.

lanta, a Bell and Howell subsidiary which developed a series of "personal growth tapes" through which encounter may be self-administered. Having placed them on the market in late 1968, only two years later HDI was reporting sales of over half a million dollars for the tapes. The most popular series, priced at three hundred dollars a set, has been the Personal Growth Groups tapes, which instruct users how to conduct their own series of ten hour-and-a-half encounter sessions. The next most popular tape offers married couples a five-session, five-hour encounter to deepen their relationship and work out a standardized set of marital problems. The couples series is available on tape cassettes for $59.50, or on records for $29.50.

Other tapes on the HDI list include a nondenominational religious series designed to enrich spiritual values; a two-hundred-dollar black-white encounter in five sessions; and two ten-session series for industrial use priced at $250 each, one on vocational education and one for employee team development.

Gene Ruyle, a former Episcopal minister who is now a sales representative for HDI, told me: "In the first year and a half we screened all applications for purchases on the tapes, lest they fall into the wrong hands. But on the basis of feedback about who was purchasing the tapes, we decided such screening was not necessary." He mentioned the order of frequency among purchasers: educational institutions and colleges first, churches second, government branches such as the Federal Bureau of Prisons and the Department of Health, Education, and Welfare third, and finally private training institutions and growth centers.

Ruyle and HDI often cite the studies by Lieberman, Yalom, and Miles that show the Encountertapes to be the least dangerous leadership style. But though tapes may be the "least dangerous" method, there is no evidence that they are particularly successful either. In the studies by Yalom and his co-workers, a group that slavishly followed the tape's instructions was rated lowest in generating positive change. The other tape-led group, third highest in positive change, had talked back to the canned voice, made fun of it, disobeyed it, then finally played the whole thing at once and picked out the exercises that they felt like trying.

The use of encounter tapes came in for public twitting recently when the Concord Hotel, a New York resort famous for singles weekends, advertised an encounter weekend for twenty-five dollars above the regular hotel bill. In a *New York Times Sunday Magazine* article, Judy Klemesrud reported that her group could not keep up with the timed instructions, and with much high comedy treated readers to the image of a Bell and Howell sales type interrupting a group busily working at loving, by saying, "Hurry up—you people are supposed to be doing anger now."

Some of the advertising for the encounter tapes might be mistaken for dime-store romances. The brochure for the Marriage Enrichment Program features photographs of a handsome young couple, clearly professional models, conveying so much love that any couple would be envious. It includes testimonials from satisfied customers, saying that the experience "was totally positive" and deepened and enriched their marriage. Such advertising gives no hint of the hostility and other emotions actually dealt with in the tapes.

It's hard to estimate the impact of these tapes, since consenting couples use them in the privacy of their own homes. The closest parallel I've seen in action is Group Therapy, a widely sold board game. After each player's turn, the rest of the players vote on whether he is "with it" or "copping out" on performing the encounters, exposing secrets, and confronting everyone else present with previously unexpressed feelings. The first time I played the game, one previously happy couple broke up their "meaningful relationship" that very night.

The tapes and the game sell, and judging from the glowing testimonials by their users, some people feel that such encounter devices helped them express things they could not otherwise convey to their partners. Some advocates argue that by dehumanizing the leadership aspect, the tapes help cut out the abuses of overassertive leaders. In many cases, however, encounter leaders use the tapes in conjunction with their own techniques. Others argue that in the wrong hands, the tapes and booklets increase the destructive potential of certain people. Either way, it seems clear that encounter by tape provides no real alternative to our society's alienation. One young man summed it up when he commented, "It's bizarre and ironic that a machine should teach me to be more human."

Several encounter game derivatives have been marketed as entertainment, as literature, and as theater. Probably best known is the movie *Bob and Carol and Ted and Alice,* which by January 1972 had grossed $14,600,000. Theater treatments include the long-running play *The Concept,* and more recently, the Liquid Theatre at New York's Guggenheim Museum, where patrons paid to follow the building's spiral form through an assembly line of strokes, purrs, kisses, touches, embraces, and cuddles. Literature on encounter includes Jane Howard's *Please Touch,* Stu Miller's painfully autobiographical *Hot Springs,* and Rasa Gustaitis' trippy *Turning On.*

To the best of my knowledge, only one author, Bernard Rosenthal, has pointed out encounterists' inconsistent approach to the handling of monetary issues. He sees in the encounter movement a reinforcement of the monetary values that the movement "proclaims it wishes to dethrone, i.e., preoccupation with money and profiteering."

Rosenthal points out that encounterists are selling a diversion that persuades people of their capacity to be spontaneous, compassionate, and genuine. He argues that in the process, they become increasingly sanguine about the dehumanizing effects of the economic system around them, and less likely to rebel against it. In his opinion, encounter game participants are paying an elaborate form of social conscience money "for the privilege of thinking of themselves as genuinely human. Thereupon they can better sustain the deadly and depersonalizing effects of the real world, indeed often believing that the behavior in it—manipulative, hard, opportunistic, callous—is not really bad because their real selves, or substantial segments of them, are so basically benign that their day-to-day acts do not genuinely characterize their true nature."

This self-deception, as Rosenthal sees it, has as a side effect "a vast escalation of guile, double-talk, double-think, and circuses of sham and deception," all of which allow encounter participants to avoid the true humanistic issues in our society, all the while becoming more benevolent to other middle-class players at weekend workshops.

The financial picture for encounterists, especially at growth centers, is becoming increasingly grim. While national economic trends are an important factor, there is also the possibility that encounter has become a dying fad.

One other explanation for encounter's financial crisis is the encounter world ideology itself. One of the main tenets of the faith is that there shall be no craft union; that anybody can do it, and that nobody, least of all the professionals, ought to corner the market. As a result, most growth centers refuse to grant licenses or credentials, and don't even give out certificates acknowledging the training of their resident staffers. Esalen's cancellation of its residence program illustrates the discomfort growth centers feel about the training issue. Since they can't or won't enforce standards, most growth centers cop out. Their antiprofessional bias makes it difficult for them to expect their own leaders to have the same sort of formal training and credentials that they resent in mental-health professionals.

But there's the hitch. The very motive that encounter spokesmen so often attribute to mental-health specialists—the need to overcome less expensive competition—is far more likely to damage the growth centers and untrained encounterists themselves. I have never seen a competent mental-health professional who couldn't earn a comfortable living, either in private practice or with a hospital or clinic. This is not the case, of course, for the untrained encounterists. And if the growth centers can't control the source of encounter talent, they'll soon go out of business as a result of the competition.

The encounter movement must begin to solve the problems of setting standards, establishing training programs, and doing research on its own processes, if it's to have lasting impact. Such problems require money in the encounter world, just as they do in the mental-health world. Even with the added financial power that advertising and freedom from professional constraints gives the encounterists, I believe that without significant investment in research and development the future for encounter looks dismal. Should encounterists attempt to professionalize their training and develop quality-control checks, they would have to compete with establishment researchers for government funds. As I see it, the problems they face simply can't be solved if their efforts are financed solely by participants' fees.

Very few encounter leaders are in it for the money. Though

there are exploiters, they are probably a manifestation of the economic system which places a monetary value on practically every human experience. What we usually find in encounter game pro's is just misguided altruism.

Any observer of the encounter game must be struck with the dedication, the hard work, and the emotional energy of its players. They've carried their credo, their games, and their absurdities into three main sectors of our culture: industry, education, and drug abuse rehabilitation. In each sector, encounter techniques have been applied as a kind of emotional axle grease to help individuals mesh with the gears of our complex social institutions. The next chapters will examine each of these areas.

11

Sensitivity in the Executive Suite

Most players of the encounter game cite as the movement's origin an incident which occurred in Connecticut in 1946. As part of a program to implement the Connecticut Fair Employment Practices Act, community leaders were being trained in group problem solving by several prominent social psychologists, most notably Kurt Lewin and Ronald Lippitt. Observers sat silently and coded the interactions of the group members.

Early in the conference Lewin arranged for evening meetings between the training staff and the observers to pool their observations. One night some of the participants drifted in; fascinated by the observations of their behavior, they joined in the discussion. The meeting proved so exciting that soon the participants requested that the training include immediate feedback instead of after-hours discussions of their activities. At that critical moment the notion of immediate interpersonal feedback was born, and it gave staff members and participants alike the feeling that they had hit upon a technique with the potential to create great changes in social behavior.

Shortly thereafter, in 1947, several staff members of this workshop formed the National Training Laboratories (NTL), today most prestigious of the growth centers. While the attempt was made to form NTL as a research organization, their research was plainly aimed at action—changing individuals and helping them in turn to change their environments. Lewin had reacted strongly to the Nazi holocaust and in particular the excesses of Hitler's scientists. Not content to have psychologists communicate to each other, he aimed at realizing immediate social benefits from research. Though Lewin died shortly after the beginning of this process, his influence prevailed, and most of the highly trained academic professionals who helped develop NTL are still firmly committed to the notion that their activities help to democratize our society.

One problem that emerged very quickly was that the T-group experiences (as they came to be called by 1949) had such seductive emotional appeal that almost all of the more work-oriented subjects the leaders tried to introduce were rejected by the participants. Increasingly, the NTL staff had difficulty in developing a conceptual model for their work, in differentiating their work from psychotherapy, and in honoring their avowed research goals.

Teachers, industrial managers, and ministers were the participants in the early days; the groups dealt with the problems of applying what they were learning in the laboratory to typical situations in their daily work. Many of these groups failed to achieve any significant results, according to NTL leader Kenneth T. Benne, because of the difficulty in relating back-home problems to the laboratory training work. Ultimately a distinction emerged between the T-group as "therapy for normals," directed toward problems in general human relations, and T-groups focused on common problems in occupationally homogeneous groups.

Just as Esalen later earned prestige as the epicenter of the movement on the West Coast, NTL, headquartered in Washington but with its major laboratory at Bethel, Maine, has maintained a dominant position on the East Coast. More austere, prestigious, and academically oriented than Esalen, NTL has traditionally sold its services to the upper crust of American industry, education, and social service. Its early clients included American Red Cross workers, industrial managers, Puerto Rican government workers, staff leaders from national voluntary organizations, public school teachers and administrators, the Episcopal and Methodist Churches, Humble Oil, and the Aluminum Company of Canada. In later years a list of firms that sent group members to NTL labs is virtually indistinguishable from a list of the major companies in the nation. Sensitivity training became a fad, and sending executives to labs was viewed as an indispensable way to engage in the competitive accumulation of "executive talent assets."

NTL runs labs all over the country, gearing its fees to the type of client and his ability to pay. An individual who wants to enrich his potential will pay at least $325 in tuition and fees for a week, and his living costs will range from $110 to $200. Special workshops for chief executives, board members, and group vice-presidents offered in spas like Palm Beach and Nassau run to $1500 per week; and for only $900 more the corporate man's wife can join him.

NTL's sales approach is more reserved than the pitch usually found in Esalen-style brochures, but the concerns that come through are the familiar high-sounding promises. One NTL piece included a sop to anyone who might have heard that it's all a Communist plot:

> Sensitivity training is an exact opposite of brainwashing. Sensitivity training aims to provide the knowledge, skills, and sensitivities to support individual differences. It arms the individual against group pressure. . . .

NTL claims that its work is not a means for "correcting significant psychological deficiencies" and frequently warns that "persons seeking or needing psychotherapy are discouraged from participating." Such printed statements, however, are the extent of that discouragement. NTL states:

> NTL Institute records suggest that fewer than 1 percent of participants have had significant problems during training under NTL Institute auspices. In almost all cases they have been persons with a history of prior serious disturbances.

This final statement implies that if people do crack up, it's their fault anyway.

NTL's records are mostly client self-evaluations or informal comments by group leaders—notably unreliable sources of data on psychological casualties. Further, only "serious stress and mental disturbance" has been considered a negative result by NTL people. Moderate emotional upsets, reentry problems, job dislocations, and the like are not considered significant enough to record or to mention to prospective groupers.

While there is no such thing as an "accredited trainer," NTL's brochures promise that its associates have met "standards which include extensive theoretical background in personal, interperson-

al, small-group, and organizational dynamics; a high level of interpersonal competence; and supervised training experience with a
wide variety of groups and organizations." What the prospective
NTL participant is not told is that such a person need have no
particular training in individual psychology, in the recognition of
psychopathology, or in coping with emotional disturbances, or
have any experience in individual treatment. It is true that a large
portion of the NTL Network are experienced clinicians; but as
Lieberman, Yalom, and Miles point out, even experienced clinicians are unlikely to recognize significant pathology in the encounter or T-group context.

Recently industry has turned off to NTL and its offshoots. This
attitude surfaced not too long ago in a well-known article in the
Wall Street Journal, in which Byron Calame detailed some of
industry's negative reactions to sensitivity training. Among the
most frequent complaints were the loss of key employees, extra
fusses and fights on the job, and personality reactions that caused
formerly productive executives to lose the emotional head of
steam that had kept them going. Fear of suicides and breakdowns
has made many companies aware that they may be buying their
key men a toy considerably more dangerous than the "executive
sandboxes" that were popular a few years ago. Calame noted,
"One big company in the Midwest stopped all sensitivity training
after a vice-president suffered a total breakdown during a session
and had to enter a mental hospital." He also cited the following
case:

> A division manager at one big company was described as
> "a ferocious guy—brilliant, but a thoroughgoing autocrat—
> who everyone agreed was just what the division needed
> because it was in a tough, competitive business." Deciding to
> smooth off his rough edges, the company sent him to
> sensitivity training—where he found out exactly what people
> thought of him. "So he stopped being a beast," says the
> source, "and his effectiveness fell apart. The reason he'd
> been so good was that he didn't realize what a beast he was.
> Eventually, they put in a new manager."

Humble Oil, TRW, Inc., U.S. Plywood-Champion Papers,
Northwest Bancorp, Northrop Corp., Honeywell, and Aerojet-

General are among the firms that have dropped sensitivity training altogether. Henry R. Brenner, who manages employee programs for Xerox, said in a recent letter, "There is general agreement by our management that there are a number of negative considerations with respect to sensitivity training which preclude our using the technique except in extremely selective cases." Other firms such as General Electric, AT&T, and IBM have reviewed the use of T-groups and scaled down their commitments to it; some have shifted to "Organizational Development" (OD) projects run by company staff members, in which sensitivity-type activities play only a small part.

Often the newly sensitized executive runs into the reentry problem of trying to change others in his environment, sees that it can't work, and quickly goes back to his old ways. In other cases the executive simply can't integrate the experience with his job. Corporate training directors, the very men who authorize trips to NTL labs, end up coping with the negative results.

Most executives who bare their souls may get positive feedback for bravery and openness from the group. But if they are hard hit, that's not enough to put Humpty Dumpty back together. Few have access to the kind of continuing on-the-job support for which Dr. Saul Scherzer, director of management development for ITT, and others have recognized a need:

> There was a case where the group fed back to an individual that they thought he was totally untrustworthy and challenged his sense of being, his sense of worth. Later he offered an admission of stealing, of going to people's desks. He was very upset, cried, asked for help, when the others detailed specific instances where they knew about his going to others' desks and files to obtain information. His reason for doing it was that he was willing to do anything to go upward in his career—this was the first time the group had the opportunity to feed it back to him. I've tried working with him. . . .

NTL's claim that only 1 percent of participants will suffer a psychosis reveals the mind of the combat general at work, taking calculated risks with other people's lives. If we accept Carl Rogers' estimate of 750,000 people engaging in encounter in 1971, we end up with 7500 people with serious consequences including psychotic episodes. (If we extrapolate from the Yalom and Lieberman figures, we are talking about 75,000 casualties.)

In human rather than numerical terms, psychotic experiences are not easy to accept blandly. Mrs. Bernice G., an administrator in a large public social welfare institution, registered for an intensive two-week workshop run by the National Training Laboratories at Bethel, Maine. It was at this two-week workshop that Mrs. G. became psychotic; for eight months afterward she was out of work, socially withdrawn, and unable to function in her prior capacity as an administrator. She described having been verbally attacked by the group and the leader. They had particularly condemned her for her husband's suicide several years earlier, saying that she was mean enough to drive anyone to suicide.

Her upset at first took the form of continued crying in the group. During the following week she had several hallucinatory episodes, one in which she experienced a statue coming alive and talking to her, and a second during which she felt as though great cables were rooting her to the earth and connecting her to the universe. She finally arranged for a psychiatric consultation on her own, and her symptoms subsided briefly. But the repercussions continued after she returned to her job. She said:

> They keep saying, "This isn't the same as group therapy."
> Well, it is much more intense than group therapy. Unmiti-
> gated hostility and all hell broke loose and they did nothing
> to deflect it. . . . I don't think this is institutional change—I
> think it's personal change. Our leader watched me crying my
> eyes out constantly, day after day, and didn't do anything.

When I raised the question of casualties and of psychiatric protections with NTL executives, I was assured that every professional precaution was being taken. On questioning Dr. George C. Schwartz, who was supposedly responsible for NTL's psychiatric support programs, it became clear that he didn't feel especially responsible—psychiatric support meant only that he or another psychiatrist would be available to pick up the pieces. It did not mean screening or follow-up of participants or supervision of group leaders.

Until recently NTL kept on the austere side, refusing to do nude workshops and the like, but a little sex has now crept in, according to Scherzer:

In a group in which I was a participant I saw the trainer make a play for a female member. When I challenged him about it, he thought it was good for her emotional growth. It didn't jell right, that he was in a position to make that judgment of what was good for a person's emotional growth; that he took upon himself the right to do this I consider beyond ethical bounds.

Despite incidents like this and others cited by critics, NTL's efforts have been characterized by seriousness of purpose and high-level professional functioning. Most of their errors seem to stem not from malfeasance or cupidity, but from excessively good intentions, insufficient warnings to clients, and a lack of screening and follow-up procedures.

Regardless of the apparent downturn in the sensitivity business, it's appropriate to ask why industry bought the encounter game in the first place. In what is perhaps the definitive philosophical statement on "T-Groups for Organizational Effectiveness," which appeared in the *Harvard Business Review,* Chris Argyris outlined the rationale for this endeavor into changing human behavior.

What causes dynamic, flexible, and enthusiastically committed executive teams to become sluggish and inflexible as time goes by? Why do they no longer enjoy the intrinsic challenge of their work, but become motivated largely by wages and executive bonus plans?

Why do executives become conformist as a company becomes older and bigger? Why do they resist saying what they truly believe—even when it is in the best interests of the company?

How is it possible to develop a top management team that is constantly innovating and taking risks?

In Argyris' view, the problems behind each question are ingrained in corporate life. But Argyris believes that the solution is at hand: "In recent years there has evolved a new way of helping executives develop new inner resources which enable them to mitigate these organizational ills." Of course, he's referring to sensitivity training.

Several serious observers of the executive process have concluded that the rising tide of conformity must be stopped at the top decision-making level. Each corporate team must have its radical thinkers and gadflies, so that through the hammering and testing of competing ideas the company will avoid pitfalls, increase profits, and win bigger shares of its market. What Argyris is really saying is that the overall goal for sensitivity training is to make executives more "gung ho." And yet in the face of the older American ideal of rugged individualism, there is a need to conceal or at least downplay that purpose. Sensitivity training seems to have been taken up by business largely because it provided executives with a deeper commitment to the profit motive. The executive is encouraged to speak up to the boss, and the boss's capacity to listen is also scrutinized. In all, the process most often became a parody of individual growth which served to reinforce conformity by making certain previously forbidden behaviors—like anger—acceptable.

Erich Fromm and Jacques Ellul have pointed out that technocracy requires maximum efficiency and therefore minimum individuality. Magda Denes, a Gestalt psychologist, believes that the movement provides a sop to corporate malfunctions at the human level. Speaking of the rapid rise in laboratory training, Denes says:

> Half the interest was aroused by its promise: to arrest alienation and to make possible involvement with the System without abdication of human character and autonomy. The other half interest came from what it delivered: the technical adjustment of personnel into more smoothly functioning cogs.

That was the shape of industry's commitment to the T-group movement for a long time—widespread acceptance of the notion that individual executives would go to groups, come back hopped up and raring to go, and be able to make a profound contribution to the corporation. In many companies, T-group participation was viewed as a necessary step in the career ladder, like club membership or a wholesome community activity. Group attendance became a competitive issue among young executives; how many times each had been to "charm school," as the laboratory experiences were called, became a kind of one-upmanship gambit.

Then, in the late sixties, Calame's *Wall Street Journal* article caused a surfacing of dissatisfaction with sensitivity training. People had not in fact been changed, and for the most part corporate customers did not buy the T-group partisans' defense that they just hadn't done it enough.

Clinicians had long scoffed at claims that sensitivity training could change individual behavior in a short period, since in psychotherapy even the smallest personality changes seem like a victory after working with a patient for years. In 1968, Marvin Dunnette and John P. Campbell, psychologists at the University of Minnesota, undertook an extensive study of the sensitivity-training research literature. In a lengthy critique in the *Psychological Bulletin,* they pointed out that there is little or no evidence for the contention that T-grouping sessions changed anybody's work behavior. Further, Campbell and Dunnette noted the vast methodological problems that have been blithely ignored by those promulgating the encounter game ideology and in the research supporting it.

Not all advocates are disheartened by the evidence, of course. Jack Gibb, for example, tends to apologize for the limitations of current research with unwarranted optimism. Gibb briefly reported on 106 studies that had offered quantitative data on the effects of groups. His review is important because Carl Rogers and other encounter advocates have repeatedly pointed to it in their writings and to the 106 studies as supporting evidence for the movement's activities. For example, Gibb's report stated:

> While the evidence for the therapeutic and behavior change effects of human relations training is certainly controversial and open to legitimate multiple interpretations, it seems clear to the reviewer [Gibb] that changes do occur ... Because these effects are closely related to hoped-for therapeutic outcomes, the *evidence is strong that intensive group training experiences have therapeutic effects.* It is yet to be demonstrated whether the magnitude of the effects is sufficient to justify an increased use of group training, or whether the effects are therapeutically significant in comparison with the effects of more conventional methods of therapy. (italics added)

Carl Rogers frequently quotes the italicized phrase above out of context to support his pro-encounter position. Actually, Gibb goes on to say:

> When compared with the standards of research in the psychological laboratory and with the desirability of definitive statements about the effects of [sensitivity] training, the results are disappointingly equivocal.

The clearest evidence for positive effects in Gibb's review occurred in the area of enhanced self-estimates. These findings are similar to those reported by Yalom, Lieberman, and Miles, and Gibb too noted that new values and attitudes tended to wear off after six to nine months. Gibb concluded: "What we seem to have are some promising theories, some meager data, and some methodological innovations. We do not as yet have adequate tests of the theories of group growth."

The problem of carry-over to work performance has been dealt with by only one researcher, William J. Underwood (1965). His results indicate that while laboratory training seems to produce more actual changes than the simple passage of time, the relative proportion of changes detrimental to performance is also higher for the laboratory method.

Campbell and Dunnette note:

> It still cannot be said with any certainty whether T-groups lead to greater or lesser changes in self-perceptions than other types of group experience, simple passage of time, or the mere act of filling out a self-description questionnaire.

These authors lament the small number of studies using solid research methods, noting that with the current standards, no conclusions can be drawn. Further, even if a T-group changes an individual's sensitivity, there is no evidence to indicate that the change will be accompanied by improved performance on the job. Campbell and Dunnette sum it up this way: "The assumption that T-group has positive utility for organizations must necessarily rest on shaky ground. It has been neither confirmed nor disconfirmed."

The cycle has run its course on corporate encounter, and today even the words "sensitivity training" raise a frown from any training executive. It's fashionable in industry to archly put down the whole process. As a result, industrial encounterists have shifted to an emphasis on the organization's needs rather than the individual's. The new phrase "organizational development" (OD) now prevails.

The emphasis on organizational development may have made encounter somewhat easier to sell, but it moved group leaders from individual goals that were simply unlikely to corporate ones that often are impossible. The basic notion is to change the emotional climate, hence the productivity, of the entire organization, using T-groups, and changing such things as the company's predominant style of communication, decision making, and patterns of authority. Once these elements change it is assumed that the company's productivity and profitability will change.

Richard Beckhardt, one of the principal writers on OD, has noted that only thirty or so of the major American corporations have committed themselves to the requisite long-term process necessary for a successful OD program, and that in most of these cases the commitment has not been sufficient to make profound changes in the organization. Beckhardt says that it takes at least three years to humanize and democratize a sizable company, and that during the process, profitability and work relationships are likely to suffer. Few American stockholders are willing to pay that price for long-term profits, which may never materialize, and even fewer top executives are willing to risk their own necks to put such a theory into practice.

Several kinds of things can go wrong with this more palatable corporate version of the encounter game, and all of them seem to occur with surprising regularity. NTL staff and other advocates of OD usually fail to point out to prospective clients that there is as much chance of negative results as of positive ones.

One man I interviewed considered himself to have been damaged by an internally run encounter group which, though he probably didn't know it, was part of the OD program of the company. He had been an employee of the Harwood Company, often cited in professional literature because the chairman of the board is Dr. Alfred Morrow, a well-known industrial psychologist and also a director of NTL. Chuck S. said that when he was hired for an executive job in the Harwood Company's sales force, he was immediately expected to join an ongoing group; five or six other men had already been in the group for some time. For him it was a devastating experience. Because he had not been part of the group during the early months of its development, which served as a warm-up for the other men, Mr. S. felt he had been given an especially tough roasting—"an accelerated course."

He described going to Tarrytown House for an overnight two-day encounter session. Seven months later, he still had sleepless nights thinking about that experience, and during the intervening months he had numerous conversations with close friends about the experience, trying to put his feelings into some integration.

When I asked Chuck S. if he had had any choice about participating in the group, he said that he really hadn't—he had simply been directed to participate. He said he'd asked many questions prior to the experience, but all of the answers were vague, on the order of, "You'll see when you get there," and, "We'll all learn to understand each other better."

Nobody had helped him with his upset during the group experience. He explained that he didn't really want to show how upset he was, lest his image and position in the company be damaged further. In this case, the tyrannical, competitive component operating in the group clearly outweighed its capacity to be supportive of a member, and the climate of psychological safety and trust was lacking. The example takes on added importance since it occurred in a company widely touted as an example of how well OD can work.

Another example of mishandled organizational development occurred in the Urban Coalition. At one point some blacks in the organization went to its director, John Gardner, and complained that they sensed some antiblack bias within the organization. They cited the fact that Gardner's immediate staff was all white; his public-relations man, his finance officers, and others were all white; and the top-flight blacks who had been attracted to the Coalition were nestled away several levels below the top administration. Gardner, who was originally trained as a psychologist, immediately suggested that NTL be brought in to help the Coalition work out its internal race-relations problems.

Twenty-five or so top echelon members of the Coalition spent a day working with one NTL leader, himself black, and all the taboo questions were raised during the session. Whites were challenged to state how they really felt about blacks; the blacks responded with how they really felt about whites; in general, the day was devoted to questions that served to open up feelings. Period. Unfortunately, there was no time to close the feelings up again, or to do anything constructive with them. The one or two whites who made a sincere effort to come to grips with their antiblack feelings and opened themselves up were perceived as bigots. The whites were similarly shocked to learn that black men they'd liked and worked closely with held them in low regard because their skin was white. "The organization never again had what we had when we started that process," said one participant. "The team spirit disappeared, and relationships just never were the same after that."

Such results are by no means uncommon, and it is especially unfortunate that several of the most severely negative OD payoffs have occurred in organizations committed to social change activities. For example, extensive T-grouping was for several years a built-in part of the Peace Corps training program, until mounting negative results outweighed the enthusiastic support.

American business has a tradition of looking for quick results and high payoffs for its dollars. Sensitivity training can offer neither, and the readiness of business to cut sensitivity training at the first sign of economic strain proves that, as businessmen say, "It's the bottom line that counts." Since no one has been able to demonstrate any real profitability as a result of sensitivity-training work, it becomes increasingly harder to justify dollars and executive time spent. In addition, the emotional breakdowns, suicides, and organizational foul-ups that can be attributed to the encounter game make the process a high risk proposition.

The sad part is that psychological work of real value could be done if the process were not oversold, if unrealistic expectations had not been set up, and if unqualified group leadership not become the rule rather than the exception. Further, it is in the industrial setting that results could be most easily measured; and I consider it far more likely that changes in communication style, attitudes, and on-the-job interactions could be achieved in industrial groups than among individuals in growth centers.

The failure of the sensitivity movement is most clear in the industrial spectrum, and just as the movement began there, it looks like it's beginning to end there. In the face of the economic slump and reduced group participation, NTL tried many things. It advertised weekend encounters; it announced plans to start a university to train postgraduate T-group leaders; it undertook massive reorganization; but nothing worked.

As of December 1971, NTL announced that it had dissolved its membership, its association with regional groups, and its board. A new fifteen-man board, set up for "influence and prestige, not management," became the only permanent membership. While programs at Bethel are expected to continue, other programs have been dropped. Contracts are to be developed on a free-lance basis, with finder's fees of 1 to 3 percent as incentives; and membership is to be established by bringing projects to NTL for sponsorship. Clearly, there is nothing left of NTL but its name. We can imagine the internal stresses that preceded this self-destruct move, and it will be interesting to see whether other growth centers and consulting firms will follow suit.

As Wilfred Sheed recently said, "Whom the Gods would destroy they first oversell."

12

Don't Teach Us to Think, Teach Us to Feel

In the mid-sixties a crisis emerged in education, and the response to it was far different from the traditional discussion of budgets for playgrounds and buildings. Two factors brought the crisis to the attention of the public. One was the apparent failure of increasing numbers of students to master basic educational skills; the second, a widespread discontent with authoritarian classroom practices. Many observers view the two as inexorably intertwined, and to treat both have prescribed massive injections of humanism, awareness, honesty, and improved communications for the people who are responsible for the day-to-day process of education. This antidote, of course, is the encounter ideology, and to date encounter's most successful arena has been the field of education.

According to the encounter theory, while more facilities and money might be useful, what we really need to improve education is teachers who are more humanistic and relate better to students and to each other. If we improve human relations in the school, encounterists feel, learning will become more efficient.

As we've seen, encounterists like to play the role of educator rather than psychotherapist or social engineer. "It's adult education," said Aureon's Harold Streitfeld. "We're teaching people about emotions in the same way we teach them about mathematics." They've recognized that the best place to win converts is in the schools, and that the first people who need be taught about emotions are teachers, if their ideology is to gain a firm foothold in American culture.

The encounter ideology is now enormously widespread in

American education. There is no major school system in this country without teachers who have participated in T-groups. It's a rare university or college which does not have a sensitivity-training course as part of its education sequence, in many cases required. Because of the absence of a central authority and because of the number of ways students, teachers, and school administrators can participate in encounter, there is no way to arrive at an even approximate numerical estimate; but ask any teacher and you'll find that if he hasn't encountered, his neighbor in the next classroom has.

Encounter, sensitivity training, or "affective education," as it's called in the realm of education, has until now made only minor changes in educational ideology, modest changes in the verbiage of many American schools, and—in some cases—dramatic changes in individuals and in faculty relationships, not always for the better. Significant and lasting positive results have yet to be demonstrated.

At first teachers and administrators went to laboratories sponsored by the National Training Laboratories, or run by people who had gone through NTL's training programs. As the demand increased, and word-of-mouth advertising spread, the quality of leadership decreased, and the movement turned in the direction of quasi therapy. When dissatisfaction with the prevailing educational system surfaced, more and more school districts assumed that T-groups would significantly affect their functioning and sought grants for sensitivity-training programs; sometimes they found ways to allocate parts of their own regular budgets for such endeavors. Most of the projects have been funded by local, state, or federal grants, or through philanthropic organizations, since school boards have traditionally avoided the area of psychological change.

In a number of cases, clinicians employed by or acting as consultants to local systems were recruited as sensitivity trainers, or took the initiative to sell school authorities a sensitivity program. Since schools usually pay lower salaries and require less training and experience for their mental-health personnel than other institutions do, their staff therapists are among the least qualified in their field. Many have provided encounter experiences for which their backgrounds have not qualified them and which do not address specific school-related problems—the basic personal growth approach, applied in the hope that it will improve education.

School administrators have had little reason not to implement recommendations for encounter-type programs. They are aware of the chronic difficulties stemming from personality factors among teachers and between faculty and students, and are eager for any remedy to the situation. Administrators rarely question the goals and values of encounterists, largely because the movement's clichés are so similar to those of education that they win automatic acceptance. A few may question the techniques and results, but their reservations generally have to do with avoiding horror stories or "brainwashing" charges.

An example of the extent to which encounter has penetrated education is provided by the New York City Board of Education. New York's school system has a clinical arm called the Bureau of Child Guidance (BCG), actually one of the world's largest licensed psychiatric clinics, which serves the city's school population. Its staff includes 670 professionals—psychiatrists, psychologists, and social workers. The annual city budget for this bureau is over twelve million dollars, and an additional two to three million dollars in federal funds are spent annually for staff salaries.

The Bureau of Child Guidance has used encounter and sensitivity training primarily for teachers and for its internal staff. According to Dr. Simon Silverman, psychologist director of the operation, these encounter groups have been structured as "in-service courses, not for instructional purposes, but for human development." About twenty-five bureau staff members have been specially trained in sensitivity techniques under a National Institute of Mental Health grant. Almost all other staff members have at one time or another participated in or led such groups, though not necessarily as part of their regular duties.

But Silverman is by no means sold on the encountering his subordinates are doing:

> I deplore the very dramatic and the very popular kind of stuff that is being done. To me this is an entirely unprofessional approach. You don't take the profession into the marketplace and sell it like a Bedouin telling Arabs how to cure their wives' pregnancies.

Likening the encounter craze to the earlier "magic cures" of lobotomy and convulsive shock treatments, Silverman concluded, "There may be something wonderful about this, but let's put it on an experimental basis first and see what it does." But Silverman, like so many other educators, is caught in a bind. His professional colleagues and subordinates are traditionally entitled to considerable independence, and as director of this important bureau, he backs up his aides.

While Dr. Silverman feels that the use of encounter in the child-guidance setting is minimal, several members of his staff indicated that encounter has very much affected their work at the Bureau. One staff member stated that trainee psychologists feel coerced to take part in sensitivity training, as refusal would make them seem unwilling to meet the demands of the job.

Several years ago Dr. Rachel Lauer, the bureau's chief psychologist, arranged an intensive five-day workshop for twenty professional psychologists from BCG and twenty psychologists from other organizations. The workshop was held at the Princeton Inn in New Jersey, under the sponsorship of the National Training Laboratories. Scholarships were arranged, ostensibly because all of the participants were from the federally funded Headstart program. Actually, the content of the workshop had nothing to do with Headstart or working with children. The explanation for this discrepancy was the familiar though unproven notion that if the participants became more sensitive to themselves and their peers, they would automatically become more sensitive in their work.

One participant was badly shaken by this encounter experience and suffered a psychotic breakdown shortly after the workshop. A fifty-year-old psychologist and therapist, he had always thought of himself as successful, "well related," and well received by his colleagues. He made the mistake of stating this opinion to his groupmates, who then attacked him for what they perceived as his "superiority, aloofness, and unrelatedness."

By the second night of the workshop the effect of the rejection by the group was so severe that he appeared to be in a zombielike state of dissociation and blankness. Since the group was angry with him, no one tried to help him. In the encounter framework, he was responsible for himself.

On the third day he began to hit back at other members of the group. He particularly held one woman responsible for his upset, focused his anger at her, and looked to her for emotional support. She didn't respond to him, and her rejection was the final straw.

The following night he tracked her to her room and tried to force her to pay attention to him. She refused. He made several attempts to pursue her after the workshop. She was terrified of him and went out of her way to avoid him. She attributed a series of anonymous late-night phone calls, slashed tires, and slashed hoses in her car's heating system to his misplaced ardor. A psychologist herself, she later said that what this man needed was somebody to "put the lid on his id," rather than the continual opening up which was encouraged in the group. Badly shaken, the man was hospitalized shortly afterward.

People tend to assume that professionals have some built-in protection against the abuses of group process, but the evidence is quite to the contrary. What started out as an educational experience became a "heavy trip" for these two participants, and for several others who either left the group before it was concluded or experienced reentry problems back at their jobs.

When I asked Dr. Silverman about ill effects, he felt they were minimal. He explained that he'd received a complaint or two, but he felt that such incidents were isolated crank responses. His staff members did no research and kept no detailed records of growth experiences in their groups.

For the most part teachers and counselors who have participated in sensitivity programs have been volunteers, but occasionally entire schools or school units have been ordered to take part in encounter groups. In these situations, the coercion itself is usually symptomatic of existing stresses that are likely to be exacerbated, not ameliorated, by encountering.

A case in point occurred in March 1970. Reacting to the death of a fourteen-year-old by an overdose of heroin, parents at Junior High School 52 in New York insisted that something be done about addiction. City officials asked encounter "experts" from the Addiction Services Agency to undertake a crash training program for teachers, and students were asked not to come to school for two days. As described by the *New York Times*, the program was "an attempt to impel the teachers to recognize by self-examination why teenagers experiment with narcotics." About twenty-five of the hundred-odd teachers involved were offended by the techniques used and walked out. They experienced the encounters as arbitrary infringements on their privacy. Among other things, they were asked to give value statements and autobiographical capsules to their colleagues, on the basis of which they would then subject each other to criticism. The program seemed to imply that drug abuse was at least in part a result of poor communications between teacher and pupil.

Predictably, the encounter session was lauded by many of the teachers who stayed, and reports of the incident included the usual glowing statements of new understanding and insights. One teacher was quoted by the *New York Times* as concluding:

> It helped us to perceive the moral vacuum in the world. We learned that there is not much difference between the addict and the nonaddict. It's just that some of us have chosen to conceal our imperfections by insisting on being "straight" and others have chosen drugs.

This incident, I believe, is a prime example of encounter used as a simplistic solution to a complex problem. In fact, it seemed to worsen the problem.

A year after its completion, there was no significant drop in drug abuse at the school; indeed, there appeared to have been an increase. Rather than improving relations among students and staff, one teacher told me that things had gotten markedly worse. Many of the personal revelations were later used for gossip and to reinforce petty feuds. The rift between those who'd walked out and those who'd stayed for the sessions widened, and staff morale was lower than it had been. One teacher said:

> While it was all going on—the protesting at City Hall, the encounter stuff, and all the rest—we had a sense of excitement and hope that we could change things. But a year's gone by, people have forgotten about it, and most of us are just resigned.

Such divisiveness and false hopes are not uncommon results of encounter groups. At one school in the Bronx, New York, parents, aides, teachers, and school administrators spent a Saturday exchanging "honest feedback" in a series of confrontation sessions engineered by the Manhattan growth center known as W.I.L.L.

Unfortunately, the feedback was limited to hearsay stories about "bad kids," teacher complaints about their supervisors, and parent complaints about teachers not present. If the trainers had attempted to relate the experience to the school's problems, there would probably have been fewer casualties; but when the day was over, hostilities had reached the point of blood feuds, and more than a year later the participants still mistrusted each other. The group leaders, of course, had gone on to carry encounter to other schools, leaving each to work out the problems left in their wake.

Nowhere has the generation gap and the emergence of a new consciousness come to a greater though quieter clash than in American education. New teachers, especially those who have graduated from college in the past five years, are increasingly representative of Consciousness III values. Administrators and principals, most of them over thirty, have complained that the young teachers wear their skirts too short or hair too long, refuse to wear ties in favor of dungarees, and have insisted on such revolutionary practices as taking their students home with them, playing on the floor with them, and encouraging the mutual use of first names. The fact that not all young teachers take this radical approach to education leads to even greater divisions within school systems.

When well led and well planned, a T-group experience for teachers can at least begin to bridge the gap and stimulate some understanding between these generational groups. When not well run, however, such groups only solidify attitudes on both sides. While smaller, more rural school systems usually employ more conservative and somewhat older teachers, teachers in the large urban school system staffs tend to be younger, more eager to encounter, and more easily convinced that through individual growth the improved adult can improve his interactions with children.

This assumption has never been proven in any way. Reports and evaluations are usually restricted to simple tabulations of the responses of encounter participants to questionnaires distributed at the end of the group experience. Given the excitement, the newness of the emotional interchanges, and the expectancies, most people come out of groups feeling high, and respond favorably.

In contrast to its tapering off in industry, the use of encounter in the education world seems to be on the increase. It may be that traditional aspects of the education subculture have led it to an almost perfect fit with the encounter subculture. For one thing, accountability for results is not customary in education—indeed, it is vigorously resisted. In addition, there is a tradition in education of ignoring the question of "carry-over," and rarely does anyone stop to consider whether what has been done in the classroom affects future behavior. Finally, educators tend to assume that experience is equal to learning. Each of these attitudes parallels encounter thinking. Together, they have made education a fertile ground for sensitivity training.

Encounter has made some of its greatest inroads in education at the college level, in particular in the graduate training of teachers and educational psychologists. A high percentage of the individuals who have been identified as encounter casualties or dissatisfied customers have unknowingly been exposed to encounter through university courses in "group dynamics," "human development," "humanistic psychology," "human relations," and "personal growth," all alternative names for encounter. In countless numbers of colleges throughout America today, sensitivity-training courses are a required part of the curriculum, especially in undergraduate courses in education, psychology, and the social sciences.

Annabelle K., a candidate for a master's degree in guidance and counseling, described a course she took at Montclair State College entitled Interviewing and Counseling, where the intensity of the experience became threatening to students:

> One man left in tears. I was very distressed by the fact that they seemed to be ripping people apart. They tried to get us to reveal personal things and were quite nasty. Somehow the group seemed to side with the need to come forth—you've got to come forth or you don't make it. I think I would have felt okay if the leader had been a trained psychologist, but he was an educator. The other leaders of the five or six groups were instructors and guidance counselors. I had a pretty bad reaction to it and was upset for about a week afterward. The fact that I had to leave shook me up too, because I was taking it for credit.

Another woman, Margaret E., described a speech class in the adult education department of her local college. The course was divided into "speech practice" and "group dynamics":

> This grew into a sort of amateur encounter program led by the co-teacher, who was taking a course in psychology. The group opened up to each other, talked freely about personal problems, and the lack of intelligent guidance began to have an adverse effect on several of the women. One told me that she lay shivering in bed at night, shook up about her marriage and her life. Another wound up in the hospital with an unidentified attack that could not be diagnosed. She was there only a short while, but I grew alarmed when others also reported unusual physical symptoms and depressions.

Before the semester was half over, everyone in the class except Miss E. and one man had developed physical symptoms. It is certainly not impossible that a group could react to stress with a contagion of hysterical and psychosomatic symptoms.*

Because of encounter's early move into the industrial world, business schools have also offered T-group courses for their students. One young man at the Harvard Business School reported that a generally disliked student adviser became the leader of a student adjustment program in the tradition of industrial T-grouping:

> There was great enthusiasm on the part of the socially traditional people . . . a participant told me that he now realized just how inferior he had always considered black students to be. In fact he still felt that they were making demands that were unjustifiable, but he now knew why he thought so. Subsequent classroom discussion on the topic began to include patronizing concurrence among the group of those who had actively supported T-group experience. My conclusion is that the whole thing led to a glowing self-satis-

*In only one case of those whom I interviewed, was there a clear-cut hysterical conversion reaction; Katherine T., a twenty-six-year-old nurse, had gone to an encounter group thinking that it would be like a social weekend. She found herself the object of considerable punishment from the group and the leader, and left after the first day. For the two weeks following the group she experienced pain and numbness around her neck, shoulders, arms, and sides, "as though I'd been beaten and bruised."

faction, members having thought out their values—and accepted them once again.

In some fields group experiences are indispensable learning aids, especially when the focus is on the group dynamics rather than on the individual hangups. Graduate preparation in psychology, psychiatry, social work, sociology—fields where an understanding of small-group dynamics is valuable—can be greatly enhanced by a personal experience in a group. In fact, without such experience, learning about groups can become an empty intellectual exercise. The teacher of such a laboratory experience must be very clear about his goals and the differences between group dynamics and therapy. Most of the positive outcomes of such courses seem to occur when instructors set clear limits for such groups, and most of the negative results are evident consequences of the absence of such limits.

Students generally tend to be delighted with this sort of experience offered as a course. There is rarely any preparation or homework, there are no exams, absences can be explained as "fear of the group's reaction," and interest is usually greater when one's own personality is the subject of study than in other courses.

A young lecturer in educational psychology at Lehman College said that part of the rationale behind T-groups for would-be teachers is to afford faculty members the opportunity to screen out people who "don't relate well." The student's performance in the laboratory course may become a critical factor in his achieving career goals. This view is by no means unique. Faculty members in many colleges are overtly saying, "Be open, honest, and relate freely your most intimate feelings," then covertly making judgments of their students' capacity to "relate" based on behavior and revelations in the group.

The whole picture of the encounter game in some colleges amounts to a kind of state-supported psychological training program, for the most part administered by university faculty members only marginally qualified to undertake such activities. What must be questioned here is the underlying assumption that the emotional components of students' lives are subject to the school curriculum in the same way that their physical health has become the province of the department of physical education.

There are many positive qualities to the humanistic trend in education, especially at the university level. Good teachers have always recognized that student participation in the educational process enhances learning. But while a dehumanized and formalistic education is not desirable, the mastery of knowledge and the development of skills to meet new situations need not be sacrificed to a set of vaguely high-sounding goals. The trend in this direction is evidenced by the number of newly opened experimental colleges with programs that are basically extended encounter programs, complete with third-world radicalism, body courses, Eastern mysticism, and the other provinces of the growth centers.

The purpose of encounter in the field of education is, of course, to benefit students, and in a number of cases young students have been directly involved. Some seem to benefit, at least briefly and subjectively. Some are hurt, some become reflective and concerned about their own capacities, and some—even at very early ages—seem to have the strength to withstand the inordinate pressures that groups can build up.

A seventeen-year-old junior in high school, Tina R., wrote of her experience not in a group but as a result of one:

> In March my school sponsored a sensitivity weekend. I did not attend it but several of my friends did. They proclaimed it a big success and I promptly forgot about it. That is, until last Friday.
> On Friday one of my friends who went on that weekend said to me, "On the sensitivity weekend we learned to be honest about our feelings and my feeling about you is, I don't like you, and I get the feeling you feel the same way about me." I told him that wasn't so but he just went on: "I don't think that's so. I think that you're just being phony, the way you're acting." I was stunned. I've known this boy since seventh grade. I even had a sort of a crush on him for a while and I certainly don't dislike him. His honesty may have helped him (I doubt it) but it hurt me deeply.

Tina described the boy's subsequent withdrawal and the breakup of his other friendships. From what she said, it sounds as if he'd learned how to be "honest" about negative feelings but not about positive ones, and evidently all of his relationships suffered.

Another teen-age girl, Nancy B., described her involvement in a summer "Teen Action Program," which included encounter:

I was thrilled with the way they were trying to have us reach each other but only because this was the first structured attempt I was aware of toward that goal. Mixed with that feeling was a very strong dislike for the actual session. I was glad something was being done to bring people together but I thought that in actuality the sessions were extremely phony.

I rarely felt as lonely as when I was supposedly very close to my sensitivity mates. As far as I was concerned the thick masks people wear were only changed in shape and not cracked as was the intention of the organizers.

The people, myself included, were talking about things and feelings that really weren't there. I talked about wanting to be closer to a particular person because the eyes glared at me as though they wanted me to say that. In actuality I felt extremely false within myself. I really felt obliged to say things I didn't mean.

I sincerely wish these encounters would work, unfortunately they just do not.

Sixteen-year-old Bill T. had a different sort of experience:

There were eighteen kids, including myself. People were asked if they wanted to walk around with their eyes shut, and hug the other members of the group. Then we were asked to go around with our eyes open, and hug everyone.

[Next] we were put in a small room, and it seemed that the procedure was to focus on one person, and break down his "walls." When the observers found a chink in the subject's armor, they hammered at it, until the person sat there with his head down, and confessed why he was screwed up. Then someone would run up and hug the subject, and another, and another, until everyone came up and hugged in a big pile. In most cases I would not hug, and was literally pushed onto the pile by one of the supervisors.

When the time finally came for me to be questioned, I was apprehensive. I had avoided this three times, but I was the last one to be questioned, and it was inevitable that my time would come.

First, I was asked why I had avoided being questioned, and I replied that I had no hangups. This was not taken seriously. I was asked to look around the room, and say what I felt about each person, which I did. Then I was asked to physically express what I felt about each person. I refused, saying that I would do it when I felt like doing it. Then a couple of people, one observer and a co-trainer, guessed I was all screwed up, and hugged me.

My reactions were varied. I did not agree with the philosophy that man is capable of loving everyone. That was the philosophy in the group. I did not feel *love* toward all the members of the group.

There was a conformity of a different kind in the group, and this was hugging. One other member, whom I know very well, was not the hug type. Later, he said to me that he did not know why he did all the hugging that he did. . . . Many of the relationships that came out of successful experiences are now dead, for I know all of the participants.

Individuality and independence are oft-stated goals of the encounter movement, just as they are in education. The practices, though, bespeak a drive toward conformity, submission to the group, and an ethic which regards the group as the only means of achieving one's psychological potential. Bill's experience is a familiar one—in all of my experiences with encounter groups I've never seen a person's simple, positive statement about himself accepted at the beginning of his group interaction. Feeling good about yourself, encounter groups seem to feel, must come after a gut-rending emotional interchange; otherwise you're being phony or defensive.

The more common submissions to group values in varied educational settings lead me to believe that T-grouping is not an addition to the educational system but a part of the system. It fosters conformity in the guise of individuality and helps teach submission to group norms. That is, of course, one definition of the process of socialization, and education—broadly defined—is the means by which we implement socialization and perpetuate our culture. Rather than provide a cultural alternative, in the education spectrum, encounter seems to me a disguised reinforcement of the status quo.

13

Two Drug Cultures,
Two Encounter Cultures

Until now we've looked at encounter as it happens in growth centers, psychiatrists' offices, corporate retreats, and universities. There is another encounter culture, tailored to the lower-class "hard" drug user—encounter as harsh and dramatic as the needle-scarred body of the addict himself.

Middle-class encounter game players tend to use "soft" drugs—marijuana, hashish, LSD, mescaline. The encounter groups to which they gravitate are characteristically concerned with loving, relating, and growing. A player's use of drugs, if it's considered a problem at all, elicits a predictable set of comforting gestures from other players and group leaders. In general, any antisocial behavior, from dropping out to dropping one's pants to dropping acid, is considered a step toward growth and individuation.

Another style of encounter has developed for the user of hard drugs (heroin, cocaine, and morphine). This approach is fitted to the player's (usually) lower economic class background and to the likelihood that he will be black or Puerto Rican. It assumes his unwillingness or inability to earn his own encounter fees and aims first to get him off the streets, second to eradicate his "unacceptable" behavior traits, and third to get him to contribute to our economic system. Such encounter groups are most often part of a full-time residential program lasting up to several years. The participant may be locked in for the first few months; he's likely to live in the "house" for at least the first year. He'll probably undergo at least a thousand hours per year of what is unblinkingly called "encounter therapy"; but since he lives and works with his groupmates, he may actually live in the encounter world on a round-the-clock basis. For those who get through the first month or two, the average stay is eighteen months. Some programs aim to foster indefinite participation, believing that they offer the ex-addict's only alternative to addiction; that once away from the program, no matter how well prepared, the ex-addict will return to drugs.

In encounter groups made up of addicts, reactions to drug use are negative and punitive. Drugs are an evil; the pleasures to be derived from them are the subject of much derision and contempt. Such groups tend to develop a straitlaced Puritan value system, especially with regard to experiences of pleasure. The American work ethic, so conscientiously attacked in the middle-class growth center groups, is upheld if not elevated in the drug encounter groups. Further, while the middle-class groups stress individual growth, the drug groups place a greater emphasis on the group as a collective entity. Most often the addict undergoing encounter works not toward personal enjoyment of the better things but to fulfill new or existing "obligations" to the group or his family. Guilt and shame often become the key mechanisms of social control.

The two encounter cultures may be characterized by the drugs they choose and the style with which they use them. Marijuana, and to a lesser extent LSD, tends to be a shared, group experience, and users regularly report that the drugs enhance their communication. The hard drugs elicit a much more solitary form of pleasure. Once the heroin user "gets off," he's in no shape to communicate anything to anybody. Many middle-class encounters have experimented with the soft drugs, and though it is certainly not a frequent occurrence, there have been instances of groups smoking marijuana together in order to improve the quality of their encountering. That would never happen in a group for hard-drug users.

The hard-drug addict is thought by his peers (and usually by himself) to be caught in a sick, self-destructive trap. It is generally assumed he must be suffering from severe psychopathology in order to take drugs in the first place, and that his psychopathology is so extreme it is "untreatable" by ordinary psychiatric procedures. Quality individual treatment is simply not available to addicts, just as it is not available to lower-class persons generally.

Approximately 90% of the United States mental-health resources
are used by only 10% of the population—the most affluent and
well educated. They also happen to be the 10% who most resemble mental health practicioners in values, aspirations, and accomplishments. Addicts seldom make it into that 10%, and encounter
has simply filled the vacuum left by the lack of professional
services for addicts.

The literature of the drug encounter centers describes a self-
help movement like Alcoholics Anonymous, in which ex-addicts
run the program. Contempt for the professionals is characteristic
of such programs; according to the ex-addict therapists, the
methods they use call for more blood and guts than the professionals can supply. Where the professional might be too sympathetic, the ex-addict will be merciless in his contempt for a junkie.

Encounter treatment for the addict is vigorous and exciting.
Unlike the growth centers with their colorful decors, drug encounter centers bear the grim trappings of their ghetto surrounding.
Since the addicts don't pay their own way, the programs are
always short of money; but what they do have may be far more
valuable: a fantastic team spirit. Most junkies are thought of and
think of themselves as incurable. The efforts of the drug encounter
centers take on a tone of rising from the dead, fighting against
overwhelming odds. This motif is reflected in the names the
centers choose for themselves—Exodus, Odyssey, Phoenix, Man
Alive, Renaissance.

The centers have an ideological commitment to make it tough
for addicts to get in, and start by making the applicant feel
decidedly unwanted. Nobody is "laying a mental-health salvation
trip" on the addict. He has to fight for the treatment and usually
contribute to the economic survival of his new community.

The strategy of "we've got something that you want but can't
have" was developed after years of almost total failure to rehabilitate addicts through punishment or traditional methods of mental-
health treatment. After a time, the professionals gave up on the
addicts, and the addicts gave up on psychiatry. Indeed, there is
little in the addict's world that provides as much fun as mocking
the "straights" who would "save them."

With most addicts unmotivated for therapy of any sort, and

with traditional methods ineffective, somehow the game had to be reversed—if hot compresses don't work, try cold ones, as the joke goes. That's just what an extraordinary ex-alcoholic named Chuck Dederich did when he founded Synanon, though apparently it was not by design.

Dederich was running a commune for alcoholics, junkies, and other assorted dropouts in a converted armory in Santa Monica, when he was "discovered" by a research team that had been visiting drug treatment programs throughout the country. Instead of the warmth and concern usually handed addicts, Dederich loudly passed out a mélange of humor, hostility, pop philosophy, and megalomania with such power that it evidently provoked his patients into fighting back. He ran the show like a circus ringmaster; if they wanted to stay under his tent, they conformed. Apparently they enjoyed it, and in the process developed a sense of community and an almost religious worship of Dederich. Having learned to fight in their own behalf, they were able to fight the impulse to use drugs—at least that's the Synanon version.

Another way of looking at it is that the humiliations and excoriations suffered by the Synanon backslider are so painful that a relapse is just not worth it. Once dependent on the group's respect, the Synanon member risks losing everything with a fall from grace. Many have fallen and left the drug centers in the Synanon pattern. But those who stay become devoted converts who, often for the first time in their lives, experience a sense of social conformity, acceptance, and participation.

Synanon was the first even remotely effective attempt to rehabilitate addicts by changing their culture. Although in actual numbers the successes were few, until Synanon the visiting researchers had seen none. Sociologists at that time saw criminal punishment and/or psychiatric treatment as the only alternatives for the addict: clearly neither was effective, and Synanon seemed to offer a new hope. The endorsement of Synanon by social workers and sociologists led to widespread federal funding for such programs.

Synanon became a way of life for those involved, complete with its own lingo, economy, and values. According to a Synanon brochure:

The Game, the seed of Synanon . . . is a sport—an enjoyable, often demanding pastime pitting a person against opponents. . . . Synanon Games are fast-paced and exciting, with frequent wild accusations, screams of rage, and peals of laughter. Each person's decision to involve himself in a fight for his own self-image and dignity demonstrates the sportsmanship necessary to the Game.

A precursor of the contemporary marathon, Synanon "emotional stews" lasted up to thirty-six hours, with participants and moods changing, and new targets on the firing line as new players joined. The players' experience is like that of Fritz Perls' hotseaters in many ways, except that all the players take a hand in the verbal assault. "Intensely concentrated life," is how Dederich's brochure described it, and the very intensity may be the trick that generates conversion. One recent Synanon blurb explains:

> During an addict's first ninety days, a highly precarious period in which he alternately trusts and fears and persistently looks for injustices, he is provided comfort, friendship, new opportunities for communication and new viewpoints. He participates three times weekly in tribe games where he seeks new understanding and vents frustrations. After two to three months, his behavior is scrutinized more intensely during games, and he increases his constructive use and enjoyment of them.

Largely as a result of its missionary fervor, Synanon has recently claimed fourteen hundred residents and twenty-five hundred active nonresidents. While the largest group of residents consists of former addicts, alcoholics, and others in conflict with society, nonresidents include just about anybody who is willing to participate in the weekly "game club." In addition, Synanon runs a school in Santa Monica for about 130 children of its residents. It operates a service station in Santa Monica as a job-training ground and source of income, and a nationwide advertising specialties jobbing business. Synanon recently claimed anticipated sales of eighty-two million dollars, which they expected to net the foundation five to seven hundred thousand dollars. And while this point has not been confirmed, it is widely believed that at least some participants in Synanon groups have signed over their possessions to their new "family."

Almost all of the encounter-oriented drug-rehabilitation communities are modeled after Synanon. They use the Synanon style of group interaction as well as the development of business ventures for financial support and job training. They all make initiation tough, and group membership becomes an element of pride, not disgrace as in mental hospitals and prisons.

But theirs is clearly a pride of group membership, not a pride in being a junkie. There is a certain masochistic pride among junkies; it must be reversed before there is impetus to change, and at that the encounter centers are superb. Humiliation and contempt replace the camaraderie the junkie expects and most often gets from his peers.

Considered totally unreliable, the junkie is offered no pity and no help beyond what he is willing to do for himself. Rather than being pushed into treatment, he is rejected over and over until he meets clear-cut motivational criteria or passes specific tests. At Daytop Village, one of the oldest centers and a direct descendant of Synanon, the applicant is told to call on his own, rather than have a parent or social worker do it. He is turned away at the first telephone contact, and told to call at an exact time the next day. If his call is even a minute late he's told that there are many others waiting, that his name will be placed at the bottom of the list, and to call back, for example, six days running at specified times.

Given his low frustration tolerance, the lack of structure in his life, the expectation that parents and social agencies will take an infinitely patient stance with him, the addict was often thrown by this unique approach when it was new.

No more than 1 or 2 percent of the addict population ever finds its way into Synanon-type programs. Once accepted by the program, the addict is confronted with a tough and demanding subculture entirely unlike what he has come to expect from fellow addicts. He finds no support for his lies, either to himself or to others. Instead he is faced with constant attack, and no tolerance for psychological clichés should he attempt to "cop a plea" about how tough he's had it. Everyone else there had it just as tough, and if they stayed "clean," so can he.

Psychiatrist Mitchell S. Rosenthal is the director of the Phoenix House Programs in New York City, the nation's largest drug encounter program, operating fifteen houses with more than one thousand residents. In describing the Phoenix programs, Rosenthal notes that there are two cardinal rules: no drugs, no violence (or threats of violence). The street culture, with its taboo against "squealing" and its defiance of authority, is not tolerated. "Violators are subject to harsh reprimands," he says. "Their heads may be shaved, or they may be made to wear signs spelling out their particular error." Rosenthal sees the mandatory thrice-weekly encounter sessions as an outlet for the frustrations induced by the program. This is how he described a typical encounter in a recent New York City Board of Education publication:

> Ugly. A sneering indictment, hard as the street. "Just who the hell do you think you are?" A rush of supporting indictments, insults, challenges, is answered by rage, frustration, injured innocence, and defense.
>
> The indictment is usually based on an observed attitude or a specific piece of behavior; the person didn't do something, or he did do something he wasn't supposed to.
>
> After the indictment, the participants pull out pieces of information about the indicted person. They weave a "fabric of behavior" about this person, very quickly adding up an inventory of behavior and performance. Humor plays a key role here. Buffoonery, caricature, satire, ridicule, paradox, slapstick, are all used—any verbal device that gets the person "in the hot seat" to see himself. As this happens, he is busy defending himself and getting a chance to "blow off" his own feelings. While he defends himself, however, he usually underscores the very argument that's being made against him.
>
> All of this goes with considerable love and concern. If the group were incapable of tenderness, no one would reveal himself. Tears are a frequent part of the encounter: tears of loneliness, fright, joy. It's all there—the entire spectrum of emotion.

In the drug world, encounter comes closest to realizing its potential as a change process. Addicts undergoing encounter therapy are provided with several elements that have repeatedly been shown to create profound psychological change, both in intensive psychotherapy and in brainwashing: the sustained confronting and aggressive therapy; a total change of milieu, including removal from ordinary life; rearrangement of the peer-group values; the stripping of defenses; and substitution of a new morality.

These are exactly the things that do not occur for the ordinary encounterist who pops into a growth center for a weekend marathon, nor do they occur anywhere else in our society except in prisons and mental hospitals.

Many professionals and other observers have taken aim at the humiliation and denigration designed into the rehabilitory encounter groups: the programs often operate as though once an addict joined, he surrendered his basic human rights. In defense, experts in the drug encounter say that their process transcends other forms of degradation because it is offered in the hope of positive behavior change. Rosenthal, Casriel, Dederich, and other supporters of psychological karate regularly point out that the fury directed against an encountering addict conceals a higher form of love, a love with enough care to want him not to hurt himself.

A partial explanation for the higher levels of hostility in drug encounter groups may be that they provide an outlet for anti-black or anti-lower-class prejudice. Certainly we cannot determine the motivations of one person's attack on another, but considering the population of such groups and the professional studies of self-hatred among blacks, it seems likely that encounter provides addicts an outlet for class and racial animosities. The recent emergence of proud ethnicity among ghetto groups has left many with a new sense of self-worth and group membership that serves as a deterrent to drug use. Many such groups, in fact, actively forbid drug usage by their members. But for those already addicted, the anger expressed in drug world encounters may reflect a more general self-hatred, identified with hatred for being black, lower class, and without power.

There is little evidence to show that Synanon-style encounter groups provide a therapy that is finely differentiated and curative for members. Leaders in the field regularly decry the lack of training facilities and standards, and recognize the inadequacy of graduation from a program as the basic training credential for ex-addict therapists. A New York City Addiction Services Agency report (1971) notes:

> ... informed, sensitive use of group dynamics skills, which are basic staples of many aspects of prevention and treatment programs, can either be an extremely powerful or potentially destructive tool, depending upon the skills of the practitioners.

On the whole, encounter programs have not demonstrated enough success to warrant blanket approval, but occasional programs seem to combine the best elements of encounter treatment and competent psychotherapy.

New York's Exodus House, in Spanish Harlem, has many of the characteristics of the Synanon-type program: confrontations (but not attacks) are encouraged; no evident dishonesty or "copping out" is allowed; the leaders—at least for the initial stages of the treatment program—are ex-addicts; and the language is that of the slum world.

But here the similarity stops. Unlike most programs, Exodus House has adopted many of the principles of psychotherapy, and a variety of professional controls have been incorporated into its operational structure. There is a clear role for professionals, who are given neither precedence over nor a back seat to the ex-addict leaders. The participants go through a carefully graded sequence of groups, "structured work experiences," and life challenges, beginning with "pretherapy groups" led by ex-addict therapists who have received intensive training within the Exodus House program.

The psychopathology theory of addiction causation is the basis of the Exodus House program. After several months of "pretherapy," when it is clear that the addict—who had to be off drugs for at least a week before beginning the program—has begun to take responsibility for his addiction, he may move up the ladder into the "C groups," the first therapy groups led by professionals. Real accomplishments in relation to his family, work, and love problems allow the ex-addict to progress through "B" and "A" therapy groups.

The most important feature that differentiates this program from many others in the drug world is the individualized treatment given each participant. The Exodus House staff believes that knocking out the addiction brings to light the addict's underlying problems, and their program is geared to dealing with and treating his psychopathology, not simply eliminating his symptoms.

The program does not engender as many reentry problems as most others, since there is no extended period of confinement for its members. From the beginning, addicts go out on passes and participate in the community. At regular stages each member moves toward getting his apartment, returning to his wife or family, and developing relationships outside the milieu that drove him to addiction.

While the program is tough, humiliation is not considered therapeutic. Participants must conform closely to the rules in order to demonstrate their progress in moving away from drugs. Failure to conform carries a clear-cut system of punishments, including being "set back" or "shot down" to lower levels of the program.

Except for a few individual cases, there is almost no evidence to support claims by encounter advocates that encounter is an effective method of addiction treatment. The vast majority of addicts will have nothing to do with encounter. Many addicts see that encounter programs are designed to "adjust" them to the very society from which they have dropped out, and will have none of it. Others, who might like to go the encounter route, can't stay drug-free long enough to qualify for admission.

It is notoriously difficult to get accurate figures from the drug centers. It is clear that many centers slant their statistics to make the programs look good. Some, for example, count as "admissions" only those who've stayed for over thirty days; the majority of "splitees" take off within the first two weeks. Others tend to equate staying in the program with success. While, given the nature of addiction, it is in fact remarkable for an addict to stay anywhere for any length of time, no one would reason that an extended stay in a mental hospital is equal to a cure.

The field of addiction treatment is so new, and government programs so recent, that, for example, New York City's Addiction Services Agency did not have an official in charge of program evaluations until the summer of 1971, although the agency is responsible for over 170 treatment programs.

Perhaps the failure of drug encounter is best illustrated by figures released by the Phoenix Houses programs, for many years the main weapon of New York City's Addiction Services Agency, and the nation's largest encounter program. At a time when the city death toll from heroin overdoses was averaging thirty per week, the *New York Times* lashed out at ineffective government programs and leveled a barrage at the ASA. Calling the operation slipshod, wasteful, and perhaps even harmful, the *Times* editorial (May 15, 1970) noted:

> The ASA has been heavy in personnel, with 605 staff members on the payroll, and light in achievement. After four years' operation and the expenditure of more than $50,000,000, it has only about a thousand of the city's estimated 100,000 addicts living in therapeutic communities and only another 2000 being treated on an outpatient basis. *Even by its own reports, it has rehabilitated only about 130 addicts.* Pathetically small as this figure is, it is still suspect because the ASA has no follow-up program to determine whether those supposedly rehabilitated actually remain off drugs. [Italics added.]

In spite of all the recent criticism, encounter-type programs are still a part of more than half of the drug rehabilitation programs in America, though methadone has recently emerged as the most frequent treatment. According to the most recent summary of narcotics-addiction treatment agencies, 142 of the 183 centers in the nation devoted to rehabilitation were using encounter or group treatment as a prime modality. Only nineteen centers did not use group or encounter techniques at all, and these facilities focused primarily on the use of methadone, religious counseling, individual therapy, and other forms of treatment.

As a nation, we spend a lot of money on drug rehabilitation. In 1968-69, the combined annual budgets of drug centers ranged from $17 million to $21 million, for smaller individual centers; in addition, twenty-three larger centers each reported annual budgets of over $1 million. More recently the expenditures have increased dramatically. New York's Addiction Services Agency budgeted $97 million in fiscal 1971-72, and is angling for another $50 million. Approximately half of those millions is earmarked for Synanon-type encounter programs.

Given the questionable results, and the fact that encounter programs seem to involve only 2 to 3 percent of the addict population and to be successful with only a small fraction of those involved, it is extremely doubtful whether spending money on encounter programs is spending it wisely.

Is there an alternative? A comprehensive discussion of the controversial subject of methadone treatment for addicts is not within the scope of this book. Still, a comparison of the remission rates of encounter and methadone programs shows that encounter is not the best answer.

Dr. Harold Trigg, head of the nation's largest methadone program, at the Beth Israel Medical Center in New York, has said that for years he found it hard to believe his eyes about the results of methadone, but now he's convinced. Speaking of a report by the Columbia University School of Health and Administrative Medicine which indicated a success rate of 77-80 percent for methadone programs, Dr. Trigg said:

> We measure "cure" by abstinence from drugs other than methadone, absence of antisocial behavior, measured primarily by arrests, convictions, and by employment. These [cured] 77-80 percent are on methadone, are employed or are homemakers, and show virtually no other drug abuse.

Unlike the eighteen to thirty-six months of withdrawal from society characteristic of the encounter programs, "the same day a patient starts on methadone, he is able to return to society," says Dr. Trigg. Contrary to the psychopathology theory of addiction, Dr. Trigg believes that a good two thirds of addicts have no definable pathology other than that which results from their addiction. Even for patients with serious psychopathological problems, eighteen months of outpatient psychotherapy is the exception—compared to most encounter programs, where eighteen months is more like a minimum for inpatient treatment.

I am concerned about both the methadone and encounter methods of addiction treatment because in emphasizing the responsibility of the individual addict, both are in danger of overlooking social and cultural causes of addiction. The problem we now face—aside from the social factors—is the design of programs of individualized treatment for given kinds of drug users.

In all likelihood, the next several years will see an increasing integration of encounter, psychotherapy, and methadone treatment for addicts. Such combinations have proven most effective in the past, and certainly all new alternatives deserve further exploration and a great deal of encouragement.

Encounter alone is not enough to treat more than a very small percentage of addicts. But integrated with methadone treatment and individualized psychological planning, encounter probably has a greater value than in any other context.

14

A Peculiarly American Dream

Encounter is many things to many people. It can be a set of new techniques in psychotherapy, or the emotional axle grease to make a business more profitable or a school system more "meaningful." For the individual it may mean a weekend adventure, a source of new sexual contacts, a substitute for psychotherapy, or a new religion. For the culture as a whole, encounter seems to offer instant psychological growth—like instant mashed potatoes, with all the flavor boiled out in the packaging.

Most people interpret the significance of encounter from the vantage point of their own experiences. If an encounter session was an eye-opener and an emotional high for them, they assume it is that for everyone; if it provided them with a "breakthrough" that they were then able to use in their psychotherapy, they tend to see it that way for everyone; if it amounted to a week-long vacation where they played at being sensitized, then it's that for everyone; if it gave them the chance to do their own thing, to have an affair, or to level with the boss, they tend to view it in those terms for everyone else. To Steve D.'s parents encounter is a killer; to Bill Schutz and Dan Casriel it's a way of life with a handsome income; and to the body cultists it is the route to the holy grail hidden within our neurotically tensed muscles.

Encounter is all of these things and none of them. Despite the variety of encounters and encounterers, the casualties, the joys, the fun, and the pain, I feel that certain generalizations can be made. Let's consider two basic questions: What social needs have made the encounter phenomenon possible? and, How does the movement meet those needs?

Writers and critics both in and out of the movement have emphasized that contemporary America has suffered a loss of intimacy and a consequent increase in alienation, depersonalization, and loneliness. Carl Rogers cites urban crowding, the death and burial of "the God of authoritative answers," and increasingly stereotyped behavior in interpersonal relationships as social factors which have caused the need for encounter. Rogers explains the movement's grass-roots character thus: "I believe it is because people—ordinary people—have discovered that it alleviates their loneliness. . . ."

This view is common in psychiatry as well, but is rarely used as a rationale for actual treatment. In his recent text on group psychotherapy, Irvin Yalom, no blind encounter advocate, accepts the loneliness argument; he sees encounter groups and professional group therapy as parallel phenomena. "Loneliness, confusion, and alienation haunt T-groups and therapy groups alike," says Yalom; and he names as the common cause the decline of social institutions which in former times provided us with the intimacy we needed. Supermarkets, TV sets, broken homes, teaching machines, and parental occupations incomprehensible to children have caused widespread confusion. The result, says Yalom, is a growing sense of personal inadequacy. "The individual's sense of personal worth is inversely proportional to the size and power of the megamachine in which he is ensconced."

Rogers, Yalom, and the others who explain the advent of encounter with this theory of social malaise have overlooked the fact that such conditions are by no means unique to this century. They occur with such regularity that the phenomenon of *anomie* was described in detail by Emil Durkheim, the French sociologist, in 1897. Durkheim, one of the founders of modern sociology, first observed that suicides increased when social crises upset the force of tradition. He described *anomie* as the condition of normlessness, the moral vacuum that results when the usual rules of behavior are suspended and appetites seem to know no limits. Durkheim cited ancient Rome and Greece and the first French Republic as cultures that went through periods of *anomie:*

Nothing can calm it, since its goal is far beyond all it can attain. Reality seems valueless by comparison with dreams

of fevered imaginations; reality is therefore abandoned. . . .
A thirst arises for novelties, unfamiliar pleasures, nameless
sensations, all of which lose their savor once known. . . .

The encounterists accept this picture of widespread social
decline and offer a world redemption fantasy as an antidote. It's
not one that contemporary philosophers would find creditable,
though; indeed, if encounterists ever sought a philosophical touch-
stone for their position, they'd have to go back to Rousseau and
his noble savage. A passage from Rousseau's *Emile** might serve as
the philosophical root of the encounter movement's anti-
intellectual and determinedly ahistorical view:

> The first thing I learned from these considerations [of
> philosophy and history] was to restrict my inquiries to what
> directly concerned myself, to rest in profound ignorance of
> everything else, and not even to trouble myself to doubt
> anything beyond what I required to know.
> I also realized that the philosophers, far from ridding me
> of my vain doubts, only multiplied the doubts that tor-
> mented me and failed to remove any one of them. So I
> chose another guide and said, "Let me follow the Inner
> Light."

Fortunately for our intellectual history, Rousseau didn't take
himself too seriously on this point. Yet it is with a rationale such
as this that encounter advocates justify their methods and seem to
equate men's psyches with man's condition. Instead of focusing on
changes in society's moral structure, its legal and economic constraints, or its very real social problems, the encounter movement
aims at personal salvation for those who, compared to others with
more serious, problems, least need the help.

"GROUP THERAPY," says the lead of the quarter-page ad in
New York magazine, placed by a restaurant chain offering more
than the usual menu:

> For relevant encounters, with people, salad, steak and
> beer, it all happens here. . . . The vibrations are so good,

* J. J. Rousseau, *Emile*, translated by Barbara Foxley (New York: E. P. Dutton,
1950).

everyone relates. The touch, the feel, the taste, they're all there. Tell your analyst to drop his notes and drop in. He can use a little Steak and Brew, too.

Clearly, after loneliness, the second major need to which the encounter movement appeals is man's perpetual search for psychic emancipation. The very force that sends increasing numbers into psychotherapy may be the reason others seek therapy in the form of encounter. Though some encounterists now believe there is no difference between encounter and psychotherapy, the prevailing position among those both in and out of the movement has been that emotional growth must be distinguished from the treatment of emotional illness. Increasingly, though, the lines of differentiation are becoming blurred.

Like religion, encounter offers comfort through confession, unity, subordination to a value system, and maintenance of the status quo. The people who most need such group support are, of course, those in psychic stress. And since the movement focuses on individual psyches, it is guaranteed a permanent though recycling supply of patients.

As currently constituted, the encounter game population is predominantly urban, middle-class, white, aged twenty to forty, and well educated. Clearly, players come from the very class with sufficient leisure and income to participate, with value orientations that favor personal improvement, and with the highest degree of social dislocation as a result of urban technology. It is the middle class that's hardest hit by Alvin Toffler's future shock, it is their children who are greening America, and it is consistent with both Toffler's and Charles Reich's theses that encounter should rise at this time as an apparent response to social pressures.

Given the overall rate of emotional illness in America, one can easily assert that any population group suffers from emotional stresses. The urban population aged twenty to forty has been estimated to have a psychiatric impairment rate of 23 percent. "Impairment" includes the incidence of patients rated by psychiatrists as having "marked" or "severe" symptom formation, or who, because they were hospitalized or unable to function, were rated "incapacitated." Mild to moderate psychiatric symptoms—the range that would commonly be called "neurotic"—occur in over 58 percent of the urban population. Impossible though it seems, by commonly accepted professional standards, this leaves only 19 percent of the urban population with no definable psychiatric stress.

Another surprising fact that is evident from studies of mental health in the urban population is that this "impaired" group had never had any contact with a mental health professional. Yet for the most part these troubled people reject psychiatric therapy. Encounter appeals because it generally seems cheaper and faster than traditional therapy, and because it does not carry the same stigma. Most encounter participants feel they have a "hang-up" they want to get rid of, such as "relating to the opposite sex," "dealing with anger," "experiencing feelings," and "self-assertion." In the view of most professionals, each of these statements is likely to reflect a deeper emotional disturbance.

One New York growth center is running spot advertisements over WNCN-FM, a local classical music station. After giving the usual spiel about "awareness, communications, and increased potential," the announcer in all seriousness commented, "Sounds like a pretty easy way to get rid of your hangups."

Participation in formal religious activities is on the decline in America, and church-going is increasingly viewed as an outmoded and unrewarding exercise. The falling off in church membership—especially among the young—demonstrates this trend, as do the frequent bouts of self-criticism and increased social activism reported among the clergy. For many Americans, religion has been focused on man's relationship with man, rather than on man's relationship with the Deity.

Nevertheless, man clearly needs to believe in ideals and values beyond his immediate grasp. The humanistic ethic of the encounter movement seems to offer many players a convenient way to fulfill their sense that one ought to believe in something. This trend has not gone unnoticed by the clergy, and it is no coincidence that a significant percentage of American Christian clergymen is seriously committed to encounter as a means to rejuvenate organized religion.

In *Please Touch*, Jane Howard noted that "four thousand Episcopal priests had been to encounter groups, and two thousand were qualified to lead them." She described a 1968 conference in Washington, D.C., in which five hundred clergymen participated in a microlab. This new look in godliness was also documented in a feature story by Edward Fiske in the *New York Times*. Fiske quoted clergymen from the National Council of Churches (which estimated that at that time over twenty-five thousand members had already participated in encounter groups), from the two-million-member United Church of Christ, and from the World Council of Churches, all of whom advocated encounter. The Reverend Gerald J. Judd, education director of the United Church of Christ, said:

> It's a way of helping members get in touch with their feelings and learn to love. I predict it will be for us what revivalism was for religion on the frontier.

An encounter group in Michigan is considering becoming a formal congregation. A minister described encounter as an attempt to conserve the essence of Christianity. A Queens housewife reported that church-sponsored encounter weekends "helped me to discover that Christianity is really about loving people." The Reverend David Watermulder, a Presbyterian pastor, saw encounter methods as consonant with the "man-centered" ministry of Jesus:

> Tough men like Peter, shrewd characters like Matthew, sensitive spirits like John, doubting people like Thomas—in his presence all of these found themselves opening up, letting go of their fears, and discovering that it wasn't so bad to be a person.

Evidently, for this minister, Jesus was the first encounter group leader.

Other churches are not that happy with encounter. The Episcopal Diocese of Oklahoma banned it, and Fiske noted that Dorothy Faber, editor of the conservative Episcopal publication *The Christian Challenge*, has attacked the movement in a series of articles. Comparing the evils of encounter to those of sex education in the schools, Mrs. Faber noted: "We know of sessions with clergy participation that ended up with people dancing nude around the altar."

It is the Protestant denominations that have most readily taken encounter to the altar, though in fact most church-sponsored groups have been relatively tame. Catholic groups have only gotten their feet slightly wet with encounter, and Jewish groups have shown almost no interest in it. Perhaps this is a reflection of the familiar observation that Protestant groups generally provide their members with minimal emotional rewards as compared to the warmth and emotional contact characteristic of the Mediterranean religions, Judaism and Catholicism. Or perhaps the difference stems from the greater family cohesiveness and more intense emotional expressiveness associated with American Catholics and Jews.

Although most encounterists put down organized religion as ritualized and dehumanizing, they often demonstrate a great sympathy for those committed to the religious way of life. Most groups are exceptionally protective of members who wear the cloth; and while that deference may betray a less than kind concern for their emotional fragility, even a stereotyping of individuals because of their religious devotion, I've sensed that in such protectiveness lies a very important validation of the group's activities. The presence of a minister or nun often seems to encourage the other members to believe that the group is devoted to spiritual, humanistic purposes, and such groups have often taken on a more pronounced spiritual quality than usual, not because of the contributions of the religious member, but perhaps because members unconsciously aspired to communicate with the higher human values.

The other side of this coin can come up as well, with group members baiting and attempting to shock the religious persons. For the religious persons such encounters can often be extremely painful. I remember one Catholic nun who fled a group after one man started elaborating on his lifelong fantasies about intercourse with nuns. She seemed able to handle the man's frank sexuality all right, but evidently the group's kindly affection and sympathy for her stress that followed was too much for her.

There are as yet no data on the incidence of encounter casualties among the clergy, but my guess is that the cloth provides no special psychological protection. Members of the clergy may even face increased emotional risks. While for many membership in a religious order provides ties far stronger than those of the transitory group experience, for others identification with their religion has served to compensate for a low self-esteem. I once saw a middle-aged minister, after a moderately intense confrontation from a group about his stuffiness, weep bitterly: "Without my collar, I'm nothing."

Whether the churches need encounter to rejuvenate their membership and clergy, or the encounter movement needs a spiritual handle, is a chicken-and-egg question. Probably both sets of needs interact, and both may be indicative of deeper needs for group membership, or for an ideology with which to identify. Just as the presence of clergymen seems to legitimize encounter, the social approval of openness, letting down one's hair, and touching may legitimize basic human needs among clerical encounterists.

Another explanation of the roots of the encounter movement suggests that people today feel an intense and frequently unmet need for group membership and a sense of belonging. Few of us have the powerful identification with a group characteristic of religious life. If we work in office jobs, teach in an urban school, run a small business, or follow a husband from job to job, most of our relationships are transitory, and our memberships in small groups are short-lived or superficial. With our looser family structure and work relationships, our need for group participation is unmet, and encounter groups seem to be a source of fulfillment for these needs.

Speculations about man's need for group membership, and the various forms of expression that such needs find in modern society, have recently received considerable attention from the new discipline called ethology, probably best defined as the study of animal behavior at the group level. Encouraged by the writings of Konrad Lorenz and Robert Ardrey, ethologists have identified certain characteristic behavior patterns of animals and men, including the processes of dominance ordering, sexual selection, and group identification.

If we accept their premises, several puzzling characteristics of the encounter phenomenon become more understandable. Assertiveness and withdrawal can be related to animal behavior of dominance and submission; the emotional stroking and support is similar to grooming behavior; arm wrestling, falling, and lifting games are akin to primate play; the sexual seductions and leadership styles have a ritual pattern. In this sense, encounter groups may be viewed as an intensified imitation of life, a practice session with few real risks.

In *The Territorial Imperative*, Robert Ardrey describes the phenomenon he calls a *noyau*, a social group in which antagonisms seem to serve the function of providing exercise and stimulation. The callicebus monkeys, for example, go to the edge of their territory every morning, shout and scream at each other—but never really fight—and then go away, having gotten off a lot of steam and apparently feeling better. Encounter may serve a similar purpose for humans. To the extent that groups may enhance mating and reproduction, provide support for useful economic and social behavior, improve a participant's ability to deal with others, and reduce anxiety in ordinary situations, encounter can be seen as the practice of behavior patterns characteristic and necessary to all primates.

So far, aside from the biological theory, we have considered hypotheses that explain encounter at the individual level. There are also several explanations of the encounter phenomenon at the social-cultural level. To my knowledge, no serious sociologist has taken a positive view of the encounter movement. Charles Reich probably came closest to that position—but only if his thesis is stretched a bit. While Reich does not deal with encounter per se, his general thesis of Consciousness III can be viewed as a description of the changing culture, and encounter can be seen as consonant with the new form of consciousness. My quarrel with Reich is essentially the same that I make against Rogers' and Schutz's arguments for encounter: both views are generalizations based on very small segments of the culture, and in both cases the evidence that our culture is turning around is meager. The youth revolution is dead, according to the *New York Times* (October 24, 1971); and as judged by the recent decline in gate receipts at the East Coast Esalen shindig, the encounter culture is also faltering.

Alvin Toffler, also writing in the vein of popular sociology, comments on encounter at several points in *Future Shock*, seeing it variously as a natural outgrowth of our accelerated culture, a function of the need to speed up friendships, and an anonymous packaged experience. Toffler limits his suggested "strategies for survival" to changes in society's institutions. Unlike Schutz and Rogers, he does not seem impressed with encounter's capacity to protect us all from the emotional ravages of the future.

Magda Denes, one of the few politically sophisticated psychologists to examine the social factors in encounter groups, sees the encounter wave as a response to materialist, industrial, and technocratic pressures in our culture, a response that is far from benign. To Denes, encounter prevents man from realizing his higher goals by offering him a false and tawdry social pacifier. Denes develops a picture of encounter as the whore of industry, draining off passion while, as she puts it, reintroducing "the individual as a Mechanical System into the Megamachine in the service of organizational efficiency." Denes says of encounter group membership:

> [It] serves conscious strivings for relevance. It serves the felt need to be affective, to matter, to have palpable personal impact in some human arena.

Denes suggests that the underlying cause of encounter's popularity is the need to feel "consciously visible, known, effective, self-expressive," a need which identification with an artificial subculture can gratify. Interesting in this light is the fact that encounter's rise parallels the "reverse melting pot" theme in contemporary culture, the *risorgimento* of ethnic pride and group identification.

Herbert Marcuse has taken note of the encounter movement, saying:

> I read the catalogs of the Esalen Institute. This administration of happiness is nauseating to me. They teach people to touch each other and hold hands! If somebody cannot learn that by himself, by trial and error, he may just as well give up.

Marcuse acknowledges that he knows little about the groups, but he has argued that psychological pacifiers are provided by the culture so that individuals will go along with the system. The production and availability of consumer goods serves this purpose, and the value we place on material acquisitions proves how effectively the economic system makes willing multiple-car, multiple-TV-owning dolts of us all. Marcuse argues that, likewise, sexual permissiveness serves as a social safety valve to keep the populace from exploding under pressure to produce. The structured intimacy of the encounter group ultimately serves to maintain the status quo, as well.

As though to support Marcuse's view, millions of tax dollars are being spent on programs that are fundamentally encounter. There have been training programs for the Peace Corps, numerous police departments, and countless groups of correction officers, poverty workers, and welfare officials. While the largest total dollar allocations are in education and drug-abuse rehabilitation programs, there are (or have been) significant bundles of dollars spent at the federal level in various programs, most notably those of the Office of Economic Opportunity and the Department of Labor. The Job Opportunities Business Sector (JOBS) programs of the Department of Labor includes strong recommendations for sensitivity-training components. Contractors who bid for the programs have noticed the greater likelihood of acceptance of proposals that include sensitivity training.

In many cases the term "sensitivity training" is anathema to governmental officials, probably because of the "Communist brainwashing" cries that have been raised on the far right. Robert J. Brown, associate manpower administrator at the Department of Labor under the Nixon administration, assured me that their "Office of National Projects has never been involved in the encounter group type of training program, nor do we intend to become involved in such programs in the future." Yet in his letter he states:

> However, the Department of Labor did have a contract with an organization to provide "sensitivity" training to organizations participating in the National Alliance of Businessmen's Job Opportunities in the Business Sector (NAB-JOBS) program.
> This contract was with the Human Development Institute (HDI) in Atlanta, Georgia, whose purpose was to help prepare companies (particularly management, support person-

nel, and first-line supervisors) for the successful addition of
the hard-core unemployed into their productive work force.
This contract was executed on May 17, 1968, and termi-
nated on September 30, 1970, at a cost of $1,443,273.

To date, there has been no indication of a cutback in government funds for encounter programs in the drug or education worlds.

Does the human-potential movement fulfill its promises? With
certain minor exceptions, the answer is a resounding no.

There is no evidence to support the encounter movement's
claims of profound and lasting psychotherapeutic effectiveness.
The studies by Yalom, Lieberman, and Miles indicated that only 8
percent of participants show significant positive changes, and only
about 25 percent of participants show positive results of any sort;
about 10 percent become enduring casualties, and the remaining
65 percent either drop out or have negative or unrewarding experiences.

It is clear that many people, at least briefly, *feel* as though they
have changed as a result of encounter experiences, and this in itself
may be a significant benefit. People tend to fulfill their own
self-concepts, and a change in self-concept, no matter how minimal the verifiable results, may lead to increased confidence in
facing emotional challenges.

Another possible benefit of the movement is the frequency
with which people who've been to encounter groups undertake
psychotherapy. Many do so to pick up the pieces after a shattering
encounter trip, but others have used their encounter experiences
as a starting point for serious psychotherapy. Similarly, for those
already undergoing psychotherapy, informal reports suggest that
encounter experiences—if well chosen and well conducted—may be
useful.

John P. Campbell and Marvin Dunnette found some evidence
that people who've had group experiences become more accurate
in their perceptions of others. They suggest that "training in the
'art' of forming accurate stereotypes about people in general or
about persons belonging to various subgroups in society" may be a
way of improving the perception of group participants. Another
strategy for improving awareness is the concept of "assumed
similarity." Campbell and Dunnette state: "T-group advocates

might be distressed if they were charged with training for conformity, but assumed similarity has been repeatedly shown to be an important component of accurate interpersonal perception." The argument for encounter here is simple: in an increasingly mechanized and homogenized world, accurate stereotyping may be a socially useful tool. Though it contradicts the humanistic ideology of the movement, encounter groups may indeed offer players a valuable social skill by enhancing this ability.

Along the same lines, group experiences can be successful in improving communication skills. Workshop participants often become aware of irritating mannerisms (like interrupting others) or bad communications habits (like not listening to others), and try to change them. We don't need hypotheses about intimacy and honesty to explain results of this sort—the simple educational value of interpersonal feedback is sufficient.

This is the extent of the positive results that can realistically be claimed by the encounter movement. Now let's consider some of the fallacies of encounter ideology which cause the movement's ineffectiveness.

Despite the "human potential" the movement ascribes to each of us, the encounter position includes a subtle yet basic put-down of people's capacity to relate to each other and to their own feelings. Encounterists assume that most people need the encounter group in order to be honest. William Coulson illustrates this elitist view:

> People cannot manage to encounter one another if they are simply thrown together ... they are unable to assume *permission* to talk differently than in ordinary social discourse. People need an excuse at first to speak honestly.

The generalization is drawn from the stereotype of the WASP businessman who is uptight, lonely, and afraid of all emotion, especially his own. Encounterists fail to recognize that even the most uptight businessman conforms to this pattern only in certain clearly defined situations; they seem to forget that the behavior they view as uptight is entirely consistent with American norms for behavior among strangers.

Encounter advocates often justify the movement with the assumption that man is pathologically lonely. Carl Rogers has said:

"I believe that individuals nowadays are probably more aware of their inner loneliness than has ever been true before in history." Rogers believes that, when struggling for physical existence, man has neither time nor inclination to pursue his emotional and spiritual needs, and that as society allows individuals to satisfy their basic needs more easily, they can pay more attention to transcendental needs. This argument assumes that relationships in the past were more intense, and individuals less lonely as a result—clearly one of those cultural myths based on dreams of the Good Old Days. Historical evidence of short life spans, widespread disease, long working hours, and primitive technology make it unlikely that people of previous eras had time or energy to concentrate on affection and intimacy.

Like most encounterists, Rogers seems to believe that the momentary expression of kindness or physical affection in the T-group provides the solution to an individual's loneliness. I fail to see how such brief contact between two people who never see each other again after the encounter session can alleviate anyone's loneliness. Usually just the opposite occurs—the loneliness is deepened, and through such shams one recognizes more sharply the true extent to which he is alone. Perhaps this is the reason participants keep returning to encounter groups—for the momentary antidote of a touch, a handshake, or a hug.

Encounterists tend to speak of love as though it were an antidote to loneliness, and invariably speak of love rather than of being liked, appreciated, admired, or momentarily comforted when under stress. There seems to be no time dimension in the encounter view of love, nor is there much expectation that love can endure. It has often seemed to me that encounterists label all brief feelings of warmth and affection as love without differentiation. Generalizing from hundreds of brief responses, Carl Rogers says:

> It is only as a person discovers that he is loved for what he is, not for what he pretends to be, that he can begin to feel that he is worthy of respect and love. It is one of the commonest results of an encounter group that a person no longer feels he is a walking fraud or must continually deceive others in order to be liked. This increased respect and liking for oneself does not always last after the group experience. Sometimes it needs to be renewed.

Rogers has also described the way in which encounter can alleviate loneliness:

> When two real selves reach out to each other in a group, there is the I-thou encounter that Buber has so well described. In that instant loneliness is dissolved, and the person feels himself in real contact with another, and the estrangement which has been so much a part of his life vanishes.

Unfortunately, this is not what Buber sees as the I-thou encounter, nor is Rogers really writing about existential loneliness. The loneliness described in the literature of the existentialists—which encounterists purport to remedy—is a far more pervasive condition, a feeling of chronic separateness which cannot be mediated by social contacts. Existential loneliness is not the same as not having a date or a friend. Indeed, it can be most frightening at the times when one is in the company of friends.

Several critics have refused to accept Rogers' use of Buber's concept of the I-thou encounter in regard to the groups. Max Rosenbaum pointed out that encounter participants treat each other as objects, that their exchanges are essentially I-it experiences, and that "there is no authentic mutualism, as the encounter therapies are primarily forced in nature." Rollo May agrees on this point, and commented in a recent letter that while the groups may do some real good, they "are simplistic and they destroy Buber's and my sense of intimacy."

Martin Lakin, a psychologist who has often written on the ethical problems in the encounter movement, noted, "A legitimate case could perhaps be made for the temporary alleviation of loneliness . . . but the [sensitivity] training experience as cure is absurd."

The assumption that loneliness and alienation are the primary motives of the estimated six million encounter game players is really the assumption of a collective unconscious motive. We would have to infer that all of man's social contacts are a defense against loneliness—not necessarily an untenable thesis but one which eliminates the possibility that encounter groups offer a unique antidote. Most encounter advocates deny the existence of unconscious forces in individuals. While to the best of my knowledge encounterists have not hypothesized a collective unconscious, the mass-loneliness thesis ultimately comes down to that. Furthermore, the fact the encounter movement is not universal proves that its appeal does not lie in universal motives—evidently members of minority groups and the lower economic class are never lonely, and people of other continents are not undergoing the stresses of modernization, or there would be encounter groups everywhere.

Regardless of the percentage of people we presume to be motivated by loneliness, it is clear how little the encounter movement does about it. Emmanuel K. Schwartz, reviewing several books on encounter groups, noted the "bankruptcy of the movement as a social force for overcoming alienation," and came to the conclusion that so many observers of the groups have reached, that encounter experiences

> seem to encourage, promote, and reward instantaneous affect of no duration. Human relationships in such a context must be essentially superficial.

When Bill Schutz hurries groupers through the eyeballing and fanny-patting exercises in a microlab, the intent is surely not to get them started on a relationship, but to deindividualize each and to foster relationships to the group. The facelessness of modern society is reproduced in the groups, and the fact that most people never see their groupmates again after the encounter points to the fact that encounter is not a solution, but the symptom of a problem. The brevity of encounter groups, the brevity of the relationships derived from them, and the significant number of "encounter addicts" indicate that if encounter has any effect upon loneliness, it's merely a hedge. Even a superencounter player like Jane Howard, who spent a full year touring from group to group to collect experiences for her book, concluded that while many stirring things happen, the effects don't last.

> Fond though I often felt of people I encountered in groups, none of them has come to be really important to me, nor have I to any of them. Most of them I have not even seen again, and probably won't.... It would be sad and futile, I think, to confuse the feelings born in these laboratories with genuine friendship, but people do.

Just as the encounter movement is no real answer to mass

loneliness, it is no answer to mass psychopathology. There is a difference between the common social malady, the so-called cultural neurosis, and the disturbances and stresses which psychiatric patients undergo. "The common social malady is woven into the fabric of their personality but is not synonymous with their psychopathology," says Yalom, and almost all mental-health professionals would agree.

Professionals routinely distinguish between an enduring neurosis requiring psychotherapy and personality traits that may be annoying or unacceptable to the patient. Unfortunately, most encounter groups do not make that distinction, and usually aim for a change in personality. The focus on change very quickly makes anyone a patient, not because he is necessarily sick, but because the process of change—if it is to have any effect at all—must tap significant chords in a person's psyche. For this reason, I believe that encounter groups are always *implicit* psychotherapy.

Many professionals hold that for a program to be psychotherapy, it must be called by that name. Milton Berger defines psychotherapy as a contractual situation in which one party acknowledges himself as a patient and the other as therapist. However, psychotherapeutic contracts are set up all the time in the encounter world. A person who approached a psychotherapist in his private office with the same goals as most encounter players have would certainly be accepted as a "patient." Only the context, the brevity of the contract, and the prevailing rubrics make it an encounter group.

A basic premise among encounter advocates which sets the tone for their programs is the belief that man is basically good. Carl Rogers, the philosopher emeritus of the movement, has carried over this view of man from his client-centered counseling, where he first made his name. Max Rosenbaum, in a detailed critique of the philosophy behind encounter, points out that Rogers' endorsement of encounter groups is a derivative of his view of man as essentially good. The cumulative good of the encounter group, in his view, helps each person tap the basic goodness in himself. During a confrontation between Buber and Rogers, an historic event in itself, Rogers emphasized his belief in the essential goodness of all men, stating: "I would say that there is no difference in the relationship that I form with a normal person, a schizophrenic, a paranoid . . ."

The debate over good and evil is not simply an academic issue—it is at the very core of the encounter ideology. Schutz, Rogers, and their followers tend to feel a moral superiority. Seeing themselves as well intentioned, they assume that they can do no evil. This belief makes encounterists feel justified in using psychological techniques that push people beyond their emotional limits. Though Rogers imposes some limits on his style of encountering, Schutz is avowedly ready to use any human experience in his quest for openness.

What concerns me most is the potential of encounter groups to purvey evil as well as good—which, in my view, becomes greater the more one assumes there is no evil. Nothing in the encounter position limits exploration of such human capacities as pain, brutality, humiliation, or fascism. The self-assured moralist in human history has seldom hesitated to impose his morality on others, and I could not agree more with Rosenbaum when he points out that "the encounter therapies impose normative behavior on people who participate in their meetings."

Not only do the groups become potentially fascistic as they impose their morality on others, but they are ignorant of this potential. Rosenbaum notes the lack of training in ethics, theology, and philosophy among encounter therapists, and adds that the so-called humanist therapies have in their midst exponents who view their programs as corrective not only of the human psyche, but of the human soul as well.

In a recent open letter to the Association for Humanistic Psychology, Rollo May took issue with the "general aura of irresponsibility" characteristic of their activities, pointing out that the organization's tendency

> has been an anti-intellectual one and we have tended to leave out thinking, reflecting, historical man, and put in only the feeling, touching man in the "now." This is antihumanistic. It can be genuinely dangerous—as we learned in Germany in the great romantic, anti-intellectual surge on which Hitler rode to power.

Bill Schutz recently exemplified encounter's anti-intellectual tendency when he appeared on a professional panel that had been seriously considering technical and theoretical issues of creativity in psychotherapy. When Schutz's turn came to speak, he began by leading the group in some encounter-style exercises; the audience went along. The atmosphere quickly became so charged that quiet deliberation was no longer possible. Riding the wave of excitement, Schutz proceeded to advocate the use of astrology and tarot cards, the bodily experiences, and the whole host of encounter gimmicks as the route to creativity. I'm sure Schutz would say that he'd found all the words tiresome and he simply wanted to perk up the energy level of the group. But individual freedom has never flowered in the midst of screaming crowds; indeed, its greatest subversions have occurred when primitive emotion has been encouraged.

In speaking of the fascistic potential of encounter, I am not siding with the frequent right-wing attacks on the movement. I don't believe that there is any central plot behind the spread of encounter, and I am not using the word "fascist" in the social movement sense. The fascism I have observed has been very much at the "one-two-three, hug! one-two-three, relate!" level, or in cases of individuals browbeaten by the group and leader. I believe that in a misguided reflex of liberalism, the leaders of the movement have fallen prey to the same intolerance that the rightists demonstrate.

The political preferences of movement people are clear, though, and never do they raise the question of how to encounter with right-wingers. In Rogers' book only two pages are devoted to political issues, all of which are summed up by what he calls "fear created by the encounter trend." Rogers cites some examples of the innuendo and fright tactics used by right-wingers in their attacks on the sensitivity movement. He quotes from Congressman Rarick, who read into the *Congressional Record* of June 10, 1969, a 30,000-word diatribe by Ed Dieckmann, Jr., entitled "Sensitivity International—Network for World Control," and also cites the writings of right-winger Alan Stang in *The Review of News,* and Gary Allen in *American Opinion,* the official organ of the John Birch Society.

Rogers concludes flatly that encounter groups "breed constructive change . . . hence all those who are opposed to change will be stoutly or even violently opposed to the intensive group experience." With this simple dismissal of criticism Rogers falls victim to the same reasoning that he attributes to the right-wingers whom he criticized, overlooking the possibility that there can be constructive criticism not motivated by political ideology.

Having confronted the intransigence of emotional conflicts almost daily in the last twelve years of my work with patients, I am concerned about the notion common among encounterists that personality change follows automatically from encounter experiences; about the repeated failure of encounterists to clearly express the limitations of the group method; and about the extent to which encounter advocates ignore reentry problems and the quickly disappearing results of the encounter groups. Most of all, I am concerned about the current wave of anti-intellectualism, with many self-proclaimed experts willing to throw out all contemporary standards of research.

The general failure or unwillingness of encounterists to confront research issues, in particular the dangers and long-term effects of the group, brings into question the fundamental integrity of the movement as a whole. Bernard Rosenthal has noted that encounterists might be expressing

> some apprehension or, at least, disinterest in determining whether [the movement's] experiences have their purported effect in heightening sensitivity and expanding humanism in the everyday world. For if this were not found to be the case, it would put into question the movement's claimed purpose and ostensible validity, thereby revealing its own particular manipulative and commercialized use of the materialistic world it is so intent on transforming.

Encounterists have consistently ignored research that indicates psychological casualties and the briefness of most encounter "changes." It is clear that intellectual honesty and rigor are not characteristic of the movement, especially in its efforts to evaluate itself.

Carl Rogers points out that many people tend to magnify the extent to which psychological damage occurs in groups. Certainly many uninformed, overcontrolled, or defensive people would consider expressing a lot of emotion or spending a sleepless night evidence of psychological damage. Psychologists do not consider such reactions to be evidence of damage, and I certainly do not consider such incidents sufficient reason for being concerned about encounter groups. We have much firmer evidence of psychological damage in the Stanford studies of Yalom and Lieberman and in others.

Rogers decries the limitations of the research that has been done so far. He has recommended that every encounter "subject" be enlisted as "investigator" of the process of change—a bid for using subjective experience as the criterion of change. Rogers rejects tests of long-term effects and untreated control subjects in favor of methods that he knows can yield only positive results for encounter. Rogers has said:

> This personal, phenomenological type of study—especially when one reads all of the responses—is far more valuable than the traditional "hard-headed" empirical approach. It is definitely more valuable than to know that participants did—or did not—show a difference of .05 significance from a control group of nonparticipants, on some scale of doubtful reliability and validity. For me this kind of organized, naturalistic study may well be the most fruitful way of advancing our knowledge in these subtle and unknown fields.

The "deepest insights" that Rogers refers to have a surprising similarity, if not shallowness, about them. Rather than real personal change, they suggest conformity to verbal rituals and emotional expectations. Maybe there is change implicit in learning to conform to those expectations, but personality changes at this level are transient.

Relying on individual testimonials also leads observers to believe that only uptight or emotionally incompetent people can benefit from encounter. One never hears of people who are emotionally competent to begin with; what happens to them in encounter groups? Conventional wisdom has it that one can always exercise more of his emotional strength—but I wonder. Often, it is those very people who tend to view encounter groups as naïve or absurd and don't come back. True players of the game almost automatically assume that a negative response indicates anxiety or fear of involvement. I've never heard of an encounter leader who said to a player, "You're finished—you've graduated, go home."

Rosenthal has summed up several other arguments against encounter, including the movement's tendency to supply excitement and sensationalism in the face of social deterioration. He has also underscored the movement's capacity to provide

> an escape or diversion from the authentic humanistic challenge of the day-to-day world—the true arena of depersonalization and alienation—by allowing its practitioners to get their humanistic fulfillments in those weekends or seminars at which there is no serious threat to their everyday mode of life, no immediate challenge to their daily vested commitments or economic and materialistic interests, and no serious jeopardy to their social positions in the established society of which they are a part.

The illusion of temporary self-actualization in the face of far more pressing social problems can only be viewed as a grand copout—an escapism particularly insidious since it cloaks its activities with high-sounding goals.

While many have criticized encounter for not having a sensible ethic of man, I believe it does have an implicit ethic—hedonism. The sensory experience is valued above all, and all morality is based on the pleasure principle. The difficult confessions, gut-wrenching confrontations, tests of strength, and body manipulations are sought for their pleasure component, even if it is the pleasure that comes when one stops banging one's head against a wall.

In this context, the rest makes sense. The primarily middle-class appeal, the theatricalism and moneymaking, the promiscuous sexuality, the acceptance of psychedelic drug experiences, the body emphasis, the avoidance of real social issues, and the emphasis on transitory titillations—all reveal a hedonistic tendency. Even the rejection of scholarship—it's hard work—and responsibility for others—that too requires effort—support this thesis. Indeed, the rejection of intellect is consistent with a regressive if not primitive view of man, one which, as Michael Beldoch put it, places "the blame for our painful human condition on our very capacity for reason."

Rosenthal noted the movement's undifferentiated desire for emotion and sensation:

> It is ready for all experience, all states of being, and all explorations of sensation.... It is like a desperately hungry man who will eat anything, a thirsty child who will drink brackish water as well as champagne not knowing how to judge them, or a sex-starved human who will sleep with any member of the opposite or the same sex. There is much humanism—and humanness—in this, of course, but it is not clear whether it is an animal humanism, an infantile humanism, a humanism of emotional desperation and starvation, a humanism of recreation, a humanism of escapism, or a humanism of deliberate dissociated and thoughtless indulgence.

As a whole, then, the movement can be seen as a bastardization of humanistic principles, based on the faulty premise that expression of emotion and exchange of sensation will solve the ills of the world. Historians have noted that religious movements require an irrational idea at their core and are based on a complex defense of an irrational dream, be it virgin birth or reincarnation. For the encounter movement, the irrational core lies in this notion that the complexity of human growth can be reduced to programed emotional experience.

It is also at this point that the greatest fraud of the encounter movement, perpetrated by both players and leaders, occurs. Experiences purportedly spontaneous are in fact ritualized, manipulated, and entirely predictable. Bill Schutz proudly notes in his latest book that the "spontaneous" emotions generated during his "More Joy" labs at Esalen can be charted thus:

> The week usually follows an amazingly predictable emotional evolution. Sunday night: great energy and excitement. Monday: grim, earnest, a little disappointment because the larger groups don't go as well as the microgroups. Monday night and Tuesday morning: beginning of depression and anguish as problems and negative feelings are opened up. Tuesday night: very bad, anger, hostility, and sometimes several people almost leave, which they report on Wednesday morning. Wednesday: the gloom starts to lift as problems start yielding to work; dance is a relief and many find it a great catharsis and are proud that they can feel so free. Thursday: good feelings start to rise and positive feelings

emerge; joy comes about noon Thursday, and continues to grow. Friday: euphoria and tears, difficulty in leaving, sadness, joy, and ecstasy.

Yet each group believes that its workshop was unique; each has its sexual and physical contacts, its moments of tenderness, anger, fear, and joy; each group has its psychic casualties as well as its miracle cures; and each grouper makes friends he never sees again.

The magic of theater—as theater—is valued, since we all know its intent is to enlighten, amuse, and divert. When packaged as psychic growth, the magic of theater is clearly fraudulent, just like the medicine shows of old. The human need for magic is deeply ingrained and insatiable. As encounter braces before joining the ranks of earlier fads like dianetics and phrenology, new absurdities await their turn in the wings. Primal screaming and brainwave feedback are probably the next two vehicles for the psychic hucksters. Perhaps every few years we need a new wave of irrationality to feed the illusion that, given the right trick, man is perfectible.

Bibliography

Addiction Services Agency, "Comprehensive Plan for the Control of Drug Abuse and Addiction," New York City, November 1971.

American Psychiatric Association, Task Force Report, *Encounter Groups and Psychiatry*, Washington, D.C., American Psychiatric Association, April 1970.

Ardrey, Robert, *The Territorial Imperative*, New York, Atheneum, 1967.

Argyris, Chris, "T-Groups for Organizational Effectiveness," *Harvard Business Review*, vol. 42, 1964, 60-74.

Asch, Solomon, E., "Studies of Independence and Submission to Group Pressure: I. A Minority of One Against a Unanimous Majority," *Psychological Monographs*, 1956.

——, "Interpersonal Influence: Effects of Group Pressure upon the Modification and Distortions of Judgments," in *Readings in Social Psychology*, Maccoby, E. E., Newcomb, T. M., and Hartley, E. L., (eds.), New York, Holt, Rinehart & Winston, Inc., 1958, 174-183.

Beckhard, Richard, *Organization Development: Strategies and Models*, Reading, Mass., Addison Wesley, 1969.

Brownfain, John J., "The APA Professional Liability Insurance Program," *American Psychologist*, vol. 26, no. 7, July 1971, 648-653.

Brussel, James A., Letter to the Editor, *New York Times Magazine*, May 16, 1971.

Calame, Byron, "The Truth Hurts," *Wall Street Journal*, July 14, 1969.

Campbell, J. P., and Dunnette, M. D., "Effectiveness of T-Group Experiences in Managerial Training and Development," *Psychological Bulletin*, vol. 70, no. 2, August 1968, 73-104.

Coulson, William, "Inside a Basic Encounter Group," *The Counseling Psychologist*, vol. 2, no. 2, 1970, 1-27.

Corsini, Raymond J., "Issues in Encounter Groups," *The Counseling Psychologist*, vol. 2, no. 2, 1970, 28-34.

Durkheim, Emil, "Anomie and Suicide," in *Sociological Theory*, Coser, L., and Rosenberg, B. (eds.), New York, Macmillan Co., 1957.

Elkind, David, "Wilhelm Reich—The Psychoanalyst as Revolutionary," *New York Times Magazine*, April 18, 1971.

Fiske, Edward, "American Churches Are Turning to Sensitivity Training," *New York Times*, March 26, 1970.

Gibb, Jack R., "The Effects of Human Relations Training," in *Handbook of Psychotherapy and Behavior Change*, Bergin, Allan E., and Garfield, Sol L., New York, John Wiley & Sons, 1971.

Goldman, George, and Brody, Helen, "An Analytic and a Behavioristic View of an Encounter Weekend," *Group Process*, vol. 3, no. 1, Summer 1970, 101-121.

Gottschalk, Louis A., "Psychoanalytic Notes on T-Groups at the Human Relations Laboratory, Bethel, Maine," *Comprehensive Psychiatry*, vol. 7, 1966, 472-87.

——, and Pattison, E. M., "Psychiatric Perspectives on T-Groups and the Laboratory Movement: An Overview," *American Journal of Psychiatry*, vol. 126, 1969, 823-40.

Gustaitis, Rasa, *Turning On*, New York, Macmillan Co., 1969.

Howard, Jane, *Please Touch*, New York, McGraw-Hill Book Co., 1970.

Lakin, Martin, "Some Ethical Issues in Sensitivity Training," *American Psychologist*, vol. 24, 1969, 923-928.

Lazarus, Arnold, *Behavior Therapy and Beyond*, New York, McGraw-Hill Book Co., 1970.

Lieberman, Morton A., Yalom, Irvin D., and Miles, Matthew, "The Group Experience Project: A Comparison of Ten Encounter Technologies," in *Confrontation: Encounters in Self and Interpersonal Awareness*, Leonard Blank, Gloria B. Gottsegen and Monroe G. Gottsegen, New York, Macmillan Co., 1971.

Marcuse, Herbert, *One-dimensional Man,* Boston, Beacon Press, 1964.

Miller, Stuart, *Hot Springs,* New York, Viking Press, 1971.

Montagu, Ashley, *Touching: The Human Significance of the Skin,* New York, Columbia University Press, 1971.

Parloff, Morris B., "Group Therapy and the Small-group Field: An Encounter," *The International Journal of Group Psychotherapy,* vol. 20, no. 3, July 1970, 267-304.

Perls, Frederick S., *Gestalt Therapy Verbatim,* Lafayette, Calif., Real People Press, 1969.

Reich, Charles, *The Greening of America,* New York, Random House, 1970.

Rogers, Carl, "Interpersonal Relationships: U.S.A. 2000," *Journal of Applied Behavioral Science,* vol. 4, no. 3, 1968, 265-280.

——, *Client-centered Therapy,* Boston, Houghton Mifflin, 1951.

——, *Carl Rogers on Encounter Groups,* New York, Harper & Row, 1970.

——, "The Process of the Basic Encounter Group," in *Challenges of Humanistic Psychology,* J. F. G. Bugental (ed.), New York, McGraw-Hill Book Co., 1967.

Rosenbaum, Max, "Responsibility of a Psychotherapist for a Theoretic Rationale," *Group Process,* vol. 3, Winter 1970-71, 41-47.

——, "Responsibility of a Group Psychotherapy Practitioner for a Therapeutic Rationale," *Journal of Group Psychoanalysis and Group Process,* vol. 2, Spring 1969-70, 5-17.

Rosenthal, Bernard G., "The Nature and Development of the Encounter Group Movement," in *Confrontation: Encounters in Self and Interpersonal Awareness,* Leonard Blank, Gloria B. Gottsegen and Monroe G. Gottsegen, (eds.), New York, Macmillan, 1971.

Rosenthal, Mitchell S., "Phoenix House: A Three Year Report," *Pathways in Child Guidance,* New York, Bureau of Child Guidance, Board of Education, June 1971.

Rousseau, Jean Jacques, *Emile,* Barbara Foxley, trans., New York, E. P. Dutton, 1950.

Schutz, William C., *Joy: Expanding Human Awareness,* New York, Grove Press, 1967.

——, *Here Comes Everybody,* New York, Harper & Row, 1971.

Schwartz, Emanuel K., "To Group or Not to Group," *Contemporary Psychology,* vol. 16, no. 7, 1971, 423-425.

Shepard, Martin, *The Love Treatment,* Peter H. Wyden, Inc., New York, 1971.

Sherif, Muzafer, "Group Influences upon the Formation of Norms and Attitudes," in *Readings in Social Psychology,* Maccoby, E. E., Newcomb, T. M., and Hartley, E. L. (eds.), New York, Holt, Rinehart, & Winston, Inc., 1958, 219-232.

Srole, L., et al., *Mental Health in the Metropolis: The Midtown Manhattan Study,* New York, McGraw-Hill Book Co., 1962.

Stoller, Frederick, quoted in "The Group: Joy on Thursday," *Newsweek,* May 12, 1969.

Toffler, Alvin, *Future Shock,* New York, Random House, 1970.

Underwood, W. J., "Evaluation of Laboratory Method Training," *Training Directors Journal,* vol. 19, 1965, 34-40.

Yalom, Irvin D., *The Theory and Practice of Group Psychotherapy,* New York, Basic Books, 1970.

——, and Lieberman, Morton A., "A Study of the Encounter Group Casualties," *Archives of General Psychiatry,* vol. 25, July 1971, 16-30.

Index

Index